The Accidental Library Marketer

Kathy Dempsey

Information Today, Inc.
Medford, New Jersey

First Printing, 2009

The Accidental Library Marketer

Copyright © 2009 by Kathy Dempsey

Library of Congress Cataloging-in-Publication Data

Dempsey, Kathy, 1965-
   The accidental library marketer / Kathy Dempsey.
      p. cm.
   Includes bibliographical references and index.
   ISBN 978-1-57387-368-0
   1. Libraries--Marketing. 2. Libraries--Public relations. I. Title.
   Z716.3.D425 2009
   021.7--dc22

                                                          2009018911

Printed and bound in the United States of America

President and CEO: Thomas H. Hogan, Sr.
Editor-in-Chief and Publisher: John B. Bryans
Managing Editor: Amy M. Reeve
Project Editor: Rachel Singer Gordon
VP Graphics and Production: M. Heide Dengler
Book Designer: Kara Mia Jalkowski
Cover Designer: Ashlee Caruolo
Copyeditor: Beverly Michaels
Proofreader: Dorothy Pike
Indexer: Beth Palmer

www.infotoday.com

I dedicate this book to all librarians, information professionals, and library supporters around the world who want to understand how to promote this essential industry and how to keep it strong, respected, and funded for decades to come.

Contents

Foreword, by Judith Gibbons ix

Acknowledgments xi

About the Website xiii

Introduction xv

**Chapter 1: How and Why People Become
Accidental Marketers** 1

How Did We Get Here? 1
Where Are We Now? 2
How Accidental Marketers Are Born 3
Just How "Accidental" Are We? 5
The Need for More Marketing Education in
Library Schools 9
What to Expect From This Book 11

**Chapter 2: Starting With the Basics
of Communication** 13

What, *Really*, Is Marketing? 13
The Cycle of True Marketing 14
The Missing Link Revealed 15
Definitions and Differences 16
The Four P's 17
An Example of How Businesses Use Marketing 19
What's in a Name? Or in Any Word? 21

**Chapter 3: Assessing Your Current
Situation** 25

Your Physical Spaces 27
Your Online Environment 28
Your Printed Materials 35

Your Customer Service Environment 37
The Attitudes of Customers and Potential Users 40

Chapter 4: Using Demographic, Geographic, and Census Data ... 67

Tapping Into Demographic and Geographic Data 68
Using Data to Build a SWOT Analysis 73

Chapter 5: What Marketing Experts Think Is Most Important 79

How to Avoid the Five Most Common
  Marketing Mistakes 80
What Other Experts Think and Teach 85
Words of Wisdom From Others 93
What Surveys and Studies Have Revealed 95

Chapter 6: Getting Administrators, Managers, and Staff to Buy In 103

Basic Rules of Thumb for Achieving Buy-In 103
Getting Staff Buy-In for Extra Work on Marketing
  and Promo Projects 111
The Keys to Real Buy-In 115

Chapter 7: Making Evidence-Based Decisions With Administrators 117

Examine All of Your Data and Evidence 117
Look at Your Goals, Mission, and Vision 119
Think About Your Logo and Your Brand 122

Chapter 8: Don't Shy Away From Statistics 129

Start With Stats You've Got and Make Them
  More Powerful 129
Statistics You Might Not Record, But Should 132

The Importance of Cost/Benefit Analysis 135
Examples of Results From ROI Studies Around
        the United States 140
The Cost of Value Studies 143

Chapter 9: Understanding the Cycle
of True Marketing 145

All of the Steps in the True Marketing Process 145
Follow These Vital Steps and You Will Find Success 148

Chapter 10: Writing Your Formal Plans 161

The Proper Hierarchy of Plans 162
All About Marketing Plans 163
Five Steps to a Basic Marketing Plan 164
The Marketing Plan as Part of the Cycle of
        True Marketing 168
How a Communication Plan Can Help 170
A Word About Technology Plans 172
Sharing Plans Among Friends 173

Chapter 11: Basic Rules for Producing
Good Promotional
Materials 175

Craft Your Message Carefully 175
Design Rules for Creating Good Promotional
        Materials 178
Tracking Workflow for Promotional Materials 181
Helpful Tips for Working With Print Shops 184
It All Reflects on Your Library 185

Chapter 12: Getting the Message Out 187

My Recommendations for Communication 187
Working With the Media 190
Spreading the Library's Message Through
        Partnerships 203
A Few Words About Word-of-Mouth Marketing 207
The Time Has Come for Mobile Marketing 208

Chapter 13: Using Your Website for Public Relations and Outreach 211
What Do People Expect From Websites? 212
Make Sure Search Engines Can Find Your Site 215
Learning How People Search and See 218
You Need the "Full Monty" Website 220

Chapter 14: Finally, the Fun Stuff 223
Fun Events and Success Stories 224
"Wow Factor" Ideas You Can Try on Your Own 228
Promotion That Doesn't Feel Like Promotion 237
Snappy Comebacks for That Awful Question,
    "Now That We Have the Internet, Why Do
    We Still Need Libraries?" 241
The Final Lesson 247

Appendix A: Improving Our Media Relations via Strategic Communications Planning, by Marsha A. Iverson 249

Appendix B: Designing Promo Materials That Are Legible, by Pat Wagner 261

Appendix C: Promotion Is Not the Same as Marketing, by Christie Koontz 271

About the Author 281

Index 283

Foreword

It has never been unusual for library staff members to become accidental library marketers. In challenging economic times in particular, when budgets are tight and staff is under pressure, marketing often creeps into day-to-day responsibilities or jumps into a job description under the "other duties as assigned" category.

Author Kathy Dempsey knows that this is often the route that propels a library staff member to marketing duties. Accidental marketers start out developing handy program fliers or developing attractive computer graphics. Then, wham! Marketing, or what passes for marketing, begins to take up 30 percent, 50 percent, or possibly 100 percent of their day.

Even if this hasn't happened to you (yet), there are myriad reasons to begin implementing the principles in this book. Good marketing saves your library money in the long run, gives you a clear picture of your potential audiences, and helps enhance your stature in the community. If you begin thinking and working like a marketing manager, you will develop the tools to craft and implement a well thought out marketing plan that complements your strategic and communications plans. And, as the author points out, "When an entire organization coordinates all of its plans at the highest levels, it helps ensure that everyone involved is working in concert toward the most important goals."

So when Dempsey asks, "How did we get here?" you will know that—unlike *Alice Through the Looking Glass* or Dorothy in Oz— she will provide a clean and concise road map to help review where you were, determine where you are now, and plan for where you want to be. Although she notes that marketing is not a linear process, she gives you a practical and descriptive guide to find your way through the marketing maze. If you follow her tips, you will graduate from accidental marketer to professional and proactive marketer. Dempsey's book puts you on the fast track and helps you avoid the pitfalls that ensnare marketing amateurs.

Looking back, I wish that I'd had this reference book when I became the director of a small public library. I missed the many vital services provided by the marketing department in my previous job. So, I began my marketing career by trial and error— designing fliers and writing press releases. How invaluable this book would have been in saving me time and effort!

Dempsey understands the accidental marketer phenomenon because of her many years working in libraries, journalism, and marketing. Building on her eclectic career, she began editing the newsletter *Marketing Library Services* in 1994—and, as she says, "… soaked up an incredible amount of information and best practices." She is an author and consultant, and often shares sage advice on the American Library Association (ALA) discussion list PRTALK. She took all her professional experiences and combined these with current research, networking, and good sense to put together a highly readable and lively text.

Given her firm belief in the value of libraries, throughout the book she illustrates the many ways that marketing can demonstrate the financial and social worth of the institution. She gives ample examples and an expanded appendix, with everything put into an up-to-date global perspective. In fact, her snappy comebacks about why we still need libraries alone are well worth the price of the book. It may even nudge you down the road of becoming a fledgling accidental library marketer!

—Judith Gibbons

Judith Gibbons is a writer and consultant based in Versailles, Kentucky, and a living example of the accidental library marketer. She was recently elected to ALA Council. Judith currently serves as Chair of the ALA Advocacy Training Sub-Committee and as a member of the John Cotton Dana Library Public Relations Award Committee. She is a Past-President of Southeastern Library Association and a Past-Chair of the ALA Public Awareness Committee.

Acknowledgments

The long days and nights I spent writing this book felt pretty lonely. All the knowledge and ideas I wanted to share were locked inside my brain, and nobody could get them out but me. Still, there have been many people over the years who helped put all that info into my head, so I didn't really create this book alone.

I owe a debt of gratitude to many, starting with the very first librarians I remember (Mrs. Bower at Blain Elementary and Mrs. Hower at West Perry High). Special thanks go to the staff of Temple University's Ambler Campus library, where I worked for a number of years, especially to Linda Cotilla for believing in me enough to hire me full time, Sandi Thompson for teaching me reference and so much more, and Helene Matt for getting me more involved in the writing life. Working there solidified my desire to stay in and around libraries for the rest of my career.

Later I landed at Shenandoah University's Smith Library thanks to Christopher Bean and Kirk Doran. This moved me to Virginia, where I also worked part-time at Handley Public Library. Finally, it all came together at Information Today, Inc., where I combined my library love and experience with my journalism skills. I'm grateful to Tom Hogan, Sr., for trusting me with the *Marketing Library Services* newsletter, which has allowed me to fulfill my goal of helping librarians promote their expertise and their services so they can continue to thrive.

Many wonderful people I've met and worked with since have helped shape the thought processes that went into this book. Most of all, I want to recognize Christie Koontz for informing my beliefs so much. And thanks to all who shared their knowledge directly by answering surveys and providing quotes for this book. And of course, I'm grateful to Rachel Singer Gordon, Amy Reeve, and John Bryans for making publishing possible.

Last but far from least, I thank my supportive family and friends, most of all, my patient husband Michael for always being there with hugs and encouragement when the going got tough. I could never have done this without you.

About the Website
www.LibrariesAreEssential.com

This book contains a number of useful web links and resources for accidental library marketers. An accompanying website (www. LibrariesAreEssential.com) has been created that includes all of the links from this book, as well as some color photos from events mentioned in the black-and-white text. The site will occasionally be updated with new articles and ideas.

Please email your comments or additions to the author at LibrariesAreEssential@comcast.net.

Disclaimer

Neither the publisher nor the author make any claim as to the results that may be obtained through the use of this webpage or of any of the internet resources it references or links to. Neither publisher nor author will be held liable for any results, or lack thereof, obtained by the use of this page or any of its links; for any third-party charges; or for any hardware, software, or other problems that may occur as the result of using it. This webpage is subject to change or discontinuation without notice at the discretion of the publisher and author.

Introduction

As I type these first words of my book, it's March 17—St. Patrick's Day. I'm not really superstitious, but I figure it can't hurt to invoke the luck of the Irish as I begin this massive project. It's always good to have a little extra luck, right?

Alas, many people think that success in library marketing and promotion depends on luck—but nothing could be further from the truth. Simply making some fliers and trying to get your programs announced in the local paper aren't enough, and no amount of luck will change that.

What most library employees don't realize is that there's a way to practically guarantee success in their promotional endeavors. Oddly enough, it's called "marketing." When you really understand and follow the concepts as they're laid out in the business world, you go through certain steps that take the guesswork out of the process. This is what I've come to call "true marketing." But since most people who promote their libraries end up doing so by accident, they've never learned these steps to success. That's where this book comes in.

The Accidental Library Marketer fills a need for library professionals and paraprofessionals who find themselves in an awkward position: They need to promote their libraries and services in the age of the internet, but they've never been taught how to do so effectively.

If you're a newcomer to marketing, the following chapters will give you a solid foundation. If you've already been promoting your library, this book will deliver explanations that will help you make sense of things. Even if you've been "marketing" for years, it will help you refine your processes and strategies. And for all of you who've done promo campaigns that have fallen short of your expectations, it will help you understand why and show you how to be more successful next time.

In these pages, I'll take the essential business concepts of true marketing, translate them into words that you can understand (and even enjoy), and relate them directly to library issues. I'll blend rules with advice and real-life examples from your colleagues in the trenches. And along the way I'll provide some ideas for fun promotions and interesting projects. You'll also find ways to answer the agonizing question: "Why do we need libraries when everything's on the internet?"

In some ways, I'm an accidental marketer myself. About 15 years ago, my lifelong devotion to libraries, my years of paraprofessional work, and my journalism degree all converged perfectly when I was hired as editor of the *Marketing Library Services* (*MLS*) newsletter, published by Information Today, Inc. (Could that have just been luck?) Since I took over *MLS* back in 1994, I've soaked up an incredible amount of information and best practices. I've talked with people from all over the U.S., and some from other countries. I've read countless stories of marketing campaigns, both successes and failures. I've reviewed lots of books and written tons of articles. I've attended a great many marketing workshops and conference sessions, and have presented some of my own as well. A few years back, I started my own marketing consulting service called Libraries Are Essential (www.librariesareessential.com). In 2008, I began contributing to a library marketing blog called The 'M' Word (themwordblog.blogspot.com). And now I want to compile all of this knowledge and experience into one book, to create a clear, practical, A-to-Z summary of how true marketing can work for librarians.

I want to ensure that libraries, with their vast wealth of information, and librarians, with their incredible knowledge, will always be around. Don't you? It'll take a lot more than luck to do that. So join me on this journey to see exactly how proven, well-planned promotional techniques can raise the public's awareness of and respect for the libraries we all love.

Chapter 1

How and Why People Become Accidental Marketers

The general public just doesn't value libraries as much as it used to. That change in attitude has led to less respect and, often, less funding. You don't have to do any in-depth research to find out how our field got into this predicament, but here's a brief synopsis.

How Did We Get Here?

Back in the old days—about 20 whole years ago—most libraries were still enjoying the status they'd always had. They were important because they held information and other treasures that weren't available elsewhere. Enter the internet in the mid-1980s. It was set up to make information sharing easier and faster, initially only for organizations such as the military and research universities. Of course it's hard to keep a good thing quiet, and in 1988 the internet was opened to commercial interests. The Mosaic browser was released in 1993, and as more-user-friendly interfaces were created and more cities were wired for internet connections, usage grew exponentially. As it became easier to access and share information, libraries' proud place as The Great Repository was diminished. And now, with a solid generation of "digital natives" (kids who always had this technology growing up) in place, too often we hear the question, "We have the internet; why do we still need libraries?"

1

Hence, our current situation. When many of today's librarians were studying for their masters' degrees, there were no classes in marketing or promotion because nobody really needed them. (Ditto for classes in fundraising, business practices, computer technology, and many other subjects that matter today.) Consequently, many people who've worked their way into management positions don't have any background in the subject. Sadly, the "everything's already online" mindset has now made it absolutely crucial to promote libraries' valuable, authoritative collections and librarians' expertise in finding trustworthy info. Trouble is, many of today's library schools *still* don't teach much marketing.

Where Are We Now?

So most library managers don't have this expertise, nor do many new hires. And we're already deep enough in that budgets have been slashed, and therefore people can't afford to hire extra staff (let alone professional marketers) to fight the myth that libraries don't matter anymore. This is a Catch-22, and one that we're going to have to work hard to dig out of.

It's essential that we change this situation, and change people's minds about libraries, for several reasons. Chief among these, of course, is saving our own jobs. But it's more than that. At the risk of sounding pompous, I'll say that I think we need to save people from themselves, from their own ignorance. If the supposedly learned mayors and deans and governors and CEOs and legislators truly believe that we don't need libraries, and they stop funding them, what will happen to the world's records? All the history, the memories, and the treasures? You can't just lock them up in old buildings and hope nothing will happen to them. They need active preservation—and often digitization. And what of the new information being released today? Who will organize and interpret it?

Piling documents into computer folders isn't enough. Who will help new generations learn about their world? What about literacy? I don't want to get too philosophical, so I'll stop here. Suffice it to say that, if you're reading this book, you understand many of the reasons why libraries, in one form or another, need to continue no matter how much technology gets involved with information.

This belief that libraries aren't essential anymore pervades too much of our society. It's time to fight it as if you're fighting for your very existence—because you are.

For additional motivation, check out some examples of how society views our industry. The 2007 documentary *The Hollywood Librarian* (www.hollywoodlibrarian.com) contains a nice historical glimpse of how librarians have been portrayed in various movies. Each issue of the newsletter *Marketing Library Services* (*MLS*; www.infotoday.com/mls) includes a department called "Spectacles: How Pop Culture Sees Librarians," which mentions new movies and books and comics and advertisements that portray us to the world. "Spectacles" is written by Ruth Kneale, a special librarian who has studied society's view of librarians for years. Kneale also maintains the website You Don't Look Like a Librarian! (www.librarian-image.net), which is full of fascinating (and sometimes maddening) examples of how the media portrays librarians. I'm sorry to report that the image of the shushing spinster lives on. But Kneale's site is a fun way to learn about how the world sees you, and it even includes data from some studies of librarian images.

How Accidental Marketers Are Born

So here we are, with ugly old stereotypes still haunting the profession and few people educated in the ways to paint more complimentary, updated images. Budgets aren't what they used to be, so staff members are stretched thin by the need to fill many roles with fewer people. Still, day-to-day chores must go on.

Somewhere along the way, a children's librarian needs some signs to announce an upcoming storytime. She seeks out someone who's a little more creative than she is, or someone who knows more computer graphics programs than she does. She finds a helpful colleague—let's call her Kate—to make her signs, and they look pretty nice. So when someone else needs a program flier, this person asks Kate to design it and to print some copies on colored paper. They look good. Soon, people start leaning on Kate not only for the computer work, but also for the text: "Should we name the program this or that? Would it work better at 11 AM or 3 PM?" Now Kate is giving what seems like casual advice but is actually shaping the library's offerings and outreach. Kate gets herself labeled as the "expert" on fliers and eventually that translates into being the expert on promoting programs. And you all know what happens then to someone like Kate, who has an aptitude for a little extra duty—suddenly it's part of her job. As her coworkers involve Kate earlier and earlier in the process, she becomes the go-to girl, and suddenly she's seen as "the marketing person." Yet she has no background in or real knowledge of marketing. After all, she only started out by changing some typefaces and pasting in clip art to make some nice-looking signs ... and another accidental marketer is born.

This, of course, is only one example. Sometimes a staffer will man a library table at a local fair, and thereby become the expert on outreach. Or the person who arranged for the library to be included in new-student orientation finds himself dubbed the new freshman liaison. Or the woman at the regional co-op who types up simple news releases for the members is seen as the PR person. Accidental marketers can be born in many ways; you get the idea.

Since the people who fall (or are pushed) into this extra work are often below the management level, these important tasks end up being done by someone who's paraprofessional or entry-level or part-time. Or they're done by a degreed librarian who's also working the reference desk and overseeing staff and serving on committees, and just doesn't have much time to spare. What's more, when tasks just fall into people's laps like this, the work isn't seen as essential, and the "position" (such as it is) doesn't really have any official standing to decide what should be done or to ask for resources. Consequently, even though promotion and marketing should be cornerstones of an organization's mission and strategic plan, in the library they end up being afterthoughts tacked onto an already-full job description. This is one the biggest problems with the way libraries are run today. And while the situation *has* improved over the years, it's still nowhere near as good as it needs to be.

Just How "Accidental" Are We?

As I explained in the Introduction, I've been the editor of a newsletter called *Marketing Library Services* since 1994. In that time, I've spoken with countless library promoters, many of whom admitted that they never intended to become marketers, or that they had no training in marketing, or both. This lack of background shows. It's not that someone without formal training cannot become a good marketer; it's more that they don't have the time or will or energy to really understand what marketing is about. Plus, as long as someone is complimenting them on their work, they think they're doing just fine. So, many people plan library events and make fliers for them and believe that they're *marketing* when, really, all they're doing is planning events and making fliers. Technically, that's more like *promotion*. And while many, many librarians—even experts and speakers and writers—use the "M" word for those basic tasks, that doesn't make it accurate. As you'll learn in this book, promotion is just a tiny part of marketing. True marketing is a process of asking people what they want, then creating and delivering it, then asking people how well you did. I'll dig into that in later chapters.

At any rate, I had all of this anecdotal evidence that many librarians and information professionals lack training, but I wanted to substantiate it for the purposes of this book. So I sent out an online survey to some email discussion lists. It wasn't exactly scientific, and I got just 89 responses. Yet, the answers and comments jibed pretty well with what I've come to believe over the many years I've been in the field. Let me share some results.

The first question I asked my colleagues was what percentage of their jobs involved marketing and promotion. I wanted to know because most folks I've talked to are either part-time employees or full-timers who got this work tacked on to their regular jobs. Just 26 percent of my respondents said that "pretty much all" of their jobs was marketing or promotion. The rest of the answers were spread across the board. What this tells me is that plenty of library managers don't assign marketing work as a full-time, high-value, priority task. (According to my results, 72 percent of the respondents were full-time employees. So most people in my sample were full-timers who had marketing as just part of their jobs.) Table 1.1 shows all of the answers for these two questions.

The big question—whether respondents had intended to become marketing/promo people—was split down the middle. Exactly 50.6 percent did intend to and 49.4 percent did not. The accidental marketers' comments on how they ended up doing this work were interesting. At least half a dozen enterprising individuals said they saw a need for it and so they just started doing it. A handful of solo librarians commented that if they didn't do it, nobody else would. Some admitted that their jobs had morphed to include promotional activities. One specifically said she had "started as a programming person, began promo on my own, because existing PIO [public information officer] was overloaded.

Table 1.1

Question: About how much of your job is library marketing or promotion?	
Choices	**Response**
Less than 25%	19%
25 to 40%	16%
Roughly half	13%
55 to 75%	11%
76 to 90%	15%
Pretty much all of it	26%
Question: How many hours a week are you employed by this library?	
Choices	**Response**
Less than 20 hours	2%
20 to 29 hours	7%
30 to 35 hours	19%
36 to 40 hours	72%

Did not get good media coverage. I applied for and received a PIO position, which morphed into marketing and fundraising over the years." Another admitted that when the job was created, "this aspect was lumped into" it. Here are a few paraphrased comments I'd like to share:

- I fell into it. Not much had been done previously.

- Fear of losing the library altogether to a contracted-out service company. I was disappointed to find out our customers did not know about services.

- I felt it was important due to the changing users in a 21st-century library.

- The director felt I was talented/creative with publicity.

- As people left the department, my job expanded to include those responsibilities.

- Anytime you are providing a service, you end up promoting it.

- I was encouraged to take marketing and PR courses because I love writing.

- All front-line staff have the responsibility of promoting the Library Resource Centre. As a group, we decided that every encounter could be a chance to promote the LRC's services.

When I asked survey participants whether they had had any formal training in marketing before their current jobs, 52 percent of them said they had. Of those, 76 percent said their training had been "very helpful," while nearly 22 percent rated the training "somewhat helpful." This is a testament to the value of real marketing education.

The next question asked whether respondents had had any formal training *after they began* doing marketing work. About 67 percent had. Those who hadn't gotten any education since starting cited the answers "no money" and "no time"; these were tied at 14 percent each. Only four people (out of 22) chose the answer I feared most, "administration doesn't think it's important." I was relieved to see so few give that reason for lack of training. Table 1.2 shows the percentages for each possible answer.

Table 1.2

Question: If you haven't gotten any formal training since you started doing marketing work, why not?	
Choices	Response
No time	54%
No money	14%
No desire	14%
Admin doesn't think it's important	18%

Author's Note: For these questions, I defined "formal training" as classes, workshops, seminars, or a degree; "anything other than reading or learning on your own."

Finally, I asked these staff members what they did on their own to learn about marketing, and gave them six choices of answers; they could mark as many as applied to them. Every possible answer scored between 80 percent and 92 percent, with "read articles" at the top of the spectrum and "ask colleagues" at the bottom. Other choices were "read books," "read listservs," "read websites or blogs," and "attend conference sessions."

The Need for More Marketing Education in Library Schools

One reason I was so interested in whether library staff members who do promo work had had much education in the field is that I haven't found much evidence of this incredibly important topic being taught in MLS or LIS programs, even today (at least not in the U.S.). My limited research found few schools teaching real marketing courses. Most schools include bits of marketing in other classes, like those on library management. But I'm here to tell you that a few days' or weeks' worth of lessons in the midst of another topic does not prepare anyone to do solid marketing. (If it did, I wouldn't be writing this book or editing my newsletter or contributing to the blog.)

My own small survey looked at 89 people who range from very new librarians to old pros. Just over half had library school degrees. Of the rest, 17 claimed degrees in marketing or business, and of the 28 who wrote in "other" degrees, about a dozen had degrees in journalism and/or communications. So half the folks doing this work have some public relations background but no library degree. This side of the coin presents its own challenges, because it's hard to be an expert communicator about something you don't fully understand. Although they're lucky to have writing or PR or business knowledge, the nonlibrarians I've talked with need a good bit of time to get to know the library world. I've heard them jump into conversations to ask a colleague what abbreviations such as LC or MLA or OCLC mean. These are terms that librarians take for granted. There's an awful lot for outsiders to absorb.

But I want to get back to the other side of the coin, the respondents who reported having library school degrees. Of those 49 people, only nine had any marketing or promotion classes while in library school. That's barely 20 percent. Even if a better sample showed twice that number, it wouldn't be enough. As those on the communications side would tell you, there's just as much librarians don't know about their field. There's a lot to absorb if you want to be good at publicity or promotion. So those rare people who have both library and PR-type knowledge are especially dear. Our world needs many, many more of them.

If libraries are to stay in business, marketing should never be tacked on to the end of a job description or handled by part-timers who don't have the right knowledge base. Could you imagine a major corporation doing that? What if the companies that manufactured Coke or Pepsi or Macs or PCs treated marketing as an afterthought? Libraries are businesses, too. They have managers and budgets and products and services and customers just like the big brands do. And they also have serious competitors, now more than ever. So marketing is absolutely essential, and serious skills are necessary to do it right and to keep your business afloat.

It's because I believe this so sincerely that I decided to write this book. Library schools don't prepare their students to do professional-level promotion, and most libraries don't have the money to hire extra employees who do have the necessary education. Consequently, there are lots of accidental marketers out there. Rest assured, accidental colleagues, I understand you. This book is intended to be your A-to-Z guide for all those things you sort of picked up but never properly learned. It delves deeply into a few essential topics to provide you with a rock solid foundation of knowledge, and it explores many other topics and points you to further info on those for whenever you're ready.

What to Expect From This Book

While I could not completely cover all marketing-related topics here, I think you'll find *The Accidental Library Marketer* to be a very practical, useful, and I hope even interesting guide that will explain all of those things you've been wondering about (plus a few things you didn't even realize you *should* be wondering about). And while you can obviously choose to start with a certain section to learn about a particular thing, I've written the book to be read in full. If you study each chapter in order, you'll learn the basics first, then build from there to end up with fairly complete knowledge of marketing as it applies specifically to libraries. Along the way, you'll find lots of fun, fresh ideas to use for your own marketing tasks, no matter what type of library you work in.

Oh, and I'm funny too. Very, very funny.

Chapter 2

Starting With the Basics of Communication

Don't be fooled by the boring title of this chapter—this is where I'm going to reveal the missing link that has long kept library promotions from being really successful. But first I must explain a few important, underlying facts.

What, *Really*, Is Marketing?

It's essential to start by defining some key terms. Even if you think you know what these words mean, don't skip this section! Some of these terms are constantly misused; some also have various interpretations. To make sure we're speaking the same language through all of the pages to come, please pay careful attention to the next few paragraphs. Once you understand these terms, you will have taken the first step in becoming a real marketer.

One of the most widespread problems I see in this field is misuse of the word *marketing* itself. People use *marketing* to refer to any sort of promotion or outreach activity, event programming, news releases, and a whole plethora of other things. But in the business world, where many of these concepts originated, there is but one meaning, and that's the one we're going to stick with here.

Marketing is a process where the ultimate goal is moving goods and/or services from the producer and/or provider to a consumer. But it's more than that. True marketing always involves a number of steps that ensure that the consumer *will* end up with those goods and services. How? You start by asking the consumer what he or she wants. This is why luck doesn't matter much (as I mentioned in the Introduction). Questioning people and gathering their responses takes the guesswork out of the process.

The Cycle of True Marketing

Here are the steps that make up the cycle of true marketing. I expand on this list and explain each step in depth in Chapter 9, but for now I just want to introduce you to the process.

1. Do some research to learn about the people in your service area.

2. Acknowledge that you have many different types of customers. Each is its own "target market" that needs to be treated separately.

3. Set qualitative and quantitative goals for each group you want to reach.

4. Get to know members of a chosen target market and ask them what they want and need from your organization (and what they don't!).

5. Identify (or create) products and services that will benefit each target market according to the wants and needs expressed. Figure out what people are currently using (instead of your library) to fulfill these needs.

6. Think about ways you can evaluate the effects of giving the people what they want. How will you know whether you're satisfying them?

7. Promote the products and/or services to their respective markets in ways that the target audience will be aware of and responsive to.

8. Deliver the products and services with your evaluative tools in place.

9. Get feedback from individuals in the group to ascertain whether you've really met the needs they expressed earlier; evaluate the honest feedback against the customers' original requests and your original goals. Have you done what you set out to do?

10. Use your evaluations to tweak your products, services, approaches, actions, or goals as necessary. Then go back to whatever step you need to improve and continue through the cycle again.

The Missing Link Revealed

Can you see why things done via this process are practically guaranteed to work? How can you go wrong by asking people what they want, then delivering it to the best of your ability, then asking customers for feedback, then improving your offerings accordingly? In my professional opinion, this cyclical process is the missing link that librarians need to know about. It's easy for services to fail when you don't follow these steps. It's hard for them to fail when you do.

Sit back for a minute and think about how books, programs, events, and services are chosen at your institution. How often do staff members create programs that they *think* will interest patrons? Do you order books and DVDs according to which titles are most-often checked out? Do managers ask you to organize specific programs or events because (you suspect) they're part of a pet project or a political agenda? How many things are simply repeated seasonally or annually because you've "always" done them? Now think: How often has a colleague requested a program by presenting evidence saying: "This survey shows that 40 percent of senior citizens are interested in this," or, "I know that 63 percent of residents between 18 and 25 years old love to do this." Have you ever heard that? Can you even imagine it happening?

I don't want to scare you away, but the bad news is that the process of true marketing does take some hard work and serious preparation. (But you're probably already working hard to do things that flop.) The great news is that, with some actual evidence behind you, you can waste less time on failed ideas and get way more bang for your buck on the good ones.

Definitions and Differences

Now that you've seen what the true marketing process is, you can see why the word *marketing* doesn't apply to everything. Let's define a few oft-heard words and make some distinctions among them:

- **Marketing** is taking steps to move goods from producers to consumers. It's determining what people want, delivering it, evaluating consumer satisfaction, and then periodically updating that whole process.

- **Public relations** is a planned, long-term communication program (via various media) with a goal of convincing the public to have good will toward something. It's helping people to think well of an organization, product, or concept.

- **Publicity** is sending a message via official channels such as news releases, newsletters, and press conferences.

- **Promotion** is furthering the growth or development of a product or service. It's not just aiming toward good will; it's encouraging people to use that product or service by telling those people how it would benefit them.

- **Advertising** is calling attention to something through paid announcements.

- **Branding** is a process with dual objectives: 1) establishing a strong link between a company and its logo/typeface/

picture or name/phrase, and 2) developing the "personal-ity" of your product and service, establishing the charac-teristics that should come to mind when people think of you. Branding helps build loyalty.

- **Advocacy** is getting people who have good opinions of your organization to speak to others on its behalf, to con-vince other people of its value.

Using these definitions, you can now see that the word *market-ing* really refers to the specific, planned-out process that includes evaluating and retooling strategies until they work well. Many of the other words define actions that are *part of* the marketing process. So you can see why you shouldn't say, "We're having an event to market our library," but you can say, "This event is part of our public relations plan." In the same manner, you could say "We're publicizing our weekly storytimes to promote the library as a place where young children can learn and have fun, even if they can't read yet." See the sidebar "How All of the Terms Fit Together" on page 18 for another example of correct definitions and usage.

The Four Ps

With those definitions straightened out, let's move on to some key-words that are the basis of business-oriented marketing. The big-gies are known as the Four Ps: Product, Price, Place, and Promotion. Their definitions are pretty self-explanatory:

1. **Product** (or Service) – These are the materials, services, or knowledge that you're offering.

2. **Price** – For services you do charge for, determine the price by factoring in your cost to offer the service. For services that patrons don't directly pay you for, the price is the patrons' cost in time, measured by convenience (or lack thereof), ease of use, etc.

How All of the Terms Fit Together

As part of our **marketing** strategy, we identified college freshmen as one segment of our customer base. To **promote** online databases to these students, we recruited three groups of them to tell us about their current research habits. We asked how they preferred to find information for writing papers, and they told us they only wanted to search in one location. So we worked with our info tech librarians to gather many of our general online databases under one portal with a basic keyword search box on the front page. Once we'd set up this requested, simplified way to search, we used **publicity** (announcements in the school newspaper and signage in the library) to tell the freshmen that we'd delivered for them. Afterward, per our **marketing plan**, we surveyed them to see if they really preferred this search strategy. After evaluating their comments, we tweaked a few things in the search interface, then proceeded to **promote** our new "Simple Search Screen" by telling them how much faster they could finish their research if they started with this tool. As part of our **public relations plan**, we decided to **advertise** it by buying pens that said "Simple Search Screen: www.AeiouLibrary.edu/Simple Search" and giving them away just before midterms. And we **branded** the service by using the same colors and fonts on the pens as we had on the search page itself and on the other **promotional** materials we'd created. After asking some of the students from our original study to be **advocates** for the service by spreading the word to their friends, we're now noticing that more freshmen are beginning to identify that "Simple Search Screen" logo with easy-to-find, helpful information from the library. Mission accomplished!

3. **Place** – This is the location where people can obtain the product or service. (Yes, *online* counts as a place in this sense.)

4. **Promotion** – These are the actions and techniques you use to develop or increase the demand for a product or service.

It's important to realize that users do pay a price for your services even when they don't directly hand you money for them. In the case of libraries, the price is the patrons' cost to use your products instead of an alternative (i.e., driving to the library instead of logging on to the internet). The price they pay is measured in the time it takes them, in convenience (or lack thereof), in the distance traveled (and its direct costs), in ease of use, and so on. For instance, if a businessperson needs to check a fact while preparing a proposal, and it's hard for her to use the library because it's across town or it's rarely open or there's not enough reference help on staff, then the cost of her using the library for that task is too high, and she's likely to turn elsewhere.

An Example of How Businesses Use Marketing

Now that we're all using the same terminology, let me quickly tie these concepts into real-world marketing as businesses do it. Let's run through a quick example, using all the terms I just identified.

The Sweet Soda Corp. (SSC) is up against big-name competition in the soft-drink market. The managers want to create a drink that will make them rich. So they begin with market research: Who drinks soda (demographics)? How much do they buy, and when? What features are most important to them (taste, price, packaging)? Do the consumers react to special promotions, coupons, events? Then they choose a target group of people who are most likely to buy their product, Sweet Soda.

Next, SSC marketing staff members write a public relations plan outlining how they will reach their intended audience through messages that will appeal to them, sent via means that the target market uses. They also work on branding to find a logo and type-face that will appeal to the intended audience. They test their messages, logos, colors, etc., with focus groups to get real reactions. Things are a little off the mark, so they rework parts of the strategy and test again until they see that their promotional methods will be successful.

Then SSC begins to advertise its new drink in the media that the target group reads or watches. It also runs a basic soft-drink-industry campaign by holding a press conference and by sending press releases to trade journals and newspapers. Once they've built some buzz around this new brand of soda, SSC's public relations plan calls for changing the ads to feature target-audience people espousing the delights of Sweet Soda. Later, if the ads are successful, the company might move toward building the support of advocates by asking for user-generated content. Perhaps they'll ask Sweet Soda junkies to write in with reasons it's their favorite beverage, or invite them to submit videos of themselves gulping it down.

It's important to note that the SSC managers have all these steps planned out from the beginning; they're not just guessing about what to do next.

Think for a moment about how much product personality is portrayed in a simple name.

> If you heard about a new brand called Sweet Soda, who would you imagine it was for?
> > A. health-food nuts
> > B. babies
> > C. teens

What would you imagine to be the main ingredient?

    A. soy protein

    B. vitamins

    C. sugar

Where would you expect to buy it?

    A. organic grocer

    B. high-end coffee shop

    C. convenience store

What's in a Name? Or in Any Word?

As you ponder more about what names really say about a product or service, think about the names you've given to your own. Do they appeal to—or even make sense to—the people you're trying to reach?

Back when librarians were the only ones who searched libraries' collections, the lingo worked fine because nobody else had to understand it. But now, since stacks are open, people search on their own, and vast collections are represented by mere lists of words on computer screens, your users might not have much idea of what your library is offering.

Think about some of the words you use every day. Which do you consider to be library lingo?

- Books

- Collections

- Resource

- Stacks

- Database

- Serial

- Journal

- Holdings

Of that list, most of you would probably flag *serial* and maybe *holdings* as lingo related to the field. But guess what? Various studies of patrons searching for information have discovered that they don't automatically understand the word *resource* or even *database*. Surprise!

Terms That People Don't Understand

Terms most often cited as being misunderstood or not understood by users are:

- Database
- Library catalog
- Ejournals
- Index
- Interlibrary loan
- Periodical or Serial
- Reference
- Resource

Terms most often cited as being understood well enough to foster correct choices by users are:

- *Find books, Find articles,* and other combinations using natural language "target words"
- Terms accompanied by additional words or mouseovers that expand on their meaning

From www.jkup.net/terms.html, used with permission.

The best place I've found to learn about library lingo and how it affects the success or failure of people who use libraries is a website called Library Terms That Users Understand (www.jkup.net/terms.html). Assembled by John Kupersmith from the University of California–Berkeley, it's a clearinghouse of data on usability studies and lingo, and it's essential reading for anyone who tries to communicate with library users. See the sidebar "Terms That People Don't Understand" on page 22 for other shockers from studies listed on Kupersmith's website.

Also remember the basic rule that your users don't necessarily understand brand names, vendor names, and acronyms. Why would they know words like *Ulrich's, EBSCO, WebCat, ALA,* or *MLS*? You need to translate all of these terms that are familiar only to library insiders. Kupersmith's site helps with lists of best practices and tools, so you'll realize what you need to translate and how to say it better.

In addition to minding your lingo, you also need to remember to speak the language that's appropriate to whatever target market you're communicating with at the time. Use business terms for organizations, "kewl" (cool) words for teens, plain talk for everyday folks, and industry-specific terms for various faculty members (get help from subject liaisons).

Speaking of kewl, if you do chat or IM reference (that's instant messaging, in case you don't know the lingo), you'll enjoy the huge list of acronyms on the AOL Instant Messenger (AIM) website (www.aim.com/acronyms.adp). Sure, you know that BTW means "by the way" and that IMO means "in my opinion." But do you know other current conventions like these?

> BBS = be back soon
> JTLYK = just to let you know
> PCM = please call me
> Q = question

Using the right terms for online conversations shows that you "get it," and that's an important point to make to digital natives (young people who have always had computers) if you want their respect. Seriously, dude.

Remember that your every word—every message you compose, every webpage you touch, every email you type, every press release you write—will be more effective if it talks the talk of its target audience. (No pressure or anything ...) Sure, it takes a little more time and effort to customize everything, but it makes your communication more user-friendly and more effective, so it's worthwhile. And essential.

Chapter 3

Assessing Your Current Situation

So now you've mastered the terms of true marketing and denounced the lingo of libraries. You're fired up and ready to start making some improvements to your library's various promotional and publicity vehicles. Where should you begin?

In order to get where you want to go, you need to know where you already are. So your first task is to take a good, hard look at your organization from a lot of angles. Assess what you're already doing, so you can decide what's fine and what you'll need to work on. In this chapter I'll go over the myriad physical and virtual factors that affect how others view your library. Remember, to effectively communicate with your target customers, you have to see things through their eyes

I had my own eye-opening experience about six years ago when I took a local Feng Shui class. I was curious to learn some basics about Feng Shui before putting any serious money or time into it, so I signed up to take a six-week evening course at my local high school—one of those community classes that many townships and counties offer. My registration confirmation said that my class would meet in the school's library, which made it even more interesting to me. (Geek check!)

I arrived early for the first class and eagerly explored the tiny library. What I found was a really unpleasant surprise, despite my fairly low expectations. While the room was cramped, it was set up well enough and had colorful decorations on the walls. But the stacks themselves were just awful—really dusty, kind of smelly, and full of books copyrighted in decades long before I was born. In terms of usefulness, it was sad. And while the construction-paper decorations were meant to be bright and cheerful, they actually highlighted how dingy and old everything else was. They also made the room seem very juvenile (even for a high school) and rather unprofessional.

As I spent time in this room over the six weeks of class, I had a revelation: This small, poorly supported library was leaving a bad impression on everyone who entered it. Would people even wonder if other school libraries were better, or would they assume that all were similarly ill equipped and useless? That realization led me to an answer to a question that had long plagued me: How could intelligent teens go to college and shun the academic libraries that were their gateways to learning? How could they not see libraries as centers of knowledge that were essential to their education and their growth into responsible adults? One answer was staring me right in the face. Anyone who attended a high school with an obsolete library would carry away the impression that libraries were all old-fashioned and worthless. No wonder so many students thought they could do better on their own with their shiny new PCs or university-issued laptops.

What's more, if this impression stuck with them, and they never turned back to libraries again, they'd become adults who would not support or fund libraries. Could this be part of our overall image problem? I'm not going to undertake a massive study to prove it, but I will put this out as a cautionary tale. School libraries need to be better than many are now if we are ever to influence the next generation. Unless people learn from a young age that libraries have more and better research sources than they can get for free online, they are apt to ignore libraries their whole lives, thinking them obsolete.

The lesson here is to always be cognizant of what your library says about libraries in general. The average person doesn't understand the differences between a school media center and a university research center and the public library down the street. To them, we are all inextricably tied together, so your responsibility to impress people with your importance and performance is even greater than you probably imagined.

As my story illustrates, the number of tangible and intangible factors that come together to create visitors' impressions of your institution are almost limitless. Think about how you size up any new place you enter: a retail store, a park, an office, a stadium. You look for cleanliness, clarity (signage), and organization, and you also pick up sensory cues that you're not even conscious of. It's time to explore all of these factors.

This chapter will cover how to assess your library from many different angles, including some specific things to look at during these examinations. It would be impossible to list every little thing that goes into forming an impression, but I'll discuss five of the biggies here:

1. Your physical spaces

2. Your online environment

3. Your printed materials

4. Your customer service environment

5. The attitudes of customers and potential users

Your Physical Spaces

There's a great overview article called "How to Evaluate Your Library's Physical Environment" in the May/June 2007 issue of *Marketing Library Services*. Author Julia Cooper talks about creating an environment that fits your target market and provides detailed checklists of what to look at (through their eyes, of course). For this chapter, I've created even longer lists of things that experts say you should evaluate. You can use the checklists to rate areas of your library that you probably don't even think about. Better yet, have an unbiased outsider audit your organization. There are professional "secret shopper" groups that do such work; I've joined one myself and have been fascinated by the depth and detail that their studies demand.

Whether you do it yourself or hire someone, be thorough. Remember to include your exterior; people get first impressions before they even walk in the door. You should even consider staff spaces. Sometimes they really are behind locked doors, but often they are at least partially visible. We've all been in tech services departments where there are old books on the floor awaiting mending and new books piled up awaiting processing. Scattered in between, there are glue bottles, boxes of supplies, old sweaters, empty drink containers, ancient cat posters, etc. (C'mon, you know it's true!) When visitors catch glimpses of your organized chaos, what impressions do they get?

While looking through your building, always consider a few basics: Does it appear cluttered? Piles of papers and hand-written signs make especially bad impressions. Keep all of your brochures and fliers on an organized rack or shelf. Does your space look inviting enough to make visitors want to come in and stay a while? Do lamps keep areas without natural light well lit? Do you have designated quiet areas as well as group-study areas? Are there ample containers for trash and recycling, and are they in useful spots? Do you have a designated area for cell-phone conversations? Are there some plants or flowers around? Use the Checklist for Assessing Your Physical Environment on page 29 to do a complete evaluation.

Your Online Environment

Now more than ever, people judge you by your online environment. Look at everything from your webpages to your blogs to your online photos and announcements. Do they share common logos, colors, fonts, and layouts? Anyone should be able to look at a sampling of your online world and see that each piece belongs to the same organization. (Branches can have some autonomy, but still need to be clearly branded as part of the parent organization.)

Checklist for Assessing Your Physical Environment

Outdoors:

__ Area Signage: easy to find library building?

__ Signs on Site: clean, well lit, in good repair?

__ Parking Lot: clean, well lit, lines and arrows clearly painted?

__ Sidewalk: clear, safe, in good repair?

__ Directional Signage: way to main entrance clearly marked?

__ Landscaping: overgrown or well-kept?

__ Bike Racks and Benches: clean, in good repair?

__ Book Return: clean, needs painting?

__ Entrance: clear and inviting, or covered with paper signs?

__ Cleanliness: trash and recycling containers available, tended to?

Indoors:

__ Entryway: inviting, uncluttered, clear sightlines, directional signage?

__ Traffic Flow: organized for common patron movement?

__ Greeter: anyone to say hello or offer directions?

___ Coat Area: place to leave big coats, wet umbrellas, or strollers?

___ Circ/Ref Desks: easy to find, uncluttered, bright, space to put bags down?

___ Self-Check Stations: clear instructions, help nearby, space to put bags down?

___ Book Display Areas: stocked, up-to-date, interesting, covers facing out?

___ Bulletin Boards: enough tacks, up-to-date, some-what orderly?

___ Stacks: organized, clean, clearly marked?

___ Cleanliness: trash and recycling containers available, tended to?

___ Computer Area: clear signage, clean keyboards, enough workspace?

___ Seating Areas: comfortable, inviting, well-lit, enough electrical outlets?

___ Staff Areas: clean, neat, orderly, not embarrassing?

___ Meeting Rooms: neutral decor, flexible set-up, comfortable?

___ Restrooms: clean, well-stocked, functional, dry space to put bags down?

___ Café: clean, nice view, enough seats and outlets, trash/recycling bins?

While looks matter a lot, the content is clearly more important. The way it's organized and presented, the wording you choose, the features on your site, and ease of use must all be top-notch if your library is to be considered worth using. Still, the relationship between content and physical looks is symbiotic: No matter how great one is, if the other is bad, then the whole package is ruined.

Experts have written entire books about website usability, accessibility (software tools for disabled people, such as screen-reading software), format, and the more technical aspects that today's users expect. Those topics are incredibly important and are well worth reading about, but I can't go into all of that detail here. I'll let those books stand on their own merit, and I'll touch on the parts most relevant to promoting your services to customers.

If you're in a corporate, government, or academic library, or another type that lies under a parent organization, your website probably falls under that of the larger group. While you cannot change that fact, it's essential to convince The Powers That Be that your library needs to have a clear presence on the organizational home page. You need to have your link on that top-level page so that people who are looking for your information don't have to drill down to find it.

Once visitors reach your home page, it needs to be clear and uncluttered. Savvy web surfers expect to find what they want on a page within just a few seconds. So have only the most basic break-down of links on your front page, and make sure they're arranged in a fashion that's logical to laypeople (not to librarians). Here again, the site I mentioned in Chapter 2 called Library Terms That Users Understand (www.jkup.net/terms.html) is essential reading.

Here are the sorts of basic top-level links that I recommend:

> About the Library
> Get a Library Card
> Schedule of Events and Programs
> Contact Us
>
> Find Books
> Find Articles
> Find Info Online
> Find CDs, DVDs, Videos

> Stuff for Teens
> Stuff for Kids
> Stuff [for whomever your main customers are]
>
> Ask a Librarian
> News About Us
> Our Blog
> Our Photos
> Make a Donation
>
> FAQ
> Help
> Sitemap

As you can see, that list is long already. Once you add a main photo, maybe a scrolling news headline, and some icons, your page is busy enough. It's worth your time to learn how your own user population searches, even to do some surveys or studies of your own, to see how well your home page is serving them. This is especially true if you're updating your site—never release web changes without testing them on some patrons first!

I realize that designers of online environments are also concerned with keeping down the number of clicks it takes for people to reach their destinations. I still maintain that a home page shouldn't be too cluttered or intimidating. Once people click that first basic choice and get to the second-level page (the general topic they're looking for), then that page can hold more information and choices.

I'd like to address another topic here that nobody ever seems to plan for: leaving a website. No matter where you go on the site, there should be always be an option to log out or go back to the home page. This is more important, of course, when a specific log-in or authentication was required to get in. But as a web consumer myself, I'm often frustrated by how hard it is to find that button or icon. (On financial sites especially, it amazes me how they make it so hard to log in—for my own safety—and then have an itsy-bitsy button that says *log out* in some odd spot.) When you're placing your *log out* icon, remember that, in most languages, people read left to right and top to bottom. When they want to go to *Next* or *Sign Out*, they'll look at the right, then toward the bottom. If your website allows for this intuitive sort of behavior, people will use it more often.

Another important component you should have on your website is an area designed for people from the media. As a long-time writer and editor who has spent a lot of time on library websites, I can say from experience that this area is too often overlooked. Members of the media are always busy, always rushed, and always surrounded by tons of information and possibilities. To get the most coverage possible, you need to make your resources (including your staff members) easily available to them. I address the specifics of working with the media in Chapter 12, "Getting the Message Out," and even more in Chapter 13, "Using Your Website for Public Relations and Outreach."

During your overall evaluation, I encourage you to measure your media coverage. There are a couple of simple ways to do it. Try using the search engine alert services that do the work for you. Go to www.google.com/alerts or alerts.yahoo.com and type in your library's name or the word *library* plus your town, school, or company name. You can enter your own email address to subscribe to alerts that will tell you whenever your library is mentioned in a source that these search engines track.

To report the value of your media attention, you might still want to measure "column inches" of coverage the old-fashioned way. Here's how: Look at the article you're mentioned in and literally measure the inches. If each column is 3″ wide and the text is 5″ long, then it's simply 3 x 5 = 15 column inches' worth of coverage. To make your

Checklist for Assessing Your Online Environment

__ Represented on parent organization's top-level page?

__ Each Page: shares common colors, fonts, general design?

__ Log-in: simple, quick, no need to type in long barcode number?

__ Home Page: uncluttered, clear choices, no lingo?

__ Deeper Pages: logical layout, no lingo, link back to Home?

__ Content: well-organized, up-to-date?

__ Search Boxes: links to search tips?

__ Sign Off: obvious link in an obvious place?

__ Usability Testing: have you done any?

__ Accessibility Testing: have you done any?

__ Broken Links: tested for regularly?

__ Media Page : link on library home page?

   __ street and mailing addresses?

   __ press contact clearly stated?

   __ news and press releases?

   __ backgrounder?

   __ staff directory with phone numbers and emails?

   __ logo to download (high-resolution, in both color and black-and-white, in various graphics formats such as .jpg, .tif, and .eps)?

   __ official photos of buildings, director, mascot, events (high-resolution, in both color and black-and-white, in various graphics formats such as .jpg, .tif, and .eps)?

report pack more punch, you can put a monetary value on this by finding out what that medium charges for advertising (by the inch). Then you'll have an approximate value of the coverage that you got for your organization. For instance, if the ads cost $20 per inch, and you got 15 inches of copy, its value would be $300.

Use the Checklist for Assessing Your Online Environment on page 34 to do a complete evaluation.

Your Printed Materials

Printed materials still matter, and the more often you use them, the more important they are. Here again, it's essential to have a clear brand on every single piece of paper and correspondence that leaves your library. Colors and fonts, especially, must be consistent across the entire organization. Most brochures should have the same basic setup, which can then be tweaked if necessary. Ditto for letterhead, press releases, business cards, etc. There should be no doubt that they've all been cut from the same cloth—or in this case, printed from the same stock.

This brand identity is one of many reasons that it pays to have a professional designer, if not on staff, then at least on call. It's well worth your money to hire someone, at least to look at all your materials and design professional templates. If you can't pay a designer, barter with one. Offer to trade your research or testimonials for their work. Or ask someone who teaches design courses if they'd create a class assignment that would be actual work for your nonprofit. Once that's done, you can use those templates for a long time without needing to spend more on design until a special occasion or situation demands it. All of my experience in libraries and publishing has driven home this point: Consistency is king, and design speaks volumes. Having press releases going out from different branches on different paper with different layouts is never acceptable. It makes you look like an amateur. (Even if you *are*, never let it show, especially in such obvious ways. It does not win you sympathy or funding; it only makes you look like you don't know any better.)

I talk more about good print design in Chapter 11, "Basic Rules for Producing Good Promotional Materials," and I've included a useful article in Appendix B. But for now, start by using the Checklist for Assessing Your Printed Materials on this page to do a complete evaluation.

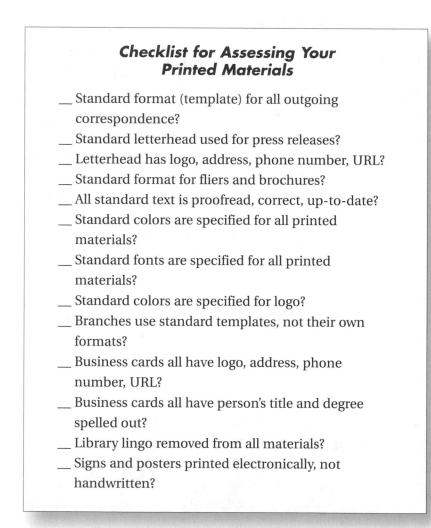

Checklist for Assessing Your Printed Materials

__ Standard format (template) for all outgoing correspondence?

__ Standard letterhead used for press releases?

__ Letterhead has logo, address, phone number, URL?

__ Standard format for fliers and brochures?

__ All standard text is proofread, correct, up-to-date?

__ Standard colors are specified for all printed materials?

__ Standard fonts are specified for all printed materials?

__ Standard colors are specified for logo?

__ Branches use standard templates, not their own formats?

__ Business cards all have logo, address, phone number, URL?

__ Business cards all have person's title and degree spelled out?

__ Library lingo removed from all materials?

__ Signs and posters printed electronically, not handwritten?

Your Customer Service Environment

We've all been in stores where the person behind the counter annoys us. As a marketing and PR consultant, I'm hypersensitive to customer service behavior. I hate it when clerks are talking to each other while ignoring me. I hate it even more when they're obviously going through the motions without any of the required emotions. Take the classic "Have a nice day." You can mumble the phrase expressionlessly, or you can bounce it out cheerfully, like you really mean it. How do your public service staffers do it?

I know it's not always easy to be cheerful when you're having a bad day, or to be courteous when a customer has been rude. I've worked at circ desks, I've worked in retail, and I've worked in restaurants. I know what it's like. But you know what? It's part of those jobs. When you're on the front lines, you need to just "suck it up" (as one colleague puts it) and be as kind as possible. Fake it when you have to. Act like you're working in a business where customer service can make or break you—because you are.

And if you hate canned lines like "Thanks for using the library" and "Have a nice day," then go with something more colloquial. Try "Come back if you need anything else" or even just "See you soon." The important thing is to train all front-line staff to be courteous no matter what. The adage is true that people who experience poor service tell many others, while people who get good service often keep it to themselves. It's a shame that good service stories don't spread like wildfire, but it's just a fact of life that we have to deal with.

Remember that personal, friendly, and truly helpful service is one of the few areas where live librarians can always outshine competitors like websites. A computer might search quickly, but it doesn't thank you for your business or open the door for you when your arms are full of books. The little things really do count.

Professional organizations that train secret shoppers and other experts who evaluate businesses work with their clients to create

Checklist for Assessing Your Customer Service Environment

Via Phone:

__ Did the phone ring more than three times before it was answered?

__ Did the employee greet you cheerfully and include his/her name? (If yes: name _____)

__ If you were transferred, did the hold music come on, and was it pleasant? Too loud?

__ Did the second employee pick up within 60 seconds?

__ Did the second employee greet you cheerfully, including his/her name? (If yes: _____)

__ Were you transferred to the correct person the first time?

__ If not, how many total transfers until you got the correct person?

__ Was the person you ultimately spoke to knowledgeable enough to help you?

__ If the employee could not help, did he/she say so and offer to find an answer, or to call you back within a specific amount of time?

__ Was your concern handled to your complete satisfaction?

__ Would you call this place for help again?

In Person:

__ Was there ample parking at the site?

__ Was the entrance easy to find and get into?

__ Were you greeted within 30 seconds of entering the building?

__ Was the greeter friendly?

__ Did the greeter tell you his/her name? (If yes: _____)

__ Did the greeter offer to direct you to what you needed?

__ Did the greeter direct you to the right place/person?

__ Did the second employee greet you with his/her name? (If yes: _____)

__ Was the second employee knowledgeable enough to help you?

__ If the employee could not help, did he/she say so and offer an alternative?

__ Was the place clean and tidy?

__ Was the public restroom clean and functional?

__ Was there a comfortable waiting/reading area?

__ Was there clear directional signage to service points, restrooms, etc.?

__ Was the checkout person friendly and efficient?

__ Did you get a farewell or an invitation to come back?

__ Was your concern handled to your complete satisfaction?

__ Would you come to this place for help again?

__ Did you feel you got the proper value/help for your money/time?

__ Did you get a follow-up call to see if you were satisfied?

lengthy checklists of specific items that the "spies" must report on. A full evaluation looks at a business' physical space and also scrutinizes its customer service. Report forms have spaces for details as small as how many times the phone rang before it was answered. The forms also demand details on whether workers followed the exact customer assistance scenarios they were trained in. And remember, even if you're not being evaluated professionally, everyday people notice these details and they base their opinions on them. As minute as some of the points may seem, they were built into the evaluation process because they've been proven to affect customers' opinions and attitudes. Use the Checklist for Assessing Your Customer Service Environment on page 38 to do a complete evaluation.

The Attitudes of Customers and Potential Users

As you assess the current state of your library from the customers' point of view, nothing is more important than—well, than the customers' point of view. If you're already soliciting feedback via a form on your website or a suggestion box, that's a great start. But those are narrow channels, and you're not controlling the questions. The only way to really get your users' point of view is to ask them for it. The main ways to do this are with surveys and focus groups.

Both surveys and focus groups can range from fairly small undertakings that you do yourself to very extensive projects that you can pay professionals thousands of dollars for. No matter where your organization goes on this scale, it's important to gather as much data as you can. I'll tell you how to handle both options here.

Surveying Library Users

There are many ways to survey your libraries' users, and in this section I'll discuss the simple methods first and work up to the more complicated ones. There are a thousand reasons to do surveys and a thousand ways to do them, so it's hard to write advice for a diverse group of readers. But all methods require the same basic steps, so I'll focus on those:

1. Decide exactly what you want the survey to accomplish.

2. Choose the target audience.

3. Carefully create your questions.

4. Test the questions on a few willing subjects and tweak as necessary.

5. Determine the method of distributing the survey and of getting it back.

6. Determine the method of tabulating the survey.

7. Choose incentives you can offer to encourage people to complete it.

8. Send the surveys out (with clear deadlines for return).

9. Send out reminders just before they're due back.

10. Tabulate survey results to create useful answers to its questions.

Now, here are some instructions and pointers for each step.

1. Decide exactly what you want the survey to accomplish. This might seem obvious, but people often skip this part or figure that "We just want to know what people think." But the more detailed your goals are, the more useful your resulting data will be. Writing down the goals of the survey forces you to be precise.

One of my favorite sayings is a simple one that serves me well in many endeavors: *Begin with the end in mind.* Think hard about how that applies to surveying people: Begin with the end in mind. What do you want this survey to tell you? If you don't know what your goal is, how will you know if you've achieved it? Do you want people to rate the services you already offer? Do you want them to suggest new ones? Do you want to see how you stack up against the internet? Do you want to see how tech-savvy customers are? Do you wonder why more people don't attend your programs? Do you want to know more about a particular target audience, or do you want to hear from everybody? Do you need to convince funders or to get permission for something?

Once you can articulate precisely what you intend to find out, you're ready for the next two steps.

2. Choose the target audience. When you practice true marketing, you'll do very little work involving the "general population," but you'll do a lot that's aimed at certain segments of it. Think about it: If you want to know why people don't come to storytimes, you only want to ask parents or caregivers. If you're trying to expand the Spanish-language parts of your collection, you want to ask Latinos what they'd like you to have. If you want to know whether your website is good enough, you'll want to question mostly off-site users.

Sure, there are times when you want to survey your entire county or client base or college. Reach out to everyone if your questions are general ones about open hours, basic perceptions of the library, or "Did you know that we do ___?" But in most cases, you need to create surveys that are customized for individual groups. (Find more details about separating people into target markets in Chapter 9, "Understanding the Cycle of True Marketing.") This allows you to keep them short and simple.

Obviously, you can't determine which market to ask until you know exactly what you're trying to learn.

3. Carefully create your questions. No matter which sort of survey you're launching, you need to begin by creating the questions. And while that may seem like the easy part, you shouldn't take it lightly. The data you get will only be as good as the questions you've asked. And nobody wants to take really lengthy surveys (more than 10 questions), so you need to pack a lot of punch into a few questions. That's another reason why you need to start by ascertaining *exactly* what you want to get out of this survey.

The most important thing about writing questions is to word them in such a way that you get the answers you want. I'm not talking about spin here; I'm talking about making them very clear. Any open-ended questions will likely result in answers that are all over the board. This is one reason why multiple-choice surveys are a bit safer. For instance, consider how people could respond to these slightly different questions:

- Do you think the library's budget should be increased? (open-ended)

- Does the library offer as many new DVDs as you'd like? (specific)

Don't ask general questions and then try to twist the responses to serve your needs. You can ask very clear, specific questions when you know exactly what sorts of answers you're seeking to accomplish your goals.

Here's another example:

- Does the library offer enough public computers? (open-ended)

- When you want to use a library computer, is one usually available? (specific)

4. Test the questions on a few willing subjects and tweak as necessary. Even if you spend hours going back and forth with your managers changing the wording of questions (and believe me, it happens), they still won't be as good as they can be. Remember, you have the background of library knowledge and the bias of knowing what you're trying to get at. Anyone who comes in cold and sees the survey for the first time could interpret your questions in a totally different way.

So, partly to avoid any one person getting his or her way on the wording, and partly to make sure that the questions will produce valid results, call in a few test subjects. They should not be coworkers, and not even family members if you can help it. (Those who live with you and hear about your work all the time will share some of your biases and interpretations of words and phrases.) Make it a point to grab a few acquaintances, or a couple of favorite patrons, or members of other organizations you belong to—book clubs, churches, scout groups, business associations—anyone who will give you 10 minutes. This doesn't need to be a formal test. Just listen and observe as your helpful guinea pigs read the questions. Ask them to talk aloud about what each question is asking and to tell you if anything is unclear.

While it's tempting to skip this step, I seriously urge you not to. Given all the time and effort that goes into a survey project, it would be awful if a poorly worded question mangled your important results. Just think, if your survey is only 10 questions long, and the answers to even one are skewed, you've lost 10 percent of your hard-earned data.

5. Determine the method of distributing the survey and of getting it back. There are many ways to distribute surveys, and your choice will be determined in large part by who and where your target audience is. But I'll list a variety of methods here to help you find one that's right for your situation:

- Mail is an obvious possibility, but you'll need to have proper addresses, spend money on printing and postage, and provide self-addressed stamped envelopes (SASEs) if you want people to respond.

- Live surveys allow you to catch people while they're in your library or at another site, like a shopping center, fairground, business meeting, school, senior center, or anywhere you're doing an outreach activity.

- Target-related surveys let you question a very specific crowd that's already present for a similar event. For instance, at a book club meeting you can ask attendees about what else they like to read, whether the meeting space is comfortable, or whether they'd be interested in related events such as author appearances.

- Piggyback distribution is when you join another organization that's already sending something to your target audience and ask its managers to include your survey. This method can save you money and effort. Of course it works best if what you're piggybacking on is something important that recipients are sure to open, like utility bills, paychecks, companywide announcements, or tax statements.

- Websites can host surveys, with a temporary icon on the home page leading to a questionnaire that people can fill in electronically. You'll need to give visitors an incentive to get them to click through and to fill it in, though.

- An email blast is a simple way to send a survey to everybody who has registered their email address with your library. Beware, though, of sending to people who don't expect a message from you, or people who did not directly give you their email address (i.e., don't use address lists from other institutions). Email surveys work best when interested people have previously agreed to receive emails from the library, which is often the case with teen groups or book clubs.

- Online questionnaires sometimes pop up at the end of a transaction, like a chat reference session or an online purchase. When people get a chance to immediately evaluate something they've just done, they're likely to do it, and you can be assured that their thoughts about the transaction are fresh in their minds.

- Survey via partnership means that other people who hold sway with your target group could hand out printed surveys for you. A teacher could give them to students (or to parents at a school event); a preacher could give them to a congregation; a businessperson could take them to a Chamber of Commerce meeting; a faculty member could distribute them at a meeting. You have a great chance to reach special populations this way.

- Telephone surveys are usually done by paid corporations, and not everyone looks upon them favorably. But if the callers are trained to immediately assure people that they're doing a short survey for the local library, results can be good.

6. Determine the method of tabulating the survey. The way you'll tabulate your survey results depends partly on how you distributed it and partly on how you set it up. Multiple-choice questionnaires are much easier to evaluate than those with open-ended questions. If you can reach your target audience online, there are survey tools you can use (like SurveyMonkey, www.surveymonkey.com) that will add up the answers for you. If you hire a group to do a professional telephone survey, they'll create a report to your specifications. If you're passing out paper, then someone is going to have to spend a good bit of time carefully tallying up the results. Again, begin with the end in mind: Make sure that you have the manpower or the money needed to collect all the data you gather into a useful report. If you don't, the survey was wasted.

7. Choose incentives you can offer to encourage people to complete it. What's appropriate here depends on your method of distribution, your target market, and the number of surveys you're putting out. To me, though, this is one of the fun parts!

Your method of distributing and collecting completed surveys impacts your choice of incentives. If you're physically dealing with people, you can give out just about anything. If a trusted associate is passing out surveys for you, be sure to ask him or her what would be most comfortable to handle wherever he or she is. If your survey is conducted via mail or phone, or if it's going out to a large group of people (say, more than 50), then it's easiest to enter respondents for a chance to win a couple of big prizes.

Here are some small, inexpensive prizes you can give out individually:

Gifts for anyone:
- Pieces of wrapped candy or mints
- Packs of chewing gum
- Pens or pencils
- Pads of sticky notes
- Coupons for goods or services
- Single carnations
- Coupons for the library café
- Reusable canvas shopping bags
- Bottles of water
- Choice of book from your book sale rack
- Golf tees or balls

- Office or desk items

- Computer screen cleaners

Gifts for youth and teens:
- Gel bracelets

- School supplies like highlighters

- T-shirts

- Coupons for a game store

- Stickers

- Balloons

- Flying discs

Anything you give out that's printable should have your library's name and URL, of course! And don't forget that you don't necessarily have to buy everything. Many of the incentives listed could be provided by local vendors in exchange for publicity or as a goodwill gesture for your nonprofit organization.

Even if you do give out small incentive gifts to everyone, it still helps to enter them in a drawing for something bigger and better! There are several valid reasons to do this. The first is to get more-accurate responses. Ask yourself: If somebody wanted you to stop what you were doing and fill out a survey in exchange for a piece of candy, how much time and thought would you put into your answers? Probably just enough to get the candy. But what if you were offered the candy *and* an entry to win, say, a $50 gift card, a pair of movie tickets, or even an iPod? You'd probably feel like you'd better bother to really think about your answers. You'd have an incentive to answer honestly and thoughtfully (hence the name "incentives"). This is especially important because, to be entered in a drawing, people need to give you their contact information.

That keeps them from quickly checking *Yes* to everything, grabbing the candy, and running away.

The second reason to have a drawing is that it gives you a chance to legitimately collect names, addresses, email addresses, and phone numbers. Collecting this data on surveys can work both for and against you, though. If the main prize you're offering is good enough, people will be happy to give you that info. But whether you dare ask for their personal info should depend largely on your survey questions. If you're asking things like "Did you know about this service?" or "Would you be likely to attend programs like these?" then respondents shouldn't mind including their names and addresses. But if you're asking about thorny issues such as, "Rate these in order of where you'd like your Local Improvement Tax Dollars to go: Library, Police Department, Parks, Downtown Development," then people might prefer to be anonymous.

A third reason to ask for names and addresses is to give you a pool of people to call on for further info. You might survey 200 people and find that 20 said they'd be very interested in attending author appearances. If your library wants to explore that option, you now have 20 people you could call in to do a focus group to help shape that new offering.

One more reason is that collecting personal data while doing a survey simply gives you more bang for your buck. You can use it to build or update databases of patron information, or to do further demographic studies to see if people in certain areas are seeking similar things.

Remember, though, to include a sentence on the form that tells people that filling in that data can give the library a right to contact them with occasional information. Provide a check-off box where they can opt in or opt out of being contacted for reasons other than prize notification.

8. Send the surveys out (with clear deadlines for return). When your surveys are finally ready to be distributed, take timing into account. For instance, if you're emailing them to businesspeople, don't do so on a weekend because they're likely to view weekend email as spam and just delete it. If you're sending the survey to people involved in any sort of school, make sure it doesn't go out just before a holiday or break, or it's likely to get lost in the shuffle.

It's essential to have a clear deadline for the surveys to be returned. In fact, I always put the deadline in two or three different spots, just to make sure that the recipients can't miss it. Here again, consider timing. It makes more sense to have something due on a Friday than it does on a Monday. Making the deadline a memorable date, like the first or last day of a month, helps as well. I once sent out a survey that I didn't need back until April 20, but I made the deadline April 15 (the date that annual U.S. income taxes are always due) because I knew that would stick in people's minds.

9. Send out reminders just before they're due back. In my experience, there are two kinds of people—those who do things immediately and those who put them off till the last minute. (Sadly, I belong to the latter group.) This is obvious when you send out surveys. When doing surveys, I always get a bunch back right away, then returns slow to a trickle. So a day or two before the deadline I email everyone to remind them "Surveys are due back this Friday; if you still want to participate, now's the time!" That always brings in a new flurry of responses.

It always pays to remind people when you can. Realistically, you know that answering your questions is not the top thing on people's minds, and so even many people who really intend to do it never quite get there. If they meant to respond, then a gently worded last-minute reminder will often get them to drop everything else temporarily because they get that "it's my last chance!" feeling. Don't be afraid to invoke that; nobody else is afraid to do it!

And don't feel that reminding people is being pushy. Respondents have often thanked me for doing it. Take the attitude that your survey really matters and is worth the time to complete. If you don't, who will?

10. Tabulate survey results to create useful answers to its questions. Finally, the data you've longed for is in your hands. You're eager to see all the answers, and it's fun looking through the surveys to see the interesting responses. But to really make sense of it all, you (or some willing soul) is going to have to slog through the task of tabulating all those answers.

If you've done an online survey, the tabulation has probably been done for you. This is really the way to go if you can. If you're facing a pile of papers and are starting by hand, you might try the method that I've used in the past. First, I swore under my breath and vowed never to tabulate a survey by hand again. Then, to tabulate multiple-choice questions, I sat down with a blank paper copy of the survey, then took completed surveys one by one and made tally marks next to the multiple choice answers.

When my returns also had open-ended questions that respondents wrote in answers for, they clearly took more effort to add up. (And yes, more swearing ensued.) The best way I found was to start typing all the responses for a given question. Inevitably, many would give the same response, although each person would word it differently. So once I'd typed out the answer, "I haven't been to a library in a couple years" I would add tally marks next to it when I came upon similar responses. Here again, begin with the end in mind. Will the managers who read your results really want to know every detail? You'll soon realize that, to report the numbers, you'll need to group them into categories. In this case they might be "Visited library within the past year," "Hasn't visited in 2 or 3 years," "Can't remember the last time they visited," and "Has never visited the library." These categories will make themselves apparent as you add up the answers.

Clearly, tabulating by hand is time-consuming and tedious, and I advise it only for small surveys (less than 50 responses). But your tabulation options depend largely on how you are able to deliver your survey to your target market. Not everyone has a computer and even some who do are not comfortable doing online surveys. If you relied on a pastor to distribute the survey to his or her congregation, you're getting paper back. If you surveyed folks who stopped by your table at the county fair, you're probably getting paper back. (Although some librarians have taken laptops to such events and asked people to do short questionnaires that way.)

Although I've admitted that you may be in for some tedious tallying, don't avoid doing surveys just because of that. The real data that you get from real live people is more than worth the effort. In fact, it's one of the only things that really gives you a basis for making important decisions about what products and services your library should offer. Consider the value of real, quantitative, personal data. Gathering and using it will help your organization waste less time and money on things that people don't want and won't use. It can prevent you from guessing which programs to offer (and fund). And it gives you a firm leg to stand on when a manager says, "But I think we should do it this way." Having info in hand helps your case when you reply, "But 84% of the patrons we surveyed said that way doesn't work for them." Touché.

Focus Groups with Library Users

Conducting focus groups is a slightly more exact science than doing surveys. It demands quite a bit of time and effort, but the results can be extremely rewarding and useful. Again, you can set up a few small groups yourself, or you can hire professional firms to facilitate lots of varied focus groups. The choice depends on your needs and, of course, your budget. But the time and money spent on focus groups *is* worthwhile. In her *MLS* article "How to Conduct a Focus Group," researcher/professor/consultant Marie Radford pointed out, "In this era of unremittingly taut budgets, people are paying more attention to accountability and assessment activities to determine whether limited funds are being spent wisely. ... More librarians are finding evaluation activities thrust upon them (ready or not!) as part of their job responsibilities" (Jan./Feb. 2008, p. 1).

There are a number of steps necessary for planning and conducting focus groups. (You'll note that many are the same as for doing surveys.) As I did in the previous section, I'll list all of the steps first then go into detail about each one:

1. Decide exactly what you want the focus group to accomplish and who can make that happen.

2. Choose the target audience.

3. Carefully create your questions, thinking ahead to how you'll be able to interpret responses to create useful data.

4. Test the questions on a few willing subjects and tweak as necessary.

5. Determine the method of recruiting participants.

6. Decide what incentives to offer to encourage people to participate; order the items ahead of time if necessary.

7. Set times and places for the focus groups to occur.

8. Invite many participants (with the promise of snacks, incentives, and a clear deadline for RSVPs).

9. Hold the actual focus groups, taking careful notes, and give participants the promised thank you gifts.

10. Study the responses and collect them into a useful report.

Here are some instructions and pointers for each step.

1. Decide exactly what you want the focus group to accomplish and who can make that happen. The key word here is *exactly.* People often say "We just want to know what the public thinks." But, as with most anything you set out to do, the more detailed your goals are, the more useful your resulting data will be. Writing down specific goals for your focus groups forces you to be precise.

As I explained in detail in step one of the survey section, it's essential to begin with the end in mind. This comes to light even more with focus groups, because you have to choose someone from outside your library to have the actual discussions with your participants. (These must always be moderated by a person who is unbiased and unrelated to your organization so participants will give honest answers.) If you can't articulate exactly what you want to learn from the group discussions, then you can't tell the moderator, so he or she cannot steer the talks in the direction necessary to guarantee your satisfaction with the answers.

Once you can articulate your goals, you have to find a moderator to work with. Professional firms are great for this purpose if you can afford one. Barring that, seek out a library consultant, or check with local college professors or business people. You need someone who can be impartial, who understands libraries, and is comfortable leading discussions. Once you find this partner, you're ready for the next two steps.

2. Choose the target audience. It seems obvious that you'll want to invite participants who can answer your burning questions. Once you know exactly what those questions are, you can decide who can answer them. And since there are a million questions, then there are a million possibilities for different focus groups.

The essential tactic here is to keep each group homogeneous. In other words, you want the same sorts of people in each group. Let me explain more clearly through some quick examples. Let's say that senior citizens are a big part of your area's population, and you want to know what sorts of services and programs they want. Make sure that everyone you invite to the focus group is a senior, but within that group of seniors, also make sure you get men and women of differing ages and abilities.

Do match your targets to your questions. If you're targeting employees of your corporation to get their overall impressions, then make sure you choose women and men from different departments who work on various levels, from administrative assistant right up to CEO. Also look for people who have been at your company for different lengths of time, from newbies to old hats. The broader your cross-section is, the more complete your data will be. Of course, if your questions are more specific, you want to narrow the field, perhaps to just the accountants or just the managers of one department. (See Chapter 9 for more details about separating people into target markets.)

3. Carefully create your questions, thinking ahead to how you'll be able to interpret responses to create useful data. Writing questions for focus groups is less tricky than for surveys, because surveys are often filled out when you're not there to help interpret questions. In a focus group, the moderator asks the initial question, but then can explain it further and can guide conversation to make sure that people give the sorts of answers you're looking for. Additionally, most of the questions can be open-ended rather than multiple choice. This means that questions are much easier to ask—but the answers are much harder to tabulate. So beginning with the end in mind will serve you well when you're trying to make sense out of a bunch of group conversations. And it's worth repeating that the data you get will only be as good as the questions you've asked.

I'll use a sample survey question from the previous section to illustrate how you can dig for deeper answers in focus groups. The question is, "When you want to use a library computer, is one usually available?" As people answer yes or no, the moderator can ask, "What time of day or what day of the week do you usually use the library's computers?" Then later you can use that information as evidence of the demand for more computers in your next budget request.

In a typical 60- to 90-minute focus group, you can cover only about 10 questions, tops, which is another reason to choose your questions carefully.

4. Test the questions on a few willing subjects and tweak as necessary. Make sure your questions are not worded in such a way as to influence the answers. They should allow your participants plenty of space for conversation and free-flowing thought. The beauty of hearing from focus groups is that people often learn their own true opinions about something for the first time as they talk it out with others.

Remember to test your questions before finalizing them. And don't test them on a fellow librarian or anyone else who knows your work well; test them on the type of people who will comprise your actual focus group. Also, if you're hiring a professional firm or an outside moderator, they need to be part of the group that has final say on the content, context, and wording of your questions.

5. Determine the method of recruiting participants. Here's the trickiest part of doing focus groups: How do you get people to bother to come? In a world where everyone seems busier than ever, why would anyone want to commit an hour or more to talk with strangers about library services or policies?

I wish I had an easy answer here, but I don't. You'll have to do some good old-fashioned hard work. And your level of success will depend largely on who is in your target market and how well you really know them. What matters to them? What makes them tick? You can learn a lot about people just by going through this recruiting process. Some groups will obviously be more difficult to lure in than others, so this step deserves a lot of thought.

Many factors will affect your success in attracting participants, including what incentive gifts you offer them and what time and place you choose to hold the events. These two are so important that I've made them their own steps in the process. Another factor to consider is, who really cares about this issue? Who has something to say? People who already have strong feelings about something are more likely to accept an opportunity to voice them.

Here are some recruiting methods that librarians have used:

- Start with in-house groups, like members of an advisory board or book club.
- Invite a ready-made group such as department heads, a project team, a particular class, or a faculty group.
- Use a social networking site to find a group of people that fits your need.
- Announce your project in your library newsletter or on your website.
- Put an ad in a newspaper or on a radio station that reaches the target market.
- Ask each staff member to find one willing friend.
- Turn to a professional group that includes recruitment as part of its services.
- Call numbers right out of the phone book.
- Try a word-of-mouth campaign.

You should know that you'll need to invite many, many more people than you'll actually want in each group. If you want 10 people, you will need to ask 30 or 40. Accept RSVPs from 15 or 18, and you'll end up with about 10 who actually show up on the appointed date.

6. Decide what incentives to offer to encourage people to participate; order the items ahead of time if necessary. Offering incentives is optional for survey participants, but it's a must when you're asking people to spend time in focus groups. Since they are committing to an event, transporting themselves somewhere, and spending at least an hour there on your behalf, it's the least you can do. Most pros wouldn't dream of skipping incentives for focus group participants. It's the norm. In fact, many people won't volunteer to do this without one.

If you're concerned about the cost, well, try putting a price on the value of the consumer information you're getting from the event. Then add the money you'll save by not running programs that would have failed. Add in the bonus value of the goodwill you'll reap just because you're showing your constituents that you care about their opinions and intend to act on them. Then ask yourself whether $10 or $25 per person is really too much to spend for those results.

When deciding what incentives to offer, what's appropriate clearly depends a lot on your target market. Put yourself in their shoes: What would you like to get? What is an hour of your time worth? This is not the time to be cheap because what you give out will reflect on your library. You don't want people to walk away saying, "They think all I'm worth is this plastic toy? Humph!" Because you know that they'll tell two friends, who will tell two other friends.

Here are a few ideas for incentives that aren't too cheap or too expensive. But I encourage you to be creative and to choose items that really fit the people who will be getting them:

- Imprinted canvas shopping bags with some goodies inside
- Movie tickets

- Gift cards for local businesses such as drugstores, card shops, grocery stores, music shops, etc.

- Products or services provided by your business partners

- As I write this, American adults would sit through just about anything to get some free gasoline!

And by all means, don't forget: Everybody likes plain old money! If you feel awkward handing out cash, you can buy gift cards from American Express or various banks that people can spend like cash just about anywhere.

If you're forced to settle for inexpensive or unexciting thank-you gifts, you can still sweeten the pot by entering all of your participants in a drawing to win one or two big pricey prizes. Try reaching out to local businesses for sponsorships. Other librarians have landed donated prizes like a camera, an iPod, dinner for two, and a bicycle. Think about fun things that people might not spend money on for themselves. What about a free limousine for a night, or something signed by a celebrity? Or something wild, like a hot-air balloon ride? The sky's the limit!

7. Set times and places for the focus groups to occur. The first thing to decide as far as time and place is whether you can hold focus groups in any of your library buildings. Do you have meeting rooms that will work, and are they private enough? For instance, don't plan to use the meeting room right next to the director's office and ask people who are sitting there to give you their candid thoughts about the library. (They might fear that the walls have ears, so to speak.) If you want to work outside your library, then where can you go? Will you have to pay to use the space?

You'd be surprised by how much your choice of time and place impacts people's decisions about whether to attend your focus group. As always, make choices based on the people you're trying to attract, and make it as convenient for them as possible. If you're trying to question county or municipal employees, then meet in one of their buildings and offer lunch as part of the incentive. If you want college students, pick a place where they are comfortable. If you're going for parents of school-age kids, maybe you can meet in a place where they'd be anyway—near their kids' soccer practice or martial arts class, or even in their school building. No matter what, if you choose a place that's not out of the way for your audience, you'll be more successful.

8. Invite many participants (with the promise of snacks, incentives, and a clear deadline for RSVPs). Plan your focus group the same way you'd plan a party. Invite your guests in whatever fashion suits the group (phone, email, paper invitations). In order to get a full house, invite lots and lots of people, because you know that many of them won't show up. Ideally, you want to gather small groups of just 8 to 12 people. In order to have a group of that size, you should invite about 40 people to start with. Hopefully you'll get 15 to 20 acceptances, and then 8 to 12 of those will actually appear. (Calling people with gentle reminders the day before or the day of is a very good idea, especially if you've invited them weeks in advance.)

In your invitations, make it clear that participants need to RSVP by a certain day and time so you can finalize your plans. And spell out exactly what you're willing to give them in return for their time. Your carefully chosen gifts should not be nice surprises at the end; they should be true incentives to attend, promised from the beginning to encourage people to help you.

It's also important that you have snacks and drinks on hand to keep them happy. Yes, on top of other incentives, it's common focus group courtesy to set out a little spread. Simple finger food and a few beverage choices are fine. And don't be afraid to highlight that in your invitations, because it *will* make a difference in whether people come. I don't advise going too heavy on the food, because after all, your guests won't talk and chew at the same time (hopefully). You want their mouths to be free for plenty of talking. But you should treat these folks as valued guests while they're helping you, and your hospitality will make an impression on them. Most will be thrilled if you offer coffee and tea, bottled water, and a few soft drinks. Add a little bite-sized fruit (grapes are perfect) and cheese with crackers, and you've got a data-filled party going on.

9. Hold the actual focus groups, taking careful notes, and give participants the promised thank-you gifts. When the big day finally comes, you need to be prepared to capture all of the information that you've worked so hard to get. This is not a one-person job.

The main worker here is the moderator, who leads the discussion where it needs to go. He or she needs to be very familiar with the questions and even more familiar with the library's goals for the event.

In addition, the pros recommend that you have someone who's tasked specifically with taking detailed notes, so the moderator can concentrate on the conversation. Obviously this "scribe" should be familiar enough with libraries to understand what everyone's saying and to record their thoughts rapidly. Nobody can (or should) record every word, which is why it helps to keep the event's goals at the forefront. The moderator and scribe should be listening especially for key words and phrases. It's much easier to note how many were for and against certain ideas than to transcribe every word of the discussion and try to assess it later.

Neither the moderator nor the note-taker should be an employee of the library. If they are, the guests are not likely to feel comfortable being honest.

Ideally, you'll also have a way to record the entire session. This not only takes some pressure off the scribe, but it also gives the scribe and moderator the chance to go back and listen again as they put together all the reactions for the final report. It lets them note intonations and times when the discussion was either heated or mellow. So if at all possible, use a video camera or tape recorder to preserve the discussion. If you're doing this, though, the moderator must tell all the participants up front that they're being recorded, and assure them that the library client will not see or hear the tape. Convince them that they'll remain safely anonymous so they won't be afraid to dish the real dirt.

One tip here: I recommend not giving folks their incentives until the event is over. Handing them out right away wastes precious discussion time. Waiting also prevents people from trying to slip out early.

10. Study the responses and collect them into a useful report. Sifting through diverse answers and thoughts from notes and tapes can be a very difficult job. If possible, specify that the moderator do the full report. If you must do it, it will help if the scribe has made some general notes to indicate how many people were positive or negative about each idea and topic. Start with those general numbers and go into more detail from there.

Note especially when participants were surprised by something ("I had no idea they would do background research for my experiment!"), because this often points to a topic that the librarians have not publicized successfully enough. Likewise, report when participants felt very positive ("I've always loved libraries since I was a kid!") or negative ("I really don't see why they're still asking for money when nobody's using the place.").

I've also found it very valuable to record some specific quotes that really drive a point home. Quotes from participants are more powerful than any sentence written by the author of a report. I'll share some good ones from focus groups I did a few years ago. (See the sidebar on page 63, "Interesting Quotes I've Gathered.") I included each of these in my final report, because I thought they'd make an impact on the administrators who would read it.

Interesting Quotes I've Gathered

These are some insightful tidbits I've gathered from various focus groups I've conducted with library users, nonusers, and staff members:

- "You can travel the world reading a book." (happy patron)
- The expanded branch is a "palatial facility," like "the Taj Mahal of Libraries." (impressed patron)
- "Barnes & Noble took over what the library used to be." (former patron)
- "Libraries are for scholars." (nonuser)
- Library has the "ambiance of a hospital." (nonuser)
- "We shoot ourselves in the foot with what we give to the public." (staff member lamenting ineffective, lingo-filled promo material)
- "For every part of your life, we have something for you." (outreach staffer)
- "Both the Spanish-speaking communities and the Orthodox Jewish communities are 'word of mouth' communities, and our current way of making the public aware doesn't work." (smart staffer)
- "I myself am often unaware of program events held in the library." (honest staffer)
- "We make it hard for people to use us by refusing to get up-to-date with technology, letting our website fall behind the times, and by not doing what we can for customers to have an easy Amazon/Google-like experience on our website." (brutally honest staffer)

The most important section of the report is the Executive Summary, because (sadly) that's the only part that most busy managers will ever read. To be a complete record of the event, however, the final report should always include the exact list of questions asked, along with the responses and notes on the discussion of each one.

A Word About Users vs. Nonusers

People who don't use your services at all are extremely important. It's tempting to think, "Let's not bother with them; we have enough trouble keeping current patrons happy." But please don't. Nonusers, in any library setting, represent several things. They are, first, potential customers. (Do you see any big businesses ignoring potential customers? No! They want everybody to be part of their market share.) Second, they are the key to understanding why not everyone values libraries—their feelings and thoughts are the holy grail for librarians who want to understand what people do and do not want, need, use, or value.

It can be difficult to get nonusers to participate in surveys or focus groups. Sometimes they see no reason to go through the exercise, yet sometimes they're happy to tell you what they feel. I urge you to tap these people for information. Sure they'll say things you might not want to hear, but isn't that part of learning, of getting the big picture?

There *are* ways to get this target market to participate. I heard of one library that was doing a user focus group (with people they knew and trusted), and organizers asked each participant to bring a nonuser friend along. Those friends went to a separate group that met in another room during the same time period. One nonuser group I ran was recruited by the librarians themselves, who asked friends and relatives to attend. (Hey, guilt can work!)

When you're doing an on-location survey out in public, make sure that one of the first questions on the page is "How often do you use the library?" and be sure to include specific questions for people who respond, "Hardly ever" or "Not at all."

Don't be afraid to hear what nonusers have to say about libraries, because we need to heed their voices most of all.

A Few Favorite Tips and Tricks

Here are some tips and tricks to help you through the work of both surveys and focus groups:

- Hold your first groups with friendly, safe, ready-made groups of people—your teen advisory board, very frequent users, Friends, appointed board, trustees, or staff members. This will help you build your confidence.

- Base your first focus group questions on hot topics that people will really want to talk about. That gets discussions going.

- For on-site surveys, have clipboards and pens to let people fill out paper forms without having to wait for a spot at your table or booth. Have a few chairs for them too. Anything that will make it physically easier for people to complete the surveys will increase your return.

- Use humor in focus groups to put people at ease.

- Promise participants that you're really going to read and ponder their opinions. Then follow through and prove that you've done that by announcing your decisions, changes, or new services to them.

- On the form you use to sign people up for library cards, have a space for an email address and a note saying that filling in the address means the signer agrees to receive occasional emails from the library. You can use these later to email surveys or to recruit people for focus groups.

An Inconvenient Truth

As you've realized by now, doing just one survey or focus group won't give you a complete picture. You'll need to do a number of them, each aimed at learning about one particular group of people, or at answering one particular set of questions. Yes, this means doing more work, but don't panic. As with many repeated tasks, once you have a template and a plan, the later work goes more quickly than the initial work. And the better your initial plan is, the more smoothly everything goes thereafter. Beginning with the end in mind helps ensure that everything runs well.

Chapter 4

Using Demographic, Geographic, and Census Data

In Chapter 3 you learned how to assess your library's situation by studying your current promotional materials, your physical and online environment, your customer service, and the attitudes of your users and nonusers. All of this knowledge that you've drawn from inside your own library is very valuable and can help show you what you need to change, but there is still more data to gather. This time you need to look outside of your building and your institution to learn about the surrounding area and the people who live there. Then I'll show you one more tool you can use for an overall analysis.

It's important to get to know people if you intend to serve them well, so it makes sense to study data about them. Hey, librarians are all about knowing how to find and use information, right? And you realize that there are tons of sources out there. Here's a question for American readers: Have you ever considered using official U.S. Census Bureau data for your own purposes? What about maps and geographic surveys? They can do a lot for you if you know how to use them.

For my readers outside the U.S., I don't know the details about your versions of a census, the official governmental tally of residents. But, most countries do count their citizens on a regular basis. If you can access that data, then you too will be able to benefit in the ways that I'm about to explain.

ping Into Demographic and
Geographic Data

I never thought too deeply about U.S. Census Bureau data until the first time I heard a presentation by Dr. Christie Koontz at an American Library Association conference many years ago. She taught me just about everything I know about this aspect of marketing, and I'm still learning from her. I was so impressed with her work that I invited her to write an article for my *Marketing Library Services* (*MLS*) newsletter back in 2001, an overview called "Marketing Research Is a Useful Tool for Libraries" (Oct./Nov. issue). I invited her to become a regular contributor to *MLS*, and in 2002 we created the "Customer-Based Marketing" column, which she still writes today. Koontz's background in public relations and advertising, journalism, library management, research, and marketing has provided the perspective for her core belief that virtually all library decisions should be based on research. And when you hear her talk about it (she's an active LIS marketing teacher and presenter), it all makes incredibly good sense.

One of Koontz's many hats is that of director of the GeoLib program at Florida State University (FSU) in Tallahassee. It's part of the College of Information there, and its home page (www.geolib.org) succinctly explains what it's all about: "GeoLib's mission is twofold. First, to improve access to digital geographic information in libraries, regardless of whether the information is desired by library users or by library managers. And secondly, to apply marketing solutions to library problems." In other words, GeoLib combines geographic and demographic data and shares it with public librarians so they can understand their physical locales and can use that knowledge to serve residents better.

GeoLib offers many services to libraries, including doing studies and analysis of potential customer markets. One of its major accomplishments was creating the Public Library Geographic Database (PLGDB) with its project partner, FSU's Information

Institute. This database includes the locations of America's 16,000 public libraries, population characteristics from the Census that describe the people who use them, and library usage stats from the National Center for Educational Statistics. The Geographic Information System (GIS) data that PLGDB was built on is what GeoLib relies on as benchmarks for further studies. There's so much data that it can seem intimidating, but the ultimate goal is to introduce librarians to this geographic and demographic data so they can combine it with their own patron data to see an actual picture of the people and areas that they serve (and those they don't). Having this picture can inform everything that your organization does.[1]

How Census Data Can Help Public Librarians

How does it work? Koontz advises public librarians to learn about their current and potential customers by studying the official data about the area they serve, particularly the Census and local geographic data. The Census results tell you what sorts of people live in which places, including information on age, sex, race, ethnicity, household income, education level, number of children, etc., and the data is updated every 10 years. Since the government first began counting U.S. citizens in 1790, it has added many other questions to the long version of the Census that reflect vast changes in society. Koontz explained a few interesting additions in an article she wrote for *MLS* in 2003:

> As the nation became increasingly complex, the length of the questionnaire grew. For example, the Great Depression of the 1930s added questions regarding unemployment and income, as well as migration. The explosion of the automobile added questions about mode of travel to work, what time people left for work, and the availability of carpools. This year, there is one new question, added by the

Welfare Reform Act, concerning grandparents as care-givers. Additionally, the question on disability was expanded to cover vision and hearing impairment, and disabilities associated with learning and remembering. Finally, a revision of the question on race allows select-ing one or more race categories.[2]

So if you haven't looked at Census results in a while (or ever), I think you'll find that they contain an incredible amount of fasci-nating information. It's all been gathered and paid for already, so it's just sitting there waiting for you, and it's available in different sorts of products for different needs and levels of expertise. It all comes via internet, CD, or DVD, some goes into print, and you can download much of it for free from www.census.gov. Another thing you may not realize is how specific the Census regions can be. You can get a data set that covers the whole country, or a region, state, county, etc.—all the way down to a city block. You can look at other spatial units such as school districts, legislative districts, even traf-fic analysis zones. Amazing.

But how can you use all of this to your advantage?

Well, if you get a map of Census information and combine it with your list of cardholder addresses, you'll have a great portrait of the types of people that are using your library (and, by omission, what types are not). You might see that just a small percentage of a certain minority has library cards. You could see evidence that most families with young children have cards.

In many regions, people who share ethnic backgrounds tend to settle near each other, and knowing where there are pockets of culturally connected people can be useful as well. This can help with planning programs and with deciding where to put special collections (or multilingual staff), among other things. There's just so much data that you can simply *access*, without having to gather it on your own; it's crazy not to use it in order to better understand the people who live in your service area. But that's only the beginning.

How Geographic Data Can Help Public Librarians

Adding geographic data opens up another treasure trove of useful information. Overlaying a mapped-out version of your patron address database onto a map shows you exactly where your users live as well as areas where no users live. It can be a real eye-opener to realize that a majority of your patrons are clustered in a certain area, or that you have almost no cardholders from another location. Identifying where nonusers live can often help you figure out *why* they don't use the library. Koontz and her associates have done numerous studies[3,4] on how the location of a library affects how and if people will use it. They have found that geographic barriers, including major highways, railroad tracks, rivers, and bridges, have a huge effect on usage.

After a map reveals pockets of residential areas where you have few or no cardholders, you may discover that there is no public transportation between that area and your library. Even new construction can place barriers between you and your potential users. As more buildings and more traffic make it harder to get around towns and cities, this can cut people off from your services. Of course, understanding why they're not coming in would be the first step in changing things so that they can or will start coming in. And as you can imagine, studying maps like this can also point you to where there are unmet needs, showing you where should build your next branch or kiosk.

On the other side of the coin, this data can also explain why some library branches do so poorly that they are targeted for closure. Koontz and two fellow researchers recently finished a grant-funded study and published a paper called "Why Public Libraries Close."[5] She wrote a summary of the full-length paper for the Jan./Feb. 2009 issue of *MLS*.[6]

One reason that it's important to study public library closures is that it gives you quantitative ammunition to use if your own library is ever targeted for closure due to lack of funding. If you can combine demographic and geographic data to paint a picture of all of the people who will be affected if your library disappears, then you can show lawmakers all of their constituents who will suffer without you. Obviously that gives you a better chance of staying open.

So now you see how useful it can be to study data from outside your library and to better understand your physical location. Granted, incorporating all of this into your market research is a big step, but it's almost certain to result in big revelations. If you've ever wondered why you have few patrons from such-and-such neighborhood, or why overall usage skyrocketed after you moved to a new building across the river, or why circulation dropped once the new shopping mall was built, this sort of market research (which retailers routinely use to choose sites for new stores) can answer those questions once and for all.

If you decide to go for it, you can contact Koontz at GeoLib (CKoontz@ci.fsu.edu), or you can go directly to your local municipal offices. City/county planners, architects, and the like have the geographic maps you'd need, and they should be willing to give you copies (especially if your public library is another city/county-funded department of the local government). The planners might even already be combining the geo data with Census information as well as with predictions for growth in the area if they are considering expansion plans or approving new building construction or road work. In that case, all you need to do is ask them for a copy of their mapped-out data, then plot your cardholder addresses. In fact, if you're trying to decide where to add a new branch, your local officials are probably working all of this up anyway. And once you explain the benefits of adding your cardholder information to the maps, they might ask for your database and do all the work for you. Ideally, libraries should have a place in city or county geographic data that's equal to that of schools, fire stations, etc. Ask your municipal administrators if they'll insert a layer of library locations into their data so you can have quick access to maps and demographics. Be sure to get copies of the maps to keep for further studies and decisions, and to plan outreach to nonusers.

Imagine what you could achieve if all of that demographic and geographic data were simply handed to you, for free. It's there for the asking. What are you waiting for?

Using Data to Build a SWOT Analysis

One common tool that people use to analyze many types of organizations is known as a SWOT analysis, which stands for Strengths, Weaknesses, Opportunities, and Threats. You simply think about many aspects of your institution and decide which category they fit into. Sometimes, the same aspect can be both a strength *and* a weakness, or both an opportunity *and* a threat. When putting together a SWOT analysis, the strengths and weaknesses usually apply only to the internal environment, while the opportunities and threats apply to the external environment.

I think these analyses are kind of fun (but I'm weird that way), plus they're great for putting things into perspective. You can do these in a very serious manner of course, but they're also great for discussions and brainstorming. So if you sat down with some coworkers to think about your internal strengths, what would they be? What about your weaknesses? (Depending on the mood, it can be easier to point out weaknesses than it can be to find strengths.)

The last time I did a SWOT exercise with library staff members, they came up with a number of ideas. I've added some of my own here to help you see what kinds of things you can list. Let's look at internal stuff, the strengths and weaknesses, first. (Note that these are simply side-by-side lists, the ideas on each line don't necessarily go together.)

Strengths

- Staff expertise
- Good collections
- Good budget
- Main branch's location
- Director's vision
- Visible to public
- Quality PR materials
- Active teen group

Weaknesses

- Internal communication
- Managers disagreeing
- Not enough money
- Not enough staff
- Could use a branch for west side of town
- Not enough continuing ed for staff
- Building needs repairs
- Low staff pay and morale

Now let's look at the external stuff, the opportunities and threats.

Opportunities

- Local government upgrades GIS technology
- 2.0 website for parent organization
- Listen to people outside the building
- Civic groups help us with outreach
- Become a community center
- Good reputation/public support

Threats

- Becoming out-of-date
- Internet searches
- Dealing with change
- Bookstores
- Public doesn't know our services
- Stereotypes

Opportunities (cont.)

- Bring in vendor for a café
- Partner with local gaming groups
- Work with K–12 teachers
- Chance to attend conferences
- Build branch on west side
- Join other orgs for diversity training

Threats (cont.)

- Losing funding
- Not enough public computers
- People using Google
- TV/movies/theaters
- County budget cuts
- Don't know how to reach Latinos

These are just a few of many possible answers for each of the four categories, but they should get your brain going. Once you've done your internal audit of your printed materials, website, customer service, and building, write down all the strengths and weaknesses you see. You'll find more by studying the results of any customer surveys or focus groups you did. Looking at the maps of demographic and geographic data will tell you even more.

Strengths	Weaknesses
Opportunities	Threats

Figure 4.1 Making a simple diagram with four quadrants is one way to show a visual SWOT analysis.

Doing a SWOT analysis is not the only way to sum up your findings, but I think it is a nice one because it doesn't involve a long, formal report—it's something visual that's easy to digest. I've made sure to use enough examples here to make my columns even so they'll look good in print, but you might find in your own analysis that one set of columns, either positive or negative, is much longer than the other.

Before you take action on all the data you've gathered, read on to learn more about what's most important, and how to get others to believe your evidence and buy into the plans you'll create together.

Endnotes

1. Christie M. Koontz, Dean K. Jue, Charles R. McClure, and John Carlo Bertot, "Public Library Geographic Database: What Can It Do for You and Your Library?" *Public Libraries* 43, no. 2 (March/April 2004).

2. Christie M. Koontz, "Understand Census Data to Improve Your Library's Marketing" (Part 1), *Marketing Library Services* 17, no. 1 (January/February 2003): 3–5. See also Christie M. Koontz, "Census Data: Valuable Information on Your Library's Customers" (Part 2), *Marketing Library Services* 17, no. 2 (May/June 2003): 6–8.

3. Christie M. Koontz and Dean K. Jue, "The Location of Your Library Building: Why It Is Important, and How to Do It, Using GIS (Geographic Information System Software)," in *Library Buildings in a Changing Environment*, ed. Marie-Francoise Bisbrouck (IFLA Publications 94, 2001), 141–153, www.geolib.org/pdf/lbce.pdf (accessed January 26, 2009).

4. Christie M. Koontz, "A History of Location of U.S. Public Libraries Within Community Place and Space: Evolving Implications for the Library's Mission of Equitable Service," *Public Library Quarterly* 26, no. 1/2 (2007): 75–100.

5. Christie M. Koontz, Dean K. Jue, and Bradley Wade Bishop, "Why Public Libraries Close," (2008), www.webjunction.org/facilities/articles/content/11041525 (accessed January 26, 2009).

6. Christie M. Koontz, "Studying Why Libraries Close," *Marketing Library Services* 23, no. 1 (January/February 2009): 1, 3–5.

Recommended Reading

Sarling, Jo Haight and Van Tassel, Debra S. "Community analysis: Research that matters to a north-central Denver community." *Library & Information Science Research* 21:1 (1999): 7–29.

Chapter 5

What Marketing Experts Think Is Most Important

What mistakes do most accidental marketers make? Exactly what should you know that most librarians don't? I've done tons of reading and talked with lots of experts about these questions over the years. As you can imagine, the answers vary, but a few main points surface again and again. Here's a list of what I've come to believe are the biggest things librarians get wrong when it comes to real marketing:

1. Librarians think they know what their customers want without asking them.

2. Librarians send press releases and promote programs and call it "marketing."

3. Librarians don't separate people into different target markets and treat each group differently.

4. Librarians don't study the people who make up their user bases.

5. Librarians don't fully evaluate the results of programs and campaigns and then use that data to improve future efforts.

Not coincidentally, these oversights are tied to the sorts of major marketing tenets that you've never had a chance to learn if you haven't taken any formal classes. But don't despair; each concept is easy to grasp and to act on. Once you get through this chapter, you'll have the essential knowledge you need to do some real marketing projects.

How to Avoid the Five Most Common Marketing Mistakes

Now that you know what the most common mistakes are, I'll explain how to avoid making them.

1. Librarians think they know what their customers want without asking them. If you've ever created a program or event without any input from the group of customers it's aimed at (and who hasn't?), then you're guilty of this cardinal sin. Libraries (and many other organizations) choose and create events constantly without any public input, but that doesn't make it right. And it certainly doesn't qualify as true marketing.

"But we have no time to work public response into our planning process!" you exclaim. "We can't do a focus group every time we want to create a program," you lament. Well, OK, but then don't call what you're doing *marketing*. (Unless your program or event fills a need or desire stated by the target audience, *you're not marketing*.) Just keep this in mind the next time you're frustrated because you put together a really cool event and only 11 people showed up.

You can actually *save* time in your planning by not bothering to plan events that nobody's asking for. I realize that staffers don't want to give up on the old standards that they've "always" done, but you've simply got to stop wasting time and money on things that are not evidence-based. If no one is asking for it, and few people are showing up for it, then *stop doing it* and funnel your precious resources to more popular things. It's a very simple concept; I don't know why so many librarians ignore it.

2. Librarians send press releases and promote programs and call it "marketing." Terminology may not be the most important thing in your life (meaning that you *have* a life), but you shouldn't ignore it either. If you're going to play the marketing game, you need to know the basic rules and terminology. Let me reiterate what I detailed back in Chapter 2:

- Sending out press releases to established media outlets is called *publicity*.

- Explaining the benefits of something to encourage people to use it or buy it is called *promotion*.

- Using paid media space in newspapers, radio, etc., is called *advertising*.

- Following a long-range communications plan is called *public relations*.

- All of these are mere parts of, and tools for, *marketing*.

- When you're following a complete process in which you separate potential visitors into groups that have things in common, ask people in those groups what they want, create programs or events in response, publicize those events in ways that will reach each intended audience, have the events, and evaluate your results, *then* you can call it true marketing.

It may seem pedantic, but I think it's worth repeating these differences again and again until everyone understands the terms and uses them properly. Why? One reason is that librarians are intelligent professionals who always like to know what they're talking about. No reason to act differently here.

Another reason is, if you're talking to your managers or trustees and say, "I'm marketing my programs but still, nobody is attending," and they hear "marketing," they'll think you're doing the whole cycle. They may throw their hands up and say, "Well, I don't know what else you can do." But if you say "I'm doing publicity, but still nobody is attending" they'd have the chance to ask what your overall marketing plan is, and maybe offer some helpful input. (Note: If you don't have an overall marketing plan, back up and punt immediately! Or, if you don't have a football, just hang out till you get to Chapter 10, "Writing Your Formal Plans.")

Finally, doesn't it drive you crazy when people misuse library jargon? What if a temporary worker said to you, "I'm ordering that book" when they meant "I'm ILL-ing that book." One implies spending money; the other doesn't (or spending less tangibly, at least). One implies you'll own the book for your collection; the other doesn't. And while *ordering* a book *via ILL* is correct, just plain *ordering* means something else. Don't you expect people to say what they mean, to communicate clearly? It's no different here. So I hope you'll join me in my personal quest to get every librarian in the world to know what *marketing* really means and to say it only when it really applies.

3. Librarians don't separate people into different target markets and treat each group differently. Let's say you're creating an advertisement for a library event you've planned for senior citizens. Would you design that ad the same way you'd design one for a teen event? Or for a storytime for young parents? Would it be the same as an ad for businesspeople in your community? Or for college students? If you answered *no* to these questions, then why would you design any public relations materials the same way for vastly different groups of people?

Of course, marketing is more than designing PR materials, but the theory should carry the whole way through the process. The marketing cycle should *begin* with group segmentation, and every act after that should continue to be customized to the group you're targeting. If you want to do something to attract senior citizens to your library, and you find out what they want, you also need to find out lots of other information about them. What times of day or days of the week do they prefer? (Some don't drive at night; some have group bus transportation into town on certain weekdays.) How can you reach them to tell them what you're offering? (What newspapers do they read? What radio stations do they favor? Do they ever look at your website?)

By the same token, it doesn't make sense to send all of your press releases to the same editors at the same newspapers. That can easily lead to press-release-overload, where the harried editor says, "Oh, *another* thing from the library. What*ever*." You should have one list of places where you send senior stuff, another list for teens, another for businesspeople, etc. Sure, there will be some overlap. But you don't want to overload any one media source by sending announcements that don't apply to their readers. Take it from me, an editor who's gotten press releases about everything under the sun relating to the keywords *library* or *marketing* or *computer*. A great way to cut through everyone's clutter is targeting, targeting, targeting.

4. Librarians don't study the people who make up their user bases. Most librarians don't like being stereotyped as people who love to read, but yet many of you lean on stereotypes when you think about your user bases. You might do it subconsciously, and mean no ill will, but most think in terms of stereotypes or "the norm" just the same. But what do you know *for sure* about your customers and potential customers if you never ask them about themselves? For instance, not all teens are alike: Some play games, some make crafts, some read, some play sports. Boys and girls vary wildly at that age, and 14-year-olds are a world away from 18-year-olds. Even if you don't lump all your teens together when you're creating programs, do you assume that all of the 15-year-old girls want a knitting class? Do you assume that all of the 17-year-old boys want sports programs? Is that really the case in your community?

Likewise, do you assume that businesspeople or scientists in your organization all want to receive information the same way? Do they prefer email, text alerts, intranet info, or printed reports via interoffice mail? Do they want to hear from you daily, weekly, or just monthly? Do they even understand what function your info center serves?

I'm talking about more than simple market segmentation here. What most librarians neglect to do is to study the demographics of their user communities. What percentage of people use the info center, and of those, which ones use it regularly? Who doesn't use it (and why not)? How do older and younger employees differ in their information-seeking habits? Do in-house employees call on you more often than those in other buildings or cities? How do needs differ among users in various departments? As librarians, you encourage people to find and use valid data when they're making decisions; why wouldn't you do the same yourselves?

The more you know about the people you're supposed to do work for, the better you can serve them. You need to understand what they value, and how they make decisions about what info to use and what events to attend. When you completely understand the work they need to do, their demographics, and their personal preferences, you can customize your services to make them more relevant and more useful. This is at the heart of the true marketing cycle.

5. Librarians don't fully evaluate the results of programs and campaigns and then use that data to improve future efforts. I've been to plenty of library events where I see a staff member quietly counting the number of attendees, writing it down, and slipping out of the room to go back to work. I've been to very few where staffers hand out evaluation forms, or ask for feedback at the end, or send an email afterward asking me to gauge the usefulness or enjoyment value of the event. This is absolutely the wrong way to measure success—that is, if you ever want to increase your chances of success.

That phrase itself—*chances of success*—is silly. As I bemoaned in the Introduction to this book, you don't have to leave much to chance. Offering things that you're sure your customers want is a great start. But what makes a huge difference in your success rate is evaluating the results at the end. Take the good comments with the bad, and then read the bad ones over and over again (especially when a number of people voice the same concerns). There's your answer about how to be more successful next time. You don't have to leave much to chance when you have direct feedback telling you what can make your events better: Ask for it, gather it, use it.

This doesn't have to be a long, complicated process: Any feedback is better than none, although, of course, the more you get, the better. If you're still doing programs and never evaluating them beyond attendance numbers, you might as well quit while you're behind, because things aren't going to get much better unless you find out where you went wrong in the first place.

What Other Experts Think and Teach

To test my own theories, and to give readers of this book a wider range of expert opinions, I contacted people from around the world who teach library marketing or speak about it on the professional level. I asked them all the same open-ended questions:

- What steps of the marketing process do you think are most important or most overlooked?

- What do you think most librarians don't know about marketing, but should? (Or don't do, but should?)

- What is the most important aspect or idea that you teach in your classes?

- If you could tell the world of librarians one thing about marketing/promotion, it would be …

In this section, I'll tell you who each of the respondents is and then share his or her answers. Each replied a little differently, so by taking all of their answers into account, you will get the "big picture." (And, I was relieved to see, most of them reflect my own list in one way or another. Proof that I haven't been wrong all these years! Whew.)

Réjean Savard, PhD, is a professor at the School of Library and Information Science at the University of Montréal in Quebec, Canada. He's taught marketing for almost 20 years. When I asked what he thought was most important about library marketing, Savard told me this:

> For me, the main thing has always been to make sure the students understand clearly that marketing is not only a question of promotion. The profession in general needs to know that marketing is a process, starting with the clients' needs. Therefore marketing research is important and, as Christie [Koontz] used to say, "Any research is better than no research!" Then you have to develop a strategy based on *all* the elements of the marketing mix, not only promotion. It means you often have to change your product or invent a new one, which is sometimes difficult for librarians.

Christie Koontz, PhD, is a faculty member of the College of Information at Florida State University (FSU) in Tallahassee. She teaches marketing and management at FSU and has been conducting workshops on marketing and marketing research for colleagues around the globe. Koontz is a member of IFLA's Management & Marketing section, where she's a judge for IFLA's

International Marketing Award. Koontz also directs the GeoLib program at FSU. She told me that the main points she attempts to relay to her students are these:

- Marketing is a complex, yet common-sense-based planning tool that is essential to an organization's success.

- Marketing is not promotion; promotion is one of its tools.

- You cannot offer programs or services that are not research-based. You need to develop your offerings based on customer research.

Koontz emphasizes the importance of environmental scanning (looking at the physical environment in and around your library), customer research, and evaluation of marketing efforts.

Angels Massísimo is a professor at the Universitat de Barcelona Facultat de Biblioteconomia i Documentació (the University of Barcelona Faculty of Library and Information Science) in Barcelona, Catalonia, Spain. She is the current chair of IFLA's Management & Marketing section. Here is what Massísimo deems most important to know about marketing in libraries:

> First of all, I think the most important thing is to be aware of the idea of marketing as a whole, as many libraries believe they are involved in marketing when they actually are only *promoting* their services, programs, etc. As [IFLA's] Glossary of Marketing Definitions says, "[Marketing is] The process of planning and executing the conception, pricing, promotion, and distribution of ideas, goods, and services to create exchanges that satisfy individual and organizational goals" (www.ifla.org/VII/s34/pubs/glossary.htm#M).
>
> Second (and according to our given definition) is to understand marketing as a continuous process, or a

kind of never-ending wheel, starting with market research (knowing our clientele, both actual and potential); then segmenting the market; then designing products, programs and/or services which fit the requirements of every targeted segment. You then establish a "marketing mix" for those products, programs or services; and finally evaluate the results, thereby reinitiating the wheel.

Third is to understand that, as with every planning-based task, we must start with some previous work such as context analysis, environmental scanning, and so on. Only with a sound knowledge of our institution, its mission and goals, its strengths and weaknesses, etc.—and with a sense of our own purpose and limits—will we be able to market our services in a successful way.

Fourth is to carefully establish a marketing plan based upon our knowledge about our parent institutions and our clientele, and including a careful, realistic, and well-balanced marketing-mix strategy. This means we need to identify a target group and a specific need or want, then to design a product, program, or service that meets this specific need or want. We need to be mindful of the costs users will have to pay for receiving the goods; to find a way of distributing or providing the goods in order to minimize the cost impacts for the user. It's also essential to promote the new product, service, or program in a way that really reaches the target group (taking into account different languages, strategies, and media for different user targets).

Last, but not least, is to control the whole process in order to meet both our clients' individual goals and our own. To be aware of our mission and goals is a core requirement to ensure that we do not go beyond our responsibilities nor do we fail in them. Perhaps we don't have to meet a particular requirement; we only have to advise users about how this requirement can be met. But it is our responsibility to find out which "relevant" requirements they have and to meet those that apply to our libraries.

Pat Wagner, co-principal of Denver-based Pattern Research, Inc., is a trainer, writer, and consultant who speaks frequently across North America. Her work with Leif Smith at Pattern Research focuses on personnel, management, leadership, marketing, career, and strategic planning issues. Wagner specializes in libraries; 85 percent of her programs are with libraries and library organizations such as state and national associations, state libraries, and universities. Wagner identifies these four problem areas as the most important or most overlooked:

- Having no working strategic plan. They may have a complicated, legalistic document filled with organizational jargon, but not one that the average employee can use to determine priorities or target audiences.

- Doing no real partnering with library users; for example, planning events without having members of the target audience on the committee. The result can be a really embarrassing marketing faux pas: Dorky adults are creating publicity materials that are decades out of date; native-born Americans are insulting new arrivals with mistakes in language and context, etc.

- Having no clear idea of how projects will be evaluated. Wagner is not a fan of "quantitative worship," which is popular these days. "Who cares what the statistics say, if the greater descriptive goals are not met?"

- "Most of my library clients think they know what their library users want, particularly if they share their demographics, so most marketing decisions are met with superficial input. I think the days of relying on surveys and even focus groups are over. If I am going to create a literacy program for young Hispanic mothers, more than half of the people on the planning committee—with voting rights—should be young Hispanic mothers."

Wagner goes on to add, "Marketing is a conversation where the library user does most of the talking. Marketing is awareness of the library user, changing in responses to their needs, and then, and only then, communicating the benefits, on the library users' terms." The most important thing she chooses to teach in her classes is the concept of building relationships with library users that gives *them* decision-making power, and making sure you create campaigns using *the library users'* values, words, and points of view—not those of the library.

She also acknowledges the value of evaluating failures: "All marketing is an experiment, and it is more useful to fail than succeed—you learn more for the next time."

Liudmila N. Zaytseva is the chief of the General Planning and Reporting Department at the Russian State Library in Moscow. She has been there for more than 20 years, with more than 10 of those in the management sphere. She has significant experience in preparing statistical, information-analytical, strategic, and other materials on various aspects of library activities. Zaytseva told me this:

> IMHO, it is very useful to study marketing projects that are successful and also projects that are not very successful. Studying the experiences of our colleagues from different libraries all over the world frequently serves as a good stimulus or a reason to develop new library services of our own. And it is important not only to look at

their results but also at the methodology used in their achievements, and also at their advertising.

This is not the normal way to look at library service. But if we desire to make friendly library services, it gives the user confidence.

Concrete examples of best practices are always evident. We should make this true marketing knowledge easier for librarians to find and distribute it widely.

Judith Siess, founder of Information Bridges International, Inc., was the first chair of the SOLO Librarians Division of the Special Libraries Association (SLA). Her Champaign, Illinois-based IBI, Inc. facilitates "exchanges of ideas among librarians and information professionals around the world." Siess is the former editor of *The One Person Library* newsletter and has authored various books, including *The Visible Librarian: Asserting Your Value Through Marketing and Advocacy*. She has guest lectured at a number of library schools. Siess concludes:

> The most important thing about marketing in libraries is *variety*. You need to market to a variety of people on a variety of subjects in a variety of ways. Each audience requires a different message and a different approach and, perhaps, even a different time. This will require all of the imagination and initiative you can muster, but it will make marketing more interesting and, therefore, since you are more engaged, will provide a better result.

Stephen Abram is the VP of Innovation at library vendor SirsiDynix and was the 2008 president of SLA. He speaks around the world on library trends and the future of libraries, and often includes the concepts of marketing in his presentations. In his signature outspoken style, Abram shared his well-informed take on true marketing:

I'd say that the most important thing for librarians to know about true marketing is that it is really *sales*. When you are doing marketing well, you are truly trying to *influence* (change for the better) people to change their behaviors and thinking. If you're marketing well you do these things:

1. Change people's opinion about something (like libraries, story hours, quality databases vs. Google, etc.) and ask them to act on that opinion—support libraries, vote for that bond issue, tell their friends, etc.

2. Change their behavior (come to the library/intranet/website instead of the video store, borrow a book because it's greener than buying it, etc.).

3. Get them to buy in to something (not necessarily with money but with their time, their future success, or their prestige).

4. Learn a lifelong skill that you apply whenever it's needed because you make positive choices about underpinning your decisions with quality information.

5. The most important thing that I have learned is that we need to use their words to rattle the chairs in their attic. Our words need to be excised in a 12-step program. They work for our internal conversations but fail miserably with everyone else.

To assume that marketing is just education or informing folks is to truly deny the real goal—positive behavioral change and visible support and use. And to think informing is enough is to be naive. You have to admit that you want action, changed behaviors, and ask for it.

If our colleagues truly understood this, then we'd approach awesome success!

Well said, Stephen, well said.

Words of Wisdom From Others

When you look around, advice on marketing and promotion is everywhere. That doesn't mean it's all good, of course. But I've gathered some favorite thoughts here as well as tidbits that I've found especially insightful or inspiring.

During the months I was writing this book, I had a fortuitous opportunity to see Seth Godin speak, live and in person. By now, most people who are even remotely involved in marketing know that Godin is a popular guru who's written 10 best-selling books, including *Purple Cow*, *The Dip*, and *Meatball Sundae* (see www.sethgodin.com). His latest book is *Tribes*, and that's what he was talking about when I saw him in New Jersey in October 2008.

Figure 5.1   Seth Godin talked about how "tribes" matter in marketing, then signed copies of his new book.

a lot of interesting things into his short talk, but a
out for me. One was his claim that most libraries
effort to create an experience for people. He meant an
perience" such as the one that customers have at an Apple Store
or a Disney theme park. Most libraries come across as simple book
warehouses. So why would anyone flock there? Good point.

Even more hard-hitting was a comment near the end where he
said simply: "Amazon knows what I like—why doesn't my librarian? I'd tell her." There again is the core marketing principle—ask
people what they want, then deliver it. Sure, you may know a few
frequent customers that always come in for the latest issue of
Scientific American or a new romance novel, but what about the
other thousand people? Do you ever ask what *they* like, in a systematic and actionable way? If not, how can you wonder why they
prefer to use Amazon.com? Isn't it obvious?

I know, I know, librarians deliver personal service; websites
don't. (Well, actually, many shopping sites that offer live chat *do*.)
But many times, if people know just what they're looking for, they
don't need that personal service. In those cases, you're beat out by
the ease and convenience of Amazon.com and other such sites.
Beware your competition.

Here's another essential concept that's so simple it's often overlooked: Develop a succinct message, then deliver it concisely and
consistently. Each message should focus on just one thing, and
should be clear and complete, not clever and confusing. I like the
way Lisa A. Wolfe summarized it in her 2005 book *Library Public
Relations, Promotions, and Communications*:

> Don't try to tell people everything at once or in one
> communications effort. If you are simply trying to
> change perceptions, then your messages should com-
> municate whatever perception you are trying to create.
> But, if the aim of your message is to get people to act,

then make sure your message tells them what you want them to do. If you want them to check out more books, communicate that action: "Anytown Public Library— Check Us Out!" If you want people to think your library is a safe place, develop a message that says "Anytown Public Library—A Safe Place." Don't let clever words and slogans get in the way of your message. It is better to be clear and get the word out than to be clever and confuse a lot of people. (pp. 31–32)

And while you're telling your customers about what you have, you need to pay close attention to what they're telling you as well. Suzanne Walters said it well in *Marketing: A How-To-Do-It Manual for Librarians* (1992):

Essentially, a marketing approach to services means that we talk to our customers, and that we develop specific products and services as a direct result of listening to their needs. The listening process stimulates creative solutions to problems. It drives an honest evaluation of current serv- ices and creates an awareness of changing customer needs. Marketing is also scientific: it involves accurate research, analysis, and systematic planning. (p. v)

What Surveys and Studies Have Revealed

Of course, no one library or group has the time and money to study every aspect of customers' perceptions, attitudes, needs, or wants. Luckily, though, various associations and companies undertake studies and scans and make the results available to all of us.

The study that's gotten the most attention in the recent past is an OCLC report titled "Perceptions of Libraries and Information Resources." If you haven't seen this, run, don't walk, to your nearest

Type in www.oclc.org/reports/2005perceptions.htm. ~~~, you can download a free copy (286 pages!) or buy a bound one that will be sent to you. Either way, this tome is worth its weight in marketing-research gold.

I won't bore you by explaining too much of the methodology, but you should at least know that professionals used an online survey to contact English-speaking people of all ages from six countries: Australia, Canada, India, Singapore, the U.K., and the U.S. There were 3,348 respondents who answered up to 83 questions (including follow-ups) within five broad topics: library familiarity, usage, the library brand, advice for libraries, and whether the library brand is "universal."

There are so many fascinating findings that it's hard to know which to highlight. I've selected just a few that underscore the need for more true marketing:

- The library brand is "books," meaning that print books are what most people think of when asked about libraries. Still.

- Only 1 percent of respondents begin their information searches on a library website.

- While respondents were very familiar with email, search engines, and online news, they're not familiar with "Ask an Expert" services; 20 percent don't know about online libraries; 30 percent have never heard of online databases.

- Asked about their familiarity with and usage of information sources, people ranked library websites about halfway down the list. Worldwide, 71 percent had used Google, 46 percent had used AskJeeves, 28 percent had used Lycos, and just 21 percent had used a library website. (This is just a fraction of the full list.) Libraries did rank in the top half of the pack, above About.com, Dogpile, and a few others. But "Ask an Expert" and

"Online Librarian" were at the bottom of the list; people
are not hearing about those services.

The verbatim responses that are included in charts and as colorful quotes sprinkled throughout are especially fascinating. Two
answers to the question, "If you could provide one piece of advice
to your library, what would it be?" really caught my eye. A 30-year-
old from Australia said, "Advertise. I have forgotten about libraries
since I left school." And a 51-year-old U.S. resident offered, "Get a
website so that I can see what materials are available in the
library." Umm … I think we've covered that one.

This jibes with other things I've read, as well as with some of my
own experiences in conducting focus groups: People routinely ask
libraries to "start up" services or products that they already offer.
There's no surer sign that you're not getting the word out!

Seeing the vital importance of such surveys, I wrote my own
report about recently published research on libraries. It was a
round-up of titles that had come out in 2008, and my selection
covered public, school, academic, and special libraries. I published
the full article in *Marketing Library Services* (Nov./Dec. 2008, pp.
8–9), and am including excerpts in the sidebar "Useful Reports
from 2008" beginning on this page so you can see what's available
to inform your own data-gathering efforts.

And as you're no doubt catching on to by now, the more data
you start with, the more successful your marketing will be.

Useful Reports from 2008

These reports contain numbers on budgets, buildings,
collections, reference transactions, public computers
and filters, information literacy, salaries, opinions, and
more. This is by no means an exhaustive list; rather,

these are just a few titles I've chosen for their potential usefulness to marketing plans and projects. Many of them are available for free.

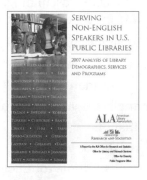

Serving Non-English Speakers in U.S. Public Libraries

From: ALA's Office for Research and Statistics

About: Spawned by U.S. demographic changes, this is the first national study to look at the range of library services and programs developed for non-English speakers. It covers effectiveness of services, barriers to library usage, most frequently used services, and most successful programs by language served. It analyzes library service area populations and patron proximity to libraries that offer specialized services. There is a companion toolkit.

To Get It: Download it for free at www.ala.org/non englishspeakers.

Research Library International Benchmarks

From: Primary Research Group

About: This 200-page study is based on data from 45 major research libraries from the U.S., Canada, Australia, Germany, the U.K., Italy, Japan, Spain, Argentina, and other countries. It covers materials, salary, info technology and capital spending, hiring plans, spending trends, personnel deployment, discount margins from vendors, relations with consortia, info literacy efforts, learning-space development, use of RFID technology, federated search, and many other pressing issues. This study contains more than 500 tables.

Data is presented separately for university, government/nonprofit, and corporate/legal libraries, and for U.S. and non-U.S. libraries, as well as by size and type of library.

To Get It: Order from www.primaryresearch.com/publications-Libraries--Information-Science.html. Paper costs $95; a PDF costs $105; a limited site license costs $210.

What Executives Think About Information Management

From: Outsell, Inc.

About: This report explains how executives perceive their organizations' information management (IM) functions and the role of information in furthering organizational objectives. It discusses executives' information use habits to reveal the gaps that IM leaders must address to fortify IM's value proposition. It also includes data from Outsell's Information Management Benchmarks survey and User Market survey, and reveals what execs don't know about IM activities, therefore pointing out opportunities for educating them. One disturbing finding: It says that 65 percent of executives use the internet as their first choice for information and that 40 percent cite the lack of competitive information as their highest-ranked information gap.

To Get It: Download the PDF for $495 at www.out sellinc.com/store/products/752 (SLA members get a discount).

Academic Libraries: 2006 First Look

From: U.S. Department of Education's National Center for Education Statistics (NCES)

About: This report presents tabulations for the 2006 Academic Libraries Survey conducted by the NCES. It summarizes data on services, staff, collections, expenditures, electronic services, and information literacy at 3,600 academic libraries in the 50 states and the District of Columbia. While this survey was done in 2006, it was just released as a free PDF in July 2008.

To Get It: Download it for free at nces.ed.gov/pubs 2008/2008337.pdf.

Libraries Connect Communities: Public Library Funding & Technology Access Study 2007–2008

From: ALA's Office for Research & Statistics and the Information Institute at Florida State University

About: This study assesses public access to computers, the internet, and internet-related services in U.S. public libraries. In addition, it discusses the impact of library funding changes on connectivity, technology deployment, and sustainability.

Data says that 66 percent of public libraries offer free wireless access. One in five libraries report that there are consistently fewer computers than patrons who want to use them during the day. The study builds on the longest-running study of internet connectivity in public libraries, begun back in 1994 by John Carlo

Bertot and Charles R. McClure (www.ii.fsu.edu/plinternet_findings.cfm).

To Get It: Download it for free from www.ala.org/plinternetfunding or order a bound copy through the ALA Store at www.alastore.ala.org for $28 ($25.20 for members).

Latinos & Public Library Perceptions

From: WebJunction

About: WebJunction, in partnership with the Tomás Rivera Policy Institute, published this research report about a six-state telephone survey of more than 2,860 adult Latinos. It details their library usage and perceptions of libraries.

The report indicates that 54 percent of the Latino population visited libraries in the past year and that they have positive perceptions of libraries. Interestingly, although Spanish-language materials are important to them, their perceptions of staff service are a stronger factor in terms of increasing visits than Spanish-language materials. You can download the survey questions to use with your own Latino communities.

To Get It: Download it for free at www.web junction.org/latino-perceptions/resources/overview.

Chapter 6

Getting Administrators, Managers, and Staff to Buy In

Getting people to "buy in" to your ideas means getting them to believe in your cause, to support you, to get behind what you're doing, and to help convince others to get behind you too. You can't go it alone, so you'll need colleagues all around you to buy in to your marketing and promotional plans. Sometimes, the more innovative or unusual your ideas are, the harder it is to get others to buy in to them, which can make it difficult to accomplish anything new. But there *are* tactics for winning people over to your way of thinking.

It's not easy to give advice on this topic, because every library and every situation is different. And many factors affect whether you can get people to buy in to your ideas: Budgets (of course), politics, a person's previous experiences, and an organization's history are only a few of the potential roadblocks. But in this chapter I'll recommend a few one-size-fits-all rules and then add strategies that other librarians have tried.

Basic Rules of Thumb for Achieving Buy-In

Despite the vast differences that exist in all sorts and sizes of libraries, I can offer you three basic rules of thumb for achieving buy-in in practically any situation:

1. Involve colleagues early in the process.

2. Communicate your ideas in a clear and complete manner.

3. Have real evidence to show there's a need for what you're proposing.

Let me explain each one in some detail.

1. Involve colleagues early in the process. Here is one of the most important things you can do to achieve buy-in: Involve your colleagues (at all levels of the food chain) right from the beginning of your project. Bring them in at the planning stage, and then keep them in the loop. Don't wait until you *need* their support before you start asking for it; that makes your task much more difficult. Get people involved in small ways right up front by asking for their opinions and advice. Make them feel like they're an important part of what you'll be doing (because they are). Once people have a personal or professional stake in something, they're more likely to support it going forward.

You don't want to come up with a great new promotional idea, plan it all out, then spring it on your bosses and expect them to support it. They'll have lots of questions for you to answer before they'll give you time and money to carry out your plan, so then you're fighting an uphill battle. Think what a difference it would make if you consulted your bosses at the beginning, sharing your ideas and asking their opinions. By the time the plan has come together, they'll not only know most of the answers to the questions they'd pose—they'll be the ones who've helped shape those answers. And once they've helped shape your project, how can they not support it?

This is a very simple rule, but a powerful one that you shouldn't overlook. You'll need buy-in from all around you, not just from your bosses or managers. You'll need it from your colleagues, from the library staff, and sometimes from your customers as well.

Again, this is part of the concept that true marketing is a never-ending circle: Ask people in advance what they want, then create it, deliver it, publicize it, and ask them how you did, so you can begin the cycle again. If you ask customers what they want, you're more likely to deliver programs, events, and information that work for them. If you ask your managers ahead of time what they want (their organizational goals, the way they want things done), you improve your chances of getting their approval for your projects. And if you ask your coworkers and staff members how they want to be involved and how they think things will work, then they'll have a stake in your success and they'll be more likely to do their part. You may even want to involve potential partners from outside your own library or information center.

I don't mean to say that you need to question and involve everyone in your organization at every step along the way. If you had to do that, nothing would ever get done. (In fact, I'm not even a big fan of committees, because I think they slow the pace of action dreadfully.) So you need to think strategically and to begin with the end in mind. Whose support will you really need, and at what stage of your work? Involve a few folks from each of the groups mentioned, but don't try to get everyone. Whenever you can, choose those who are respected, who are vocal, and who can influence others on your behalf when the time comes.

2. Communicate your ideas in a clear and complete manner.
Here's a situation we've all found ourselves in at some point, either at work, at home, or among friends: You have an idea for something that you think is really cool. You share your idea with others, but nobody else seems too jazzed about it. You can't understand why they're not jumping on your bandwagon. What's wrong with them, anyway? Why are you the only person who sees the amazing potential of this cool idea? The answer could be quite simple: You're not explaining it well enough.

Maybe your idea *is* the greatest thing since sliced bread. But before others can agree, they need to understand it completely. Perhaps you have a hard time communicating clearly. Even if you *are* a great communicator, you need to realize that, when you're explaining something you're really excited about, it's easy to skim over little details or to leave out bits and pieces. And sometimes those gaps can mean the difference between an idea sounding great and an idea sounding like it hasn't been thought through.

I've seen this very problem time and time again in my career as an editor. Librarians will pitch stories to me, telling me about projects they want to write about for my publications. Of course, I need to decide whether each idea will make a good article. I have to ask myself many questions in order to decide which are worth publishing—just as library managers have to decide which projects to support. Here are a few of the questions I ask myself:

- Exactly what will this article explain or explore? (To answer this first question, I need to be able to understand the concept from the article description or abstract that I've received.)

- Is this a new concept that people need to learn about? If it's not new, then is it at least being done in a new way? (The potential author has to make sure I know what's already been done in the field, and then present clear evidence that he or she has done it in an innovative way that's worth sharing.)

- Would this article fit the mission of my publication?

- How many librarians might be interested in reading about this? Will it serve a wide audience or only a few of my readers?

- Does this pitch convince me that the potential author will be able to write well enough that readers will be able to learn from this article? (We've all seen speakers or read

authors we know to be brilliant, yet we cannot understand what they're telling us because they can't put all
their knowledge into logical sentences and paragraphs.)
Editors and others who read your proposals see them as
samples of your work and your writing ability. If they are
put together sloppily, it stands to reason that your final
work would be too.

I've gone through this decision-making process a thousand
times. And it's relevant here because I can tell you that a majority
of librarians I've communicated with over the years have not
explained themselves clearly. They do not show me the benefits of
choosing their project to become my next article. These are people
who are trying to convince me that they've done something great,
something worth telling the world about (literally), yet they either
cannot or do not take the time to explain to me why their project
is important. So they've failed before they've even begun.

You should hope that none of these folks is ever nominating you
for an award, for you would never make it past the first round of
selections. In fact, when you're trying to get buy-in or approval or
funding for a project, you should look at it from that perspective.
What would you do if you were nominating this project for an
award? How would you explain it so the judges would understand
how amazing it is and would deem it worthy of winning? That is
essentially what you're doing when you seek buy-in for a marketing or promotional project. There are many other services and
people and products competing for the time and money that you
need. If your project is worthwhile, and if you convince others of
that, then you win the prize package, which is approval and support. So this step is one you should never skimp on.

The point is, you cannot just say, "Here's what I want to do."
Instead, you need to say, "Here's what I want to do, and here's why
it would be good for our library, and here's how it will benefit our
customers." Write down your pitch and ask others to read your

work repeatedly to make sure that your words and intentions are communicated very clearly.

Also, use common language, not marketing buzzwords, in proposals. Recognize that many librarians and staff members don't have marketing training, so they could be slow to grasp your ideas if you express them in jargon. (They might also be defensive about their lack of knowledge.)

3. Have real evidence to show there's a need for what you're proposing. It's one thing to ask for something you simply *want*, or for something that you *think* others want. It's quite a different story to ask for something when you have *proof* of people's wants or needs. Having actual evidence immediately catapults your project above others that are based on feelings rather than facts.

This is why it's essential to have assessed your environment and the attitudes and desires of potential and actual customers. You really shouldn't be asking for things that aren't backed up by evidence anyway. Once you have, say, numbers from surveys, or comments from focus groups, or suggestions from program evaluations, you can show your managers that your project will do well or be popular. That effectively erases his or her ability to say, "I don't think anyone will be interested in this."

Think about how this works with legislative advocacy. Members of library associations can't simply call their representatives and say, "Hey, you should give us more money." Nor can they call and say, "Hey, we hear patrons saying you should give us more money." They use proof and sheer numbers to communicate. They ask citizens to send emails, or they create postcards or petitions for them to sign. Then they gather all this evidence, perhaps thousands of signatures, deliver them to government reps, and say, "Hey, look how many of your constituents are willing to sign their names to a statement saying that you should give us more money."

Representatives can easily ignore a few individual requests; it's much harder for them to ignore mounds of evidence.

Another way to inject proof into your proposals is to cite best practices. If you can find other organizations that have done something like what you are proposing and have had good results, this bodes well for you. (Don't forget, you should cite work from libraries that are similar to your own. Similar, at least, in whatever ways affect the proposal at hand—same demographics, usage numbers, user populations, etc.)

A Serious Reason to Support Library Promotion: Librarians Save Lives

Some of you may have heard stories of how a medical librarian found the right answer at the right moment and kept a doctor from giving his patient the wrong treatment. Maybe you thought these were urban legends, but here's at least one story that was real enough to be reported by Reuters in 2006: "Cancer patients are more likely to find what they are looking for with a librarian-mediated search instead of 'going it alone.'"

The article, titled "Internet searches: Librarians do it better," went on to explain that professional librarian Ruti Volk, manager of the Patient Education Resource Center (PERC) at the University of Michigan Comprehensive Cancer Center, and her colleagues had done more than 2,000 searches for cancer patients during the previous five years. Each time, they asked the patients to evaluate the information the librarians had provided to them.

According to the article, "Results from 513 evaluations revealed several interesting findings," Volk noted in an interview with Reuters Health. "One of the most interesting was that 65 percent of patients said they were not able to obtain the information that we sent to them from any other source. They were not able to get it by themselves by using the internet; they didn't get it from a healthcare provider or from a cancer organization." Another 30 percent said the librarians had provided at least some new information. Only 4 percent of the PERC patients said they had found all of the same information on their own.

Volk told the Reuters reporter, "This demonstrates that even though the information is supposedly so accessible and everything is on the web, people still need the help of a professional to find information that is relevant to them that is current and accurate and authoritative." She continued to explain that "the biggest advantage is expertise in searching."

So why have a library but not give it the resources necessary for promotion? Even special librarians need to promote themselves. Show this story to anyone who doesn't believe you need a marketing plan and budget. Send them the link to the full text: www.medicineon line.com/news/12/4533/Internet-searches-Librarians-do-it-better.html.

Here's one easy way to find best practices to emulate: Look at award winners. Borrow the John Cotton Dana Library Public Relations Award entries from ALA and study them. Read articles or blogs that cover other winning projects and see what the winners did right. Ideas and evidence are bountiful!

Conversely, if you find other organizations that have tried something and failed, and you can study their plans and show that yours differ in a critical way, that too might help your cause. This shows that you're doing the legwork that's necessary for success, rather than just tossing ideas out without seriously considering how they'll work. What's more, once you gain a reputation for doing good legwork and creating solid, evidence-based proposals, managers should be more open-minded about any projects you present to them in the future.

Getting Staff Buy-In for Extra Work on Marketing and Promo Projects

Many of the recommendations I made in the beginning of this chapter lend themselves to staff members getting buy-in from higher-ups. However, it's important for managers to realize that they need to get buy-in from their underlings as well, even if they have the power to "make" staffers do things. Everyone can see the difference in performance when someone is forced into a duty versus when they *want* to be involved.

During a series of focus groups I conducted for a multi-branch public library, I gathered information from staffers on what managers should do to get staff buy-in for the extra promotional work they were planning to assign. You must realize that any time you're about to give somebody extra work, you should be prepared for some backlash. One way to cut back on that is to position the new tasks correctly, making them seem more like "helping the organization" rather than "accepting more duties as assigned." My focus groups provided suggestions from the staffers themselves about what would help them take on the extra marketing-related work without being too bitter about it:

- To give staff members time to take on extra tasks, free them up from other things. Re-examine areas that are known for red tape, or eliminate mundane old duties that don't matter much anymore. Don't be afraid to axe some things altogether. Ask yourself questions like these: What really slows down your employees' work? What keeps them from spending more time serving the public? Are there reports that could be done quarterly instead of monthly? Can you computerize something tedious that's currently being done by hand? Do you really need all of those committee meetings? Streamline to allow staff more time to do the important work of marketing and promotion. Simplify processes that are in place for writing and sending press releases, taking phone calls, updating the website, etc.

- When employees complain, tell them—and make them believe—that their voices are being heard. Staffers know that management can't change or fix everything, but when they complain of overwork, or effort wasted on tactics that fail, they feel better when they're sure that their complaints are not only being heard but also acted on whenever possible.

- Empower some higher-level staff members to take action, so that every little question or complaint doesn't have to wait for management. This is actually a common tactic in customer service: Give front-line staff blanket approval to say, "I'm sorry that happened, and I can do [this] to help make it up to you." This makes customers much happier (especially as opposed to hearing, "Sorry, I'm not authorized to do anything about that."). It also makes front-line people feel more powerful, useful, and trusted.

- Communicate constantly with staff. Before launching any initiatives, tell all staff members what you're planning to do, so it's not an unwelcome surprise. Share the goals for your plan so they are not just management's goals but staff's as well. (How can anyone work toward something when they don't know what outcome is expected?) Give employees the big picture so each one can feel invested in the library's success. Help them work toward the main goals, because just making them feel like they're in the loop helps them feel better about their jobs overall. And communicate in ways that reach every staffer at every level. Staff-wide communication is often poor in large organizations or in those that are spread over distance. The fact that libraries employ many part-timers makes all-staff communication more challenging. But if you want people to feel like they're part of the group, then it's imperative to have excellent communication processes in place.

- Set people up to succeed. Explain expectations up front, and offer training where necessary. Start with a project that's short and easy so staffers can see quick results, which will boost their confidence and enthusiasm for future projects. Remind everyone from the outset that marketing is a fluid process where plans can change in mid-stream. Finally, realize that many staffers are not used to being involved in projects with directly measured outcomes, so this will be a new (and perhaps intimidating) experience. Explain that you have to evaluate the success of each step in order to make future projects better, not in order to find fault with their individual efforts.

- Include some staffers in brainstorming and planning. Front-line workers, especially, probably have important insights about your customers that managers or outside planners and consultants would never know. Asking staff members for their expertise in appropriate situations does a lot to get their buy-in. It gets them involved "on the ground floor" so they feel more ownership of the project.

- Let staff members volunteer for tasks they're interested in before you make any assignments. Many staffers want to help make their libraries better; take advantage of that enthusiasm! Don't kill the excitement by deciding, on a management level, who must do what, and when. Ask for volunteers as each initiative starts, then go from there. This makes them feel more in control of their own destiny.

Some of these same points are discussed in a book by long-time marketer Suzanne Walters. In her Introduction to *Marketing: A How-To-Do-It Manual for Librarians* (Neal-Schuman, 1992), she explains the concept:

> There are two secrets to staff acceptance of the marketing concept, and they are crucial to success. The first is enlisting the full commitment of the executive director. This individual must totally adopt the concept of a "market driven/customer driven" institution and provide the necessary leadership to reinforce each aspect of the service. The second is the direct involvement of the staff. Staff may be hesitant at first. Why should they try to understand customer needs more clearly? It may seem laborious to understand the level of detail required for each target market. They may feel they already know what customers want. Planning takes time away from the desk and serving customers. However, when the staff is involved in the process of obtaining specific information concerning customers, they see their customers in a new and different light. This dedication and enthusiasm lead to greater commitment to the customer and improved service. A clear understanding of customer needs and measurements of customer satisfaction provide a factual basis for

increased funding, whether from public or private sources.

The Keys to Real Buy-In

As you can see, the keys to getting real buy-in at any level are involving people early on and communicating with them clearly. Both principles are very simple, yet easier said than done. Some organizations don't operate this way at all, preferring privacy to transparency. And many managers either choose not to communicate much with underlings, or they try to communicate but are just lousy at it. In those cases, all you can do is be a careful communicator yourself, in the hopes that your good habits will rub off on others. Comfort yourself with the fact that great speaking and writing skills never go out of style.

Recommended Reading

Illinois Library Association and the American Library Association. Library Advocacy: Influencing Decision Makers. August 2004. www.ila.org/advocacy/advocacy.htm (accessed January 27, 2009).

Still, Julie. "How You Can Influence Your Local Legislators." *Marketing Library Services* 18:3 (May/June 2004): 1–3.

Weinstein, Beth. "For the Best Library Marketing, Get Your Whole Staff on Board." *Marketing Library Services* 17:1 (January/February 2003): 1–2.

Chapter 7

Making Evidence-Based Decisions With Administrators

This is where you'll start to apply the information you've learned and gathered as you worked your way through the earlier chapters of this book. It's time to start making serious decisions about what direction to take with your library marketing and promotion, and all of your decisions should be based on solid evidence, not guesses or wish lists.

Examine All of Your Data and Evidence

First, let's go back to Chapter 3 and Chapter 4. Round up all of the data that you gathered when you did your own assessment, or "environmental scan," of your library:

- You looked at your press releases and other promotional materials. What did you see? Do they seem outdated? Are your messages consistent? Are you getting the sort of press coverage you're aiming for?

- You studied your physical environment. Is it comfortable for visitors? Does the layout make sense? Is it safe and easy to use? Is it clean and inviting?

- You evaluated your website and online environment. Are they easy to navigate and to use? Are they full of broken links? Are you getting much traffic?

- You asked for opinions and thoughts from both users and nonusers. What did they say? What are they satisfied or dissatisfied with? Most importantly, what services did they request that you are *already* providing? Those, clearly, are the services that aren't getting enough PR power yet.

- You downloaded Census data and combined it with demographic and geographic information. What do your maps tell you about the areas and groups that you are or are not serving?

- You did a SWOT analysis. What weaknesses and threats need to be addressed first? What are your strengths and opportunities?

Examine all of your data and allow yourself to see it with fresh eyes. What topics have come up repeatedly? Does the big picture reveal any glaring omissions? What are the main differences between what your environment actually is and what your organization wants it to be? No matter how hard it might be to face the answers, you must do it—only by assessing your library honestly can you take steps to improve it.

Once you've studied your overall assessment, you're sure to see things you want to change and improve. Of course, your bosses and/or board members will also see things they want to alter. Chances are that they won't see eye-to-eye with you on many matters. This is where the experts and the evidence come in.

First, make a list of the various marketing and promotional tasks you could undertake or different directions you could go in. Are there certain target groups that you want to pay special attention to? Has your parent organization adopted a new focus that you need to address? Are you in a situation where it's essential to seek more funding? Are there important challenges on the horizon? Is there a major anniversary or event coming up that you need to plan for? Do you need to launch a capital campaign? Do your staff members need to learn how to promote their services? Do you need to make your physical space or your online space easier to use? Have you discovered that your user community doesn't turn to you first when they need information? Has a technological shift left you in the dust? Are your communication methods out-of-date? Are you getting less press coverage than you want or need? Are you trying to do bits of this-and-that without a clear plan?

Once you have a list of all the things you could do, narrow it down to what matters the most. To help avoid arguments between you and the higher-ups you're working with, look back to Chapter 5 for guidance on where to begin. What's the most important area that your organization has not addressed sufficiently? Also look back at any requests you got from users or nonusers; their votes especially should resonate with management. (This assumes that you're working in a customer-driven organization.)

As you make your choices, consider this: Although you'll see many outreach projects that seem essential, it's often better to start internally, making sure that people at every level of your organization share the same mission and that they know how to communicate among themselves to achieve it. When that's the case, all the rest of the processes will run more smoothly.

Choose a few top priorities and assign values to others. Plan so that you're setting up the main pillars first (such as internal communication, web usability, and finances), then add building blocks in ways that make sense chronologically as well as financially.

Look at Your Goals, Mission, and Vision

Of course this is also the time to align all of your new data, hopes, and plans with your organization's purpose and mission. If you haven't studied the latter carefully, do so before you meet with any high-level supervisors. Then sit down for a frank discussion with your administrators, stakeholders, bosses, and board members of all stripes. If you're going to lead the effort to set up a sensible, useful marketing plan (this is your chance to wow them!), then have an agenda ready and have as much supporting documentation as possible.

Everyone you're talking with needs to understand what the organization's goals are. Based on those goals, then, what should your library's general marketing/promotional mission be? Is it reflected in your library's mission statement? (Do you even have a mission statement?) In addition, how do those goals relate to your vision statement? (Do you even have a vision statement?)

If you want help with crafting mission and vision statements, there are other books and resources that cover those topics thoroughly. In keeping with the marketing focus of this book, I'll just define these two terms briefly, add a bit of detail in sidebars, and refer you to titles that address these topics in more depth.

- A **mission statement** describes an organization's key purpose; the reason it exists. It should say who the library serves, what it does, and for what purpose.

- A **vision statement** describes what the library (and sometimes its community as well) will look like in the future if the mission goes well. It should paint a realistic picture of what the organization intends to become.

Marketing communication expert Linda Wallace differentiates between the two in this way: "The mission statement is present tense. It is a here-and-now statement of who we are, what we do, and why. The vision statement paints the long-range picture of where the library is going and what it wants to happen when it gets there."[1]

Wallace also provides a list of questions you can use to evaluate your library's mission statement:

- Does it communicate the most important thing you want people to know and remember?

- Does it convey the unique benefits offered by the library?

- Does it inspire enthusiasm among employees, partners, and funders?

- Is it simple and memorable? Would it pass the T-shirt test?

- Are the language and content current?

- Does the tone complement the image you wish for your library?[2]

One good example of a clear mission statement comes from the Special Libraries Association: "The Special Libraries Association promotes and strengthens its members through learning, advocacy, and networking initiatives" (www.sla.org/content/SLA/index.cfm). You can find many other examples just by looking at the websites of other libraries, associations, and companies.

By now, you have collected many things:

- Assessment data that suggests possible changes or activities for your information organization

- Census, geographic, and demographic data

- Advice from marketing experts about what matters most

- The attention of—and buy-in from—colleagues at all levels

- A list of possible projects, in priority order

- Your organization's mission statement, vision statement, and overall goals

Once you assemble all of this evidence, things should start to fall into place. You'll see numerous goals you can shoot for and

> ### Characteristics of Good Mission and Vision Statements
>
> Despina Dapias Wilson, Theresa del Tufo, and Anne E. C. Norman list these features as characteristics of a good mission statement:
>
> - Simple and clear
> - Easy to understand and communicate
> - Long-term in nature
> - Customer-focused
>
> Here are their characteristics of a good vision statement:
>
> - Concise
> - Verifiable
> - Clear and compelling
>
> From Wilson, Despina Dapias, del Tufo, Theresa, and Norman, Anne E. C. *The Measure of Library Excellence.* Jefferson, N.C.: McFarland & Co., Inc., Publishers, 2008: 174–175.

possible paths for getting you to each one. After you've agreed on how to begin your marketing improvements, you'll need to start thinking about how to send a consistent message to get the job done.

Think About Your Logo and Your Brand

Logos are sort of a touchy subject in the library world, largely because of the many diverse ways that libraries are set up in terms of organizational structures, positioning, and reporting. Some have their own logos, while others must use the logos of their parent

Mind Your Ws

Suzanne Walters says that, since each library cannot meet the needs of all people, you need to determine which needs yours aims to meet. You can do that by thinking about these "four Ws":

- Who are you serving?
- What are you doing to serve your customers?
- When are your services available?
- Where are your parameters of service?

More specifically, Walters advises, you need to explore these questions when writing a mission statement:

1. What service business are you in?
2. Who uses your products and services?
3. How well does your system work?
4. How does your library compare to other institutions?
5. What might the future hold?

From Walters, Suzanne. *Library Marketing That Works!* New York: Neal-Schuman Publishers, Inc., 2004: 4–6.

organizations (companies, municipalities, universities, law firms, governments, etc.). Some float in an uncertain world between, where they can have their own logo but it must be used along with another. It's a shame that all libraries aren't free to choose their own, because a simple logo can convey an awful lot of information or emotion. But, you'll have to do the best you can within whatever constraints you might have.

ogos that have become so identified with a brand
ey carry lots of weight on their own. Think about
s" of McDonald's, the "swoosh" that symbolizes
ull's-eye of Target stores. Major marketing cam-
stent, saturated usage over many years have
made these symbols synonymous with their corporations. And
while you won't expect to achieve that sort of recognition for your
library's logo, it's still an important symbol of who you are and
what you stand for.

You might have noticed a very simple trend in library logos over
the past decade or two. Many of them used to feature books or
something related to reading; now they've morphed (thankfully) to
include more computers and technology-related imagery. This, I
feel, is extremely important. If your logo is still based on books, I
urge you to update it as soon as possible. Aren't we all trying to get
across the idea that today's libraries are more than just books?
Don't you try to tell potential customers that you also have DVDs,
CDs, databases, internet access, research services, audiobooks,
computer labs, scanners, and more? If so, why in the world would
you settle for an old-fashioned logo?

While the symbols I mentioned earlier, like that of McDonald's,
have become so recognizable in part because they have been
around for so many years, that does not mean that logos should
never change. If you look closely at old pictures of the famous
hamburger joint, you'll see that the M's golden arches have
changed styles to keep up with the times. Think, too, about kitchen
maven Betty Crocker. While the picture of this classic homemaker
still graces countless boxes of cake mix, her look has been updated
several times. If it hadn't, modern women wouldn't be buying as
many of her products.

So if you feel you need a new logo and can't get one for some
reason, then at least update the one you've got. Don't forget, even
typefaces show their age at some point. You might not notice it

until something suddenly looks hopelessly old-fashioned, but fonts are constantly getting sleeker. (For me, the litmus test is Reynolds brand Cut-Rite wax paper. I only seem to buy a new box every 5 or 10 years, so the font on the fresh one is always different from the old one. All of the women in my family have had the same experience!)

Branding is another important aspect to consider as you look at your overall marketing picture. That's really about developing the "personality" of your product and service. How do you want people to see you? What characteristics should come to mind when people think of you?

One of the corporate books on my shelf, *Become the Brand of Choice*, explains it this way:

> In creating a new brand, the company must first define the brand's objective—what is the purpose of the brand? They then decide the "pillars" or foundation of the brand—all decisions are made based on these pillars (those physical characteristics that make the product distinguishable from its competition). They must also create the intangible aspects of the brand (such as a reputation for uncompromisingly high quality. ...) Finally, the brand's tangible aspects must be defined. The desired image must originate with the company, its marketing strategy, and the product themselves—not from the customer. The customer reacts to the brand's character, but doesn't create it.[3]

One way to help yourself understand branding is to ask yourself what brands you're loyal to and why. What does each bring to your mind? To me, McDonald's says "fast" and "fries" but not "great" or "healthy," so I'll go there when I'm more concerned about speed (and fries!) than having a scrumptious or low-calorie meal. What

What
do people think when you say your library's name, and why should they be loyal to it?

College & Research Libraries News published an interesting case study about a branding process at the Biomedical Library at the University of California–San Diego. One point the authors made was that "Every library has a brand whether the library staff realize it or not. Proactively identifying and crafting a library brand is important for attracting and retaining users, and assuring that all library services and resources are in alignment with library goals and values."[4]

I published a comprehensive article in *MLS* called "How We Built a New Library Identity."[5] In it, publications coordinator Sejan Yun related the story of how the Saint Paul (MN) Public Library collaborated with its Friends group to redefine its identity as part of a huge grand re-opening of its Central Library. The team members involved reviewed current PR materials (and found them very inconsistent!), set goals, identified its audience, and hired a professional firm to design a logo and to help implement the new overall brand. Their work included creating a "user guide" and templates for brochures and fliers along with new stationery and business cards, promotional materials, and a teacher's guide to the library. The article details all the steps involved and discloses how much money and time were spent. It notes that the process forced the staff and managers to rethink their goals, their place in the community, and even the content of their brochures and communication materials.

The reason I've brought up these topics now is to highlight the importance of being consistent. If you want your plans to work in the long term, then you need to be sure that your goals, mission, and vision are all on the same track. Furthermore, your logo and brand should reflect that same vision. The time to make sure that everything matches is now, during the planning stages, not later, when it'll be harder to change things to bring them all into alignment. And as I've said repeatedly, all of these decisions should be based on actual evidence.

All of these concepts still revolve around the central principle that I originally recommended: Begin with the end in mind.

Endnotes

1. Linda K. Wallace, *Libraries, Mission, & Marketing: Writing Mission Statements That Work* (Chicago: ALA, 2004), 9–10.

2. Ibid., 7.

3. Jason Hartman, *Become the Brand of Choice*, 3rd ed. (Newport Beach, CA: The Hartman Media Company, 2002), 169.

4. Nancy F. Stimson, "Library Change as a Branding Opportunity: Connect, Reflect, Research, Discover." *C&RL News* 68, no. 11 (December 2007), www.ala.org/ala/mgrps/divs/acrl/publications/crl news/2007/dec/brandingopp.cfm (accessed January 26, 2009).

5. Sejan Yun, "How We Built a New Library Identity," *Marketing Library Services* 18, no. 2 (March/April 2004): 5–8.

Chapter 8

Don't Shy Away
From Statistics

Statistics. The word alone can elicit groans of disgust and images of endless tedium. Yet statistics are necessary—and they don't have to be painful. In fact, you can make statistics serve you like a great army of worker bees if you know how. And they can be powerful tools to help you get what you need and want, be it more computers, more staff members, or a bigger budget.

Start With Stats You've Got
and Make Them More Powerful

The first thing you'll want to do is make a list of all the statistics your library already gathers. There are probably many, ranging from your gate counts to the number of reference questions you answer to circulation numbers for all sorts of materials. All of those have been around for a long time, and your library or information center probably already puts all of them together for annual reports and for delivery to your state library or a national association. But you might not be using them for all they're worth.

One way to make your statistics not only more powerful but also more exciting is to compare them with other numbers that people can really relate to. You see this done all the time, but do you do it for your own statistics?

The American Library Association has done a great job with this regard in its familiar red pocket-sized brochures called *Quotable Facts About America's Libraries.* (You can download the English version online at www.ala.org/ala/aboutala/offices/ola/quotable facts/quotable07_printer_010807.pdf and the Spanish version at www.ala.org/ala/aboutala/offices/ola/quotablefacts/quotable_ spanish_printer010807.pdf.) Perhaps the most-often-used quote from this brochure is this one: "There are more public libraries than McDonald's in the U.S.—a total of 16,541, including branches." That's powerful, because just about everyone can relate to the fact that McDonald's restaurants are everywhere. Another attention-getting quote is, "Americans go to school, public and academic libraries 16% more often than they go to the movies." And finally, this sad fact: "College libraries receive less than two cents of every dollar spent on higher education."

These kinds of statistics are useful, but there are ways to make them even more so. When you're dealing with huge numbers, it's hard for people to really comprehend them. Your job, should you choose to accept it, is to do a little research to help illustrate exactly what a huge number means in terms that others can grasp easily.

I once read this hard-hitting fact in a *Newsweek* article[1] on cancer: "[C]ancer is on track to kill 565,650 people in the United States this year—more than 1,500 a day, equivalent to three jumbo jets crashing and killing everyone aboard 365 days a year." Now, read that sentence again and gauge your reaction to it as you go along. Here's what I was thinking as I read it:

"[C]ancer is on track to kill 565,650 people ..." <my thought: Wow, that's more than half a million. Still, in a country this size, that doesn't seem overwhelming.>

"... in the United States this year—more than 1,500 a day ..." <me: ooh, that many?!?>

"... equivalent to three jumbo jets crashing and killing everyone aboard 365 days a year." <me: OMG!! Three plane crashes a day?!? That's a massive number of people! How can we let this continue?!?>

I'll wager that many of you had similar reactions as you read the end of that sentence for the first time, so you see how the added comparisons moved the sentence's impact from lightweight to gut-wrenching. That is how you add real power to dry statistics. Granted, you don't have to choose stats that are so upsetting, but do choose topics that have some connection to what you're discussing. Since this article was about cancer, it made sense to relate it to other tragic ways that humans can die.

So if you were writing about your book circulation numbers dropping, you might relate that to literacy levels dropping. (Be sure to make it clear whether you are stating cause-and-effect proof or simply comparing numbers.) If you're trying to illustrate how in-library computer usage has climbed, compare those stats to something like the number of webpages that exist, the number of jobs that have been lost in the area, or the local population. For instance, let's say you have 25 public computers and people need to sign up to use them, so you keep track of how many individual users you have. You might say, "In-library computer usage has climbed from 200 people per day to 320 per day. That's the equivalent of every adult in the township using our computers once a month." Or "That's enough users to fill the Libraryville College football stadium on homecoming weekend."

Front-line staff members at public libraries are often confronted by patrons who are upset about fines or fees (been there, done that), and the classic line these citizens utter is "My tax dollars are paying for that!" It's great for staffers to have comebacks, as long as they can deliver them as facts, not as fightin' words. You can contact your municipality to see exactly what the library gets, per household, from local taxes. That number may be as little as $20–$50 per year. Armed with that data, you can train public services employees to reply, "Yes, some of your tax money does support the library. But we only get about $25 per year from each household. And our operating expenses are rising, just like everyone else's. That's why we still have to charge for [fines, print-outs, whatever]."

One more way to make your statistics more powerful is to customize them for the audience that will be reading them. If you're presenting a report to your board members, then you should know what their interests and concerns are. If many are businesspeople, then compare your stats to local business growth (or lack thereof). If many are grandparents, relate the numbers to children. ("Our library still has only one public computer for every 23 children who enter kindergarten in our schools each year. That's why our goal is to add 100 more computers to the system over the next three years.") If they're sports fans, go there. ("If you count all of the reference questions we answer every week—including those asked in person, on the phone, and online—you'll get 535. That number is more than all of the home runs that are scored in all of the Major League Baseball games in a week.")

As always, you'll also want to speak the language of the people you're sending stats to. That will often mean using business terminology. Or you could be presenting these statistics to the public, or a potential corporate sponsor, to faculty, or to fellow information professionals. In every instance, if you customize your words as well as your comparisons to fit the audience, your message will carry a lot more meaning.

Statistics You Might Not Record, But Should

Given the way that society and libraries have been changing, the statistics you gather should be changing too. In addition to the aforementioned stats on circulation, gate counts, and reference questions, you probably already track things like how many people attend each of your programs and how many sign up to use your public access computers. If you loan videogames or other software, you probably note those numbers as well. But there are still more usage numbers you need to be keeping track of. I suggest you monitor the following to paint a more complete picture of how often your community takes advantage of your many services:

- **Social network popularity** – Social networks like MySpace, Facebook, LinkedIn, Flickr, YouTube, and others are major avenues of communication today for people of many ages. If you've joined the leagues of social network users, then your presence on those sites counts as official outreach activity. How many "friends" does the library have online? How much activity do your sites get in the way of comments and postings? How many notices do you post there each month? How many blogs link to your pages? You should be tracking all of this information anyway to see what tactics attract people and which things don't work. Don't be afraid to include social networking stats in annual reports and other official documents. They can demonstrate a great increase in interest in the library on the part of people who might never be counted for walking in the door or borrowing an item.

- **Café customers** – You might get reports about food and drink sales from your coffee shop vendors, but do you count the number of people who visit your café? That's a related business that increases library usage, so it's legitimate to note the people who come in.

- **In-house usage** – You know that people often enjoy your books, magazines, newspapers, etc., without checking them out. This sort of browsing is common in many libraries, but is seldom part of quantified usage. Your statistical picture is not complete without these numbers! In order to track this without exhausting the staff, one expert suggests[2] choosing just a few days per month where you post signs on tables and around carrels asking visitors *not* to reshelve anything themselves. That way, staff members can note exactly how many items were pulled from the shelves as they put them away.

- **Connections outside the building** – Making your outreach literal, by meeting people outside of your building, is more important than ever. If you set up a table at a corporate exhibition, how many people stop to talk? When you set up a booth at a community festival, how many do you connect with? What about when you attend technology fairs, academic events for incoming students, legislative information days, or book fairs? And in all these cases, you should also note how many new library cards you give out. Showing impressive numbers from these kinds of activities can help justify the time spent outside the library and might even help increase your budget for outreach.

- **Presentations given by staff members** – If your staffers speak at networking events, address the business community, present at faculty meetings, etc., be sure to report on each instance and to include tallies (and results) in your reports. Don't forget to include the fun things, too, like contests entered, appearances in parades, or performances by the book cart drill team!

- **Electronic information** – You probably already get reports from your information technology (IT) department on how many times folks access your databases and your website. But technology can automatically count a lot more specifics these days, and software can be configured to create reports you might have never dreamed of. You can learn how many times people accessed particular webpages (such as those on events), how many searches originated inside or outside the building, and much more. It's worthwhile to talk with your IT staffers to find out what sorts of new numbers they can offer you that you don't get now. (Also worth noting: Often it's only

administrators who get detailed reports from IT, but
everyone involved in marketing, publicity, and planning
should see and study these stats too!)

- **Media mentions** – Your PR employees probably clip and
save every mention you get in the media. Sure, they
make for nice archives, but are you remembering to
include these numbers in reports to prove the value of
your publicity efforts? How many newspaper mentions
did your programs receive; how many of those came
before the events (more useful!) versus *after*? How many
radio mentions? What about announcements in corpo-
ratewide or communitywide newsletters? (Note: Things
you've paid for, such as billboards or ads, don't count
here. You're just looking for whatever the media picked
up on and publicized for you.)

The Importance of Cost/Benefit Analysis

As I lamented at the beginning of this chapter, *statistics* is a word
that fills many of us with fear and loathing. The same is true for
similar terms such as *balance sheet, cost/benefit analysis,* and
return on investment, better known as ROI. But it's not hard to
learn about ROI, and once you get to know it, it can be your new
best friend.

Simply stated, ROI is the return, or benefits, realized by using a
product or service. Let's say that you spend $1 on a Sunday news-
paper that contains lots of grocery coupons. You clip some of the
coupons and use them during your next shopping trip, saving $10
on that week's food. So you spent $1 and reaped $10 in savings.
That means your benefit-to-cost ratio is 10:1, making that $1
newspaper an excellent investment.

There are plenty of resources to help you understand cost/ben-
efit analysis. I was surprised to even find some on YouTube. There
are professors giving lectures, consultants making presentations,

sorts of other videos. Sarah Long, a former ALA president still very active in Illinois, even did a "vodcast" (video pod-cast, on ROI, which you can view at www.youtube.com/watch ?v=TgqoM5ZNu3Q.

I also recommend the April 2001 report from Outsell, Inc., "The Value of Libraries: Justifying Corporate Information Centers in the Year of Accountability" by Roger Strause. (Actually, I recommend *any* report from Outsell!) This 21-page PDF costs $125, and you can order it from the Outsell website (www.outsellinc.com/store/products/76). It includes sections titled "The Call to Arms: Getting Staff, Stakeholders, and Influencers On-Board for Change" and "Telling Your Story: Using Numbers to Make Your Case" along with "Collecting Data: Gathering Information About the Library's Tangible Return on Investment." There's great stuff in there, especially for corporate and special librarians.

It can take many hours of research and work to really figure out your own library's ROI for many different services. Happily, though, work done a few years ago by some wonderful souls at the Massachusetts Library Association (MLA) has made that easy. MLA created a "value calculator," which many libraries have since adopted (www.masslib.org/LibraryValue.html). The calculator assigns monetary values to most of a library's basic products and services. For instance, every book borrowed is valued at $12.50. (According to the website, this is the "estimated average discount cost of hardcover and paperback books" when it was first calculated in 2003.) Likewise, the MLA work valued each magazine read at $2 (estimated cost of an issue of a popular periodical). Borrowing a video is listed at $3.87, taken from a basic video store rental price. The cost for interlibrary loans is $25 each (average cost from Massachusetts that year). The group even figured the more-difficult-to-estimate costs, such as answering each reference question ($7).

Once all the costs had been assigned, MLA put them into an Excel spreadsheet and posted it online. Now anyone can use this tool simply by inputting how many of each item they used, and the tool automatically calculates the total value of all the products and services. Figure 8.1 is an example from the Franklin Park (IL) Public Library's website.

These calculators are amazing tools, and I think every library should have one on its website. While they're not perfect or all-encompassing, they still provide a simple and powerful way for patrons to see for themselves just how much they can save by using library resources!

That's nice for individual users, but how can you calculate your whole library's return on investment, as in all the value you offer compared against all the income you get to run your organization? For that, you can use many of the same dollar values from these ROI calculators, but you need to factor in more data.

In 2005, *MLS* published a cover story called "How We Proved Our Library's Value with an ROI Assessment" (March/April issue). Author MaryGail Coffee detailed how she and the director of the Winter Park (FL) Public Library (WPPL), Robert Melanson, crafted their ROI process. As Coffee explained:

> In 1998, a Winter Park commissioner began expressing concerns about the financial efficiency of the city departments. Rather than wait for these concerns to impact WPPL's funding, library director Bob Melanson acted. He started the ROI process by asking a simple but crucial question: What would patrons have to pay for the same materials and services they get from the library if they had to pay for them in the private sector?

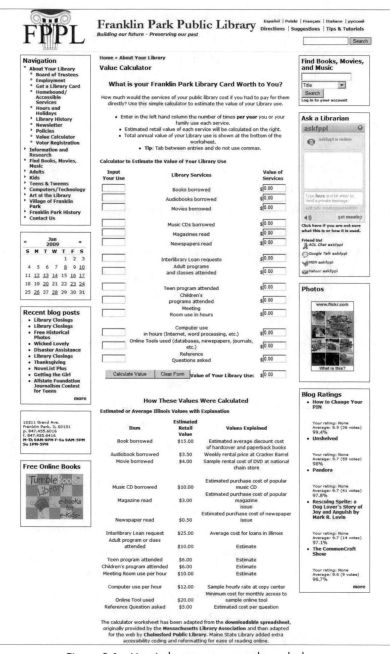

Figure 8.1   Here's the easy-to-use value calculator
on Franklin Park Public Library's website.

Coffee and Melanson came up with a four-step process:

1. Identify the audience of the report. (In this case it was the city commission.)

2. Identify collections, services, and programs that can be measured.

3. Assign valid dollar amounts that are relevant and realistic for our community.

4. Review the process regularly.

The article goes on to explain each step in the process, including where they got their dollar values. Their final number was staggering: WPPL boasted a return on investment of 620 percent! It got $1,053,865 in tax dollars and delivered materials and services worth $6,530,465. As Coffee wrote of the result, "It's proof to our community members that we are good stewards of their money and it's a powerful statement to local government that we are an efficient and trustworthy destination for their funds."

If you're wondering how they settled on dollar values for some of the less-tangible services, I'll note a couple here. For high-speed internet access, they discovered that the local Kinko's Copy Center offered similar access and so used that company's price ($12 per hour at the time). For answering reference questions, they cited the University of Central Florida's fee-based research service ($50 per hour) and calculated that WPPL's librarians spent 2.6 minutes per question, making their price per question $2.17.

By the way, Melanson was later appointed to a statewide library ROI workgroup. During a meeting, he showed WPPL's model to economists from three universities, who not only validated the model but thought its base costs were too conservative. So this is a process worth copying (adjusting for current prices, of course)!

There's an excellent book, *Measuring for Results*,[3] that I recommend if you want to dig deeper into the idea of proving your library's value in real numbers. Chapter 8 of that book has a whole section on cost/benefit analysis that goes into a lot more mathematical detail than I ever could (because I despise mathematical detail). It includes other estimated values for library products and services as well as examples of finished analyses. It also has chapters on output measures, social value, communicating value, and more. (I don't have to do any fancy calculations to know that this $40 book would give you an outstanding return on your investment!)

Examples of Results From ROI Studies Around the United States

To give you a taste of the results that other libraries have gotten from major ROI studies, I've provided some quotes and citations here from reports on libraries around the U.S. All of these reports merit further reading; the quotes are only meant to whet your appetite. You can use them as inspiration to start your own studies, and perhaps also as ammunition to help you win approval for the time and money it will take to commission a report on your own library system.

All of these reports and others are listed on a very useful Illinois Library Association webpage called Economic Benefits of Libraries (www.ila.org/advocacy/impact.htm). Reading them in full will give you valuable insight into various ways these projects can be set up, different angles they can explore, and what they can reveal. According to the page, "Several state library associations have used these studies to successfully receive major funding increases through their respective legislative bodies." Many also include discussions on the sub-topic of SROI, or social return on investment.

> Overall, Florida's public libraries return $6.54 for every $1.00 invested from all sources.

From *Taxpayer Return on Investment in Florida Public Libraries: Summary Report,* by José-Marie Griffiths, Donald W. King, Christinger Tomer, Thomas Lynch, and Julie Harrington. Prepared for the State Library and Archives of Florida. Sept. 2004. p. 5. www.ila.org/advocacy/pdf/Florida.pdf. (This study was designed to determine *the costs of not having libraries* by examining alternative sources of information that people would have to use instead, the portion of economic contribution made by public libraries that would be lost if they didn't exist, and the loss of benefits to users.)

> Pennsylvania taxpayers can be confident that their direct and indirect return on their investment in public libraries is extensive at about 5.5 to 1.

From *Taxpayer Return-on-Investment (ROI) in Pennsylvania Public Libraries,* by José-Marie Griffiths, Donald W. King, Sarah E. Aerni, et al., School of Information and Library Science, University of North Carolina–Chapel Hill. Sept. 2006. p. 14. www.ila.org/advocacy/pdf/UNC_Pennsylvania.pdf.

Summary of Economic Value Provided by Nine Southwest Ohio Libraries–2005

Library Service	Estimated Value
Circulation	$104,874,725
Reference	$64,565,102
Computer Use	$19,715,326
Computer Training	$61,900
Outreach Services	$464,197
Meeting Room Use	$310,950
GED Programs	$419,670
Red Cross Programs	$1,950
Total	$190,413,820

The application of a Household Expenditure multiplier, as published by the Bureau of Economic Analysis, U.S. Department of Commerce, to $190.4 million worth of library benefits results in a total quantifiable economic benefit of library investment equal to about $283.6 million or about $3.81 per dollar expended on library operations.

In arriving at these estimates, the quantification of economic returns from library services used conservative measures of value. For example, other economic studies of library services have used list prices of library materials as a basis for measuring value. This study used the more conservative method of library acquisition costs as the basis for the valuation of many items. This approach built in the effects of deep discounts achieved by libraries' volume purchases.

From *Value For Money: Southwestern Ohio's Return from Investment in Public Libraries*, prepared by Levin, Driscoll & Fleeter, Columbus, Ohio. June 22, 2006. p. ii. www.ila.org/advocacy/pdf/Ohio. pdf. (This study was based on the value of the materials listed in the chart and didn't include in-house use of materials. It did not attempt to quantify the value of information to its users.)

[T]he context for this ROI model is limited to grant income and does not address the value of resources to faculty in conducting their research or teaching. Using the ROI model with UIUC data produced a return of $4.38 in grant income for every dollar invested in the library in 2006.

From *University Investment in the Library: What's the Return? A Case Study at the University of Illinois at Urbana–Champaign*, by Judy Luther, president, Informed Strategies. White Paper #1 in *Library*

Connect, Elsevier. p. 4. www.ila.org/advocacy/pdf/University_ investment.pdf. (Here, the need to identify a return on a university's investment led to linking the library to income generation rather than cost savings. Since faculty use citations in their grant proposals, this study connected the use of citations in successful proposals to library resources. So these results address one component of the library's role in a university's economy—bringing grant monies to a university.)

The Cost of Value Studies

You can take advantage of the work done by those who've gone before you by adding the simple, popular MLA value calculator (www.masslib.org/LibraryValue.html) to your website or by citing existing studies. If you want to do a complete study of your own, the cost can vary greatly. One broad estimate of the costs of ROI studies comes from "Worth Their Weight: An Assessment of the Evolving Field of Library Valuation":

> The cost of implementing a study is often cited as a deterrent to doing one. It is noteworthy that the individual library studies done in Suffolk County, NY, each cost approximately $5,000. While this amount is significant to a community library, it is not exorbitant and may be worth the outlay if the report tells a persuasive story to voters or policymakers. On the other end of the spectrum, countywide studies are said to cost $50,000 or more, and statewide studies run into the hundreds of thousands of dollars.[4]

By the way, this "Worth Their Weight" study and report were funded by The Bill & Melinda Gates Foundation. As you know, the Gateses only fund work that they see as really worthwhile.

The final word here is that being able to prove your value with hard numbers is more important and more possible than ever before. Even if you choose a route that costs thousands, the results can be worth much more, not only in respect gained but in dollars gained as well.

Endnotes

1. Sharon Begley, "We Fought Cancer … and Cancer Won," *Newsweek* September 15, 2008: 44.

2. Christie Koontz, "In-Library Usage Stats Are Essential," *Marketing Library Services* 21, no. 1 (January/February 2007): 1.

3. Joseph R. Matthews, *Measuring for Results: The Dimensions of Public Library Effectiveness* (Westport, CT: Libraries Unlimited, 2003).

4. Americans for Libraries Council, "Worth Their Weight: An Assessment of the Evolving Field of Library Valuation," 24. www.ila.org/advocacy/pdf/WorthTheirWeight.pdf (accessed January 27, 2009).

Chapter 9

Understanding the Cycle of True Marketing

Now it's time to talk about the full cycle of true marketing. I briefly outlined this cycle back in Chapter 2, but now that I've explained all the prerequisite information in the chapters that followed, I'll give you the complete story here.

The essential thing for accidental marketers to realize is that this isn't a linear process. The proper steps of true marketing don't form a straight line that you follow from the starting point to the finish line; they actually form a circle that continues forever. You need to think of it that way, rather than as an action with a beginning and an end. Marketing is a process where you find out what people want, provide it, ask your people how you did, go back and tweak things to improve the process, and then go round again. It's a constant cycle of providing and improving services, according to users' needs and desires. (Isn't that what libraries have always been about?)

All of the Steps in the True Marketing Process

Here are all of the steps you need to take to be engaged in a true marketing process:

A. Do some in-depth research to learn about the people in your service area. It's essential to get demographic information; geographic data can be very useful too. Cultural understanding helps as well.

B. Acknowledge that there are many different target audiences that make up your unique user population. Explore the people; segment them into various groups; keep lists of the groups and their attributes.

C. Set qualitative and quantitative goals for each group you want to reach out to.

D. Get to know people from each group; form relationships; start conversations; ask them what they want from you.

E. Identify products and services you already have that will benefit each target market according to the wants and needs expressed. If you don't have any yet, then create them.

F. Identify what the target groups currently use to fulfill these wants and needs; realize that these alternatives are your competition.

G. Think about ways to evaluate the effects of giving the people what they want. How will you know whether you're reaching them and satisfying them?

H. Promote your products and/or services to their respective markets in ways that will definitely reach those specific groups. (Getting to know the target customers will reveal how best to reach them.)

I. Deliver the products or services, making sure you have evaluative tools in place to determine whether people are hearing your message and using your offerings.

J. Get feedback; evaluate your success by comparing your results to the qualitative and quantitative goals you'd set earlier.

K. Given the evidence you've gathered in your evaluation process, note what you did well and what you could've done differently. Plan to implement whatever changes are necessary with your next round of projects.

L. Go back to whatever step in the process you could have done better. For instance, if you discovered that your promo methods didn't work well, go back to step H and figure out better ways to reach your targeted audience. If your evaluations reported that the product wasn't quite right, then go back to step E and tweak the product.

M. From whatever point you started over, cycle through the rest of the process again until your next evaluation. Note what worked better this time, and keep adjusting to improve the products and services as you go along.

I know, I know. That's a long list of intimidating, heavy-duty steps. But try not to run screaming. You can make this process work. Remember, you're in control, and you can customize everything to fit the needs of your own library or info center, be it large or small.

The key to not panicking is to realize that, while you do need to go through every step in this cycle, you can make the process as big or as small as you want to by choosing which target market to work on. You could do something as simple as asking book club members why their numbers are dwindling, finding out what they'd like, and tweaking the club's selections or meeting times to make them happier. Or you could choose something as in-depth as running a three-year campaign to create a brand designed to change the attitudes of a whole company's employees or an entire county's population. I recommend that you start small, get comfortable with the process, and get a few successes under your belt before you tackle anything massive.

But I don't want to get ahead of myself here. Before you start choosing which projects to take on, I want to go back and explain a bit more about each of these vital steps to marketing success.

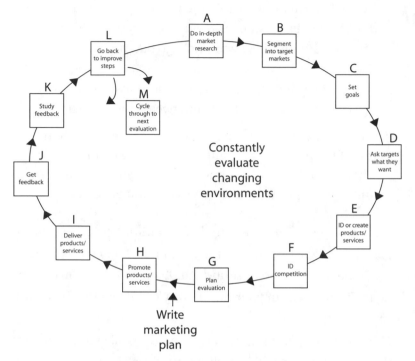

Figure 9.1   The Cycle of True Marketing

Follow These Vital Steps and You Will Find Success

Before you read through all of these steps again, take a deep breath. Try not to be scared of all the work that lies ahead. Keep a few comforting thoughts in mind:

- Doing the work involved in these steps will actually save time and money in the long run by keeping you from doing things that customers won't use or appreciate.

- All the research and fact-finding you do now will help ensure your success. Doing something right is ultimately more efficient than doing it poorly over and over again.

- Planning ahead makes everything work better. Begin with the end in mind.

OK now, are you ready to learn to do true marketing the right way? Great! Let's get into the steps. Once you see how much sense the process makes, I think you'll like it.

A. Do some in-depth research to learn about the people in your service area. It's essential to get demographic information; geographic data can be very useful too. Cultural understanding helps as well. As explained in Chapter 4, gathering demographic and geographic data about your area can be an eye-opening experience. Christie Koontz is a pioneer in this field, and the work she suggests makes wonderful sense. It's also the same sort of fact-finding that corporations and municipalities use to decide where to build their stores and institutions. (If you're ever involved in choosing a location for a new library building, these sorts of studies should be a core part of the planning process.)

You'll want to get the U.S. Census data for the area you serve and put it onto a map so you can see exactly where certain populations are. Blending this demographic data (on age, income, ethnicity, etc.) with basic geographic data gives you a whole new view of how to serve your various target markets. And if you overlay your patron address database onto the map, you can see gaps in your coverage and thereby identify whole new target audiences that you can reach out to.

If you don't work in a public library, but perhaps in an academic or a corporate one instead, you can still study data that your organization probably has just sitting around. Academic institutions surely know how many incoming freshmen there are each year; you could probably find out how many are majoring in each discipline (if they've declared), how many live on campus, what their age ranges are, and more. And companies certainly know where all their employees are, how much data access or clearance each one has, and what their specialties or primary assignments are. It shouldn't be hard to figure out that all employees who are studying, say, new adhesives are spread across a wide geographic area but they're all collaborating on one portion of the intranet. Once you realize what those people have in common, where they are, what their mission is, and how to reach them, you're well on your way to serving them better (and more proactively) than if you just kept to yourself and waited for them to send occasional questions to you.

For every type of library or research facility, information about users and potential customers exists somewhere. Since you want (and need) these people to use your services, the best way to start is by discovering the basic traits they have in common so you can segment them into groups. And you need to be digging deeper than men vs. women, young vs. old, book readers vs. music listeners, faculty vs. students, doctors vs. nurses. Because the more finely you can segment people into groups, the better you can serve each group.

B. Acknowledge that there are many different target audiences that make up your unique user population. Explore the people; segment them into various groups; keep lists of the groups and their attributes. I find it fun to think about different segments of populations because there are so many ways to categorize people. Some of the most basic ways are by gender, age, and ethnicity, of course, but you can go much deeper. To do that, you need to study more evidence and to get to know the people themselves.

Here are the main divisions to consider when grouping target markets:

- Exactly where they live or work (geographic segmentation)

- Age, gender, race, income level, education level (demo-graphic segmentation)

- Heavy users, nonusers, online-only users (behavioral segmentation)

- Interests, hobbies, activities (lifestyle segmentation)

Even within those groups, you can go deeper, breaking them up into smaller and smaller sub-segments. For instance, a sub-sub-segment could be 25- to 35-year-old women who play tennis but don't have library cards. You could partner with a racquet club to reach them or, better yet, infiltrate the group with one of your own sports-minded staffers.

To learn more about dividing people into target markets, see the May/June 2002 *MLS* article by Christie Koontz called "Market Segmentation: Grouping Your Clients."

C. Set qualitative and quantitative goals for each group you want to reach out to. Whenever you set goals, each one needs to have a component that you can measure—otherwise you'll never know if you've met the goal or not. Some things you can measure *quantitatively* (in real numbers) and some just *qualitatively* (raising the quality of something). The problem with libraries is that there's always been so much qualitative data ("I love the library; it makes me happy.") and much less quantitative information ("Circulation rose by 3% last month."). You need both, but these days you need the numerical stuff even more, because that's how outside entities (townships, corporations, boards of directors) measure your worth.

To set something you can measure, think about your goal very specifically. Do you want to raise usage of a certain something by 10 percent? Do you want to sign up 100 new people for library cards each month? Do you want to give eight bibliographic instruction courses each semester instead of the usual three or four? Do you want employees in a particular department to start using the info you provide on the company's intranet?

You can even set numerical goals for qualitative items. If you take a poll on customers' attitudes about your library, then provide useful classes, have fun events, and do some personal outreach, you can poll the same people afterward and see how their perceptions have changed. Your specific goal could be "We intend to achieve a 20 percent increase in positive answers to the statement, 'I think of the library as inviting and useful.'"

Each project or target market should have its own individual goals.

D. Get to know people from each group; form relationships; start conversations; ask them what they want from you. This can be a tricky step, but there's no end to the ways you can go about it. You can be formal, doing surveys or focus groups. You can be casual, having a pizza party to talk with students about what they think. You can be very personal, chatting with one or two customers at a time, simply asking questions when you see (or create!) an opportunity. Or you can do all of the above. You can also pass out simple evaluation forms or questionnaires, put a feedback button on your website, have a contest to bring in suggestions, or bring up questions at group meetings.

Choose your method according to the group of people you're getting to know and what works for them. But in any case, remember that this needs to be an ongoing conversation, not a once-and-done survey. You need to build ongoing relationships with people if you intend to serve them well; this is the case in any business or service organization. So you'll want to gather people's contact information to use in the future and make sure that it's OK for you to get in touch with them again. As long as you don't let your inquiries turn into constant interrogation or persistent pestering, people will often be responsive if they realize that you are making a genuine effort to serve them better. It helps too if you can make the process fun and engaging, or in some way worthwhile for the people who are helping you. (Make it sort of a party, provide food, offer prizes, have drawings for gifts, give free photocopy cards, etc.)

Once you've built good relationships, people will come to you with suggestions because they'll know you're really listening with the intent to improve. If you're really good at creating this culture of participation, you may find that you won't be able to stop it! But that would be a good problem to have.

This step, especially, shows how marketing needs to be an ongoing process. As you get to know people better, you can make your offerings fit them better.

E. Identify products and services you already have that will benefit each target market according to the wants and needs expressed. If you don't have any yet, then create them. Once you have a good grasp of what people in a certain target market want, then you can prepare to give it to them. Sometimes you already have what people are looking for, but they don't realize it. There could be several reasons for this: Maybe you're not promoting it enough or not promoting it with the right medium to reach this audience, or maybe the folks just don't ever think to look to the library for it. Maybe you're not even on their radar. (Don't worry; after you build your relationship, you will be.)

Don't be upset if everyone you survey is asking for a service you already offer; that happens more often than you'd think. The good news is that you already have what they want and don't need to invent it!

When people ask for products or services you don't offer, look into the possibilities. Sometimes, if you figure out what organizations *do* offer these, and you pass along the info, that's all it takes to satisfy the request. Don't feel as if you need to be all things to all people—in fact, that can be a recipe for disaster. Do what you can, and explain why you can't do the rest. Logical explanations can work wonders with many folks. Remember, they don't understand the inner workings of your organization. They might be upset by hearing "no," but following that immediately with a "why not" can go a long way toward fostering a positive attitude about your services.

There are times when people ask for things that you can and should do for them. It may be just a matter of tweaking an existing service or spinning it in a different way (offering home delivery for those who are *temporarily* home-bound, not on your regular list). Sometimes you'll need to start from scratch (creating a Twitter account). Sometimes you'll need to involve others (getting different features in your OPAC). The worst thing you can do is to always respond with, "Sorry, we don't do that." If enough people are asking for it, then you *should* be doing that, whatever "that" is. Remember, you exist to serve them.

When people ask for something that's easy to do, by all means, do it immediately. (Then tell them you did it, per their request!) You need to have a culture of change in your library that allows you to move forward without needing a big committee or a board meeting to address every little thing. Why can't you place a second book drop near the post office? Why can't you order a journal without waiting until the next serials budget is approved? Life changes at a fast pace these days, and your organization needs to do so too. But I digress …

F. Identify what the target groups use to fulfill these wants and needs already; realize that these alternatives are your competition. Part of getting to know people is learning how they currently work and play. Chances are their needs and wants haven't been going completely unfulfilled until you and your library came along. So what have these folks been doing without you?

Some answers are obvious: If they want movies, they've been renting from video stores or using a mail service such as Netflix or buying them outright. If they want factual information, they've likely been turning to the internet or to colleagues. All of your products and services have competition out there. You can't win business back from your competitors until you identify them, see why they've been successful, figure out what makes your version more desirable, and then communicate that value to people. In the case of movies, it's obvious what the competition is. The reason you're better here is because your service is free while the others cost money. You might also allow more films to be borrowed at one time. As for information providers, that situation is more complicated, and the answer depends a lot on what kind of information people are seeking. There are plenty of basics that the internet covers just fine. For more in-depth data, your service might be superior because your info is value-added, peer-reviewed, professionally reliable, easier to find, or again, free.

The fact is, in most cases, people who are already doing something one way are not apt to change. Remember, an object already in motion will maintain the same speed and trajectory (or something like that) unless it's acted on by an outside force. People have no reason to change unless you give them one, and it's got to be a darn good one. There has to be some tangible benefit for them that's enough to knock them off their current path. How are your offerings better than your competition's? Be prepared to spell that out.

G. Think about ways to evaluate the effects of giving the people what they want. How will you know whether you're reaching them and satisfying them? This goes back to the old "Begin with the end in mind." You're going to do something for people, then tell them about it. How will they be able to communicate back to you about whether it really worked for them? You need to build these feedback opportunities into your product planning.

For anything you're doing online, getting feedback can be easy because you can always program in a pop-up box that asks, "Did this work well for you?" or "Did you find what you needed?" Anything provided to customers in person can be simple too, because you can pass out paper survey forms with similar questions. It's the less-tangible requests and services that can be difficult to evaluate. But monitoring statistics, plus doing a little creative thinking and studying what other librarians have tried, can often do the trick.

H. Promote your products and/or services to their respective markets in ways that will definitely reach those specific groups. (Getting to know the target customers will reveal how best to reach them.) I never have to tell librarians that different sorts of people communicate in different ways. But I do have to remind them that they need to know how to communicate in all of those ways if they want to reach the various groups that they have messages for. As you question, survey, and build relationships with representatives of your many target markets, one of the main things you need to learn is how to communicate with each of them.

It doesn't take a brainiac to figure out that you can reach certain communities through their individual community newspapers or that you can reach 35- to 50-year-old men with drive-time radio. But what about, say, teenagers? Do they want emails and instant messages, or is it all Facebook and Twitter these days? (Or, are they old news already?) What about busy young mothers who don't have time for email or can't get their kids off the computer so they can use it themselves? What about executives who barely see daylight between one meeting and the next? What about doctors and nurses who can be called away at any minute?

You need to know how you can reliably get information to the many types of people who are your customers or potential customers. And you need to know not just how you *can* reach them, but how they *want* you to reach them. And there's only one way to do that: Ask them. You should never wonder or guess when you can ask.

I. Deliver the products or services, making sure you have eval uative tools in place to determine whether people are hearing your message and using your offerings. Finally, finally, it's time to launch or re-launch or announce or re-spin the products and services that people have asked you for. You've learned how to communicate with your target group and asked what they want from you. You've determined goals and given careful thought to gathering their opinions for future evaluation. You've designed things that you think will really please them. Now, put those things out there and watch your audience respond.

Be patient. Unless you're releasing some long-sought-after treasure to great fanfare, the response probably won't be immediate. Remember that other folks are at least as busy as you are. Allow time for your messages to reach the masses and then let them find time to partake of your offerings. If you've built in a mechanism for feedback or offered incentives for comments, then people who feel strongly about what you've done will respond.

J. Get feedback; evaluate your success by comparing your results to the qualitative and quantitative goals you'd set earlier. This is when you can really start to reap the benefits of all of your recent hard work. And this is when you need to know whether things are working or not, so aren't you glad you built in those evaluation methods? This is also the time to be honest with yourself. Don't discount negative comments and convince yourself that the commenter was just having a bad day. You asked for these opinions, and you need them, so listen closely to what people are really saying.

As the feedback trickles in, keep track of it and store it. Whether you collect your feedback on paper, electronically, or orally, hang onto your records for a good while after you've initially recorded the responses. Until you've gone through this process a lot, you won't know when you might want to go back to something to check a nuance or to get more info. No need to shred those surveys right away when you can store them safely in a file for at least a few months.

Be open-minded as you compare your results to your goals. Watch out for things that were just a little off, things you could've done differently, and things that are mentioned more than once. All the while, be thinking about what simple adjustments you could make that would change or eliminate negative comments.

K. Given the evidence you've gathered in your evaluation process, note what you did well and what you could've done differently. Plan to implement whatever changes are necessary with your next round of projects. It's important to make lists of things you did well along with lists of what you need to improve. Give yourself credit where it's due, and don't beat yourself up for things that weren't perfect. Remember a few essentials:

- This is a cycle; you have many chances to try again.
- This isn't a smackdown, and it's not personal.
- This is a learning experience that you want and need; it's your roadmap to improvement. Don't ignore the signs along the way.

You don't need to make changes in response to every little comment; just address those things that are requested by the majority. (And maybe a few little things that make you say, "Duh, of course!"

when you read them.) Use your evidence to start planning for next time. Aim for slow but steady improvement.

L. Go back to whatever step in the process you could've done better. For instance, if you discovered that your promo methods didn't work well, go back to step H and figure out better ways to reach your targeted audience. If your evaluations reported that the product wasn't quite right, then go back to step E and tweak the product. What will help you at this point is having good answers to your carefully written evaluation questions. If you asked yes-or-no queries ("Was this program helpful?") then you won't be sure what to tweak here. But if you asked more pointed questions ("If this program could've been more helpful, please tell us how.") then you'll be on your way faster.

This feedback will help you get the changes made, too. As I explained earlier, if you need to convince managers or colleagues that your formula needs to be adjusted, you'll now have more than just your intuition—you'll have evidence to back up your claims.

M. From whatever point you started over, cycle through the rest of the process again until your next evaluation. Note what worked better this time, and keep adjusting to improve the products and services as you go along. There's nothing new in this statement; it's just one more point in the cycle. Keep on going around until you and your customers are happy with what you're offering. This is the essence of true marketing.

Every few years, you should step back and take a look at the bigger picture. Even though you'll be constantly evaluating your efforts for each target market, you should also have a timetable for taking a fresh look at your processes as a whole. Major changes may occur in your environment that will affect the way you work:

- Demographics shift over time, as people move and populations change.

- New construction of housing, shopping, parks, businesses, or infrastructure will change the area you serve.

- Management may decide on different priorities, or management may change altogether.

- Your library or parent organization may write a new mission statement.

- Your library's physical building ages and may be replaced—or not.

- Your financial status changes.

- New technologies affect the way people work with information.

So you should set a time every two or three years to re-evaluate the big picture. That schedule should be written into your overall marketing plan. "What overall marketing plan?" you ask. Well, guess what the next chapter is about ... read on.

Chapter 10

Writing Your Formal Plans

The idea of writing a formal plan can be intimidating, but a little knowledge can go a long way. Once you understand the differences between various types of plans, things will look a lot clearer. So let's start by defining the major ones, in the order they should be tackled:

- A **strategic plan** spells out the vision for the whole organization. It lists your primary products and services, your main customers, and the overall strategy for where your organization wants to go and how it plans to get there.

- A **marketing plan** defines how you intend to move your goods or services to the intended audience. It includes the "marketing mix" of the Four Ps, which are product, price, place, and promotion. A marketing plan is a guide for how you're going to do the research on each target market and how you're going to reach those people based on what you learn about them.

- A **communication plan** is the one in which you outline just how you're going to communicate with the world. There are both external and internal communication plans (because you need to spread your message within your organization too). But external plans usually center around establishing long-term relationships with the media. You might write several mini communication plans as part of your larger marketing plan.

The Proper Hierarchy of Plans

Everything that happens in your library or information center should be based on your parent organization's strategic plan. Everyone who makes visionary decisions about where the library is headed needs to read, know, live, and breathe that strategic plan. If that's not happening, then you're already out of alignment with your main goals (and maybe with a few planets, too).

If your library or info center is part of a corporation, school, university, or other larger entity, then you must base your actions and decisions on its plan. That doesn't mean that you shouldn't also write a strategic plan just for the library. It will still be based on the bigger entity that you're serving, but you can boil down its goals and strategies to spell out exactly what *you* need to do to support them. The library's own strategic plan will be your guiding light for everything else you do.

Marketing plans should always be written *after* the strategic plan and should spell out the goals you want to reach and actions for getting you there. While you'll have one major plan, you'll probably end up with many smaller sub-plans that detail individual projects.

Communication plans are the last ones you should write, because they outline how to get the word out about what you're doing. And of course, you don't know exactly what you'll be doing until you've finalized your strategic and marketing plans. Once you've decided on what to do and how to do it, you'll know when you'll need to use the media, and your communication plan will guide you through disseminating that information to your public.

Here's a simple example of plan hierarchy for an academic setting. Your own strategic plan says that you want to make your library the first place people on campus turn to for all their information needs. Your marketing plan says you need to court faculty members, to convince students to use your resources, and to communicate more with staff members university-wide. All three are big jobs, so you'll need to write specific sub-plans for each group. For faculty, you might decide to flatter them by setting up a system in which you buy a copy of every book that members publish, then offer each author a forum to do a book talk in the library. You might also set up meetings between faculty and subject liaisons prior to each semester to ask how the librarians can best support the professors' upcoming courses. To reach the faculty, you might choose to use a faculty/staff newspaper or email list. Then you'll do more mini-plans to accomplish your goals with the student and staff groups as well.

Sound like mega-planning-mania? Well, maybe it is. But plans lead to results. And a lack of plans usually leads to floundering around and working piecemeal, which often accomplishes a whole lot of nothing.

The good news is that most strategic and marketing plans are written to cover three-year or five-year increments. So once they're written, you follow them for a good while before you need to update and rewrite them for the next time period.

All About Marketing Plans

This book being what it is, I'm going to concentrate on marketing plans. Every organization probably tackles them a little differently, but I can tell you the necessary steps and let you mold them to fit your own needs.

I teach a half-day workshop called Create Your Own Customized Marketing Plan. I begin by defining lots of basic words and concepts to make sure that everyone who's there is speaking the same language. (There's still a lot of confusion about the difference between the words *marketing* and *promotion*.) I also highlight various marketing tools (surveys, testimonials, sound bites, good website positioning, etc.) and talk a bit about marketing materials. (People don't think of things like business cards as promotional items, but they really are. Ponder: How unimportant do you look if you *don't* have business cards?)

Next, I speak briefly about mission statements, because if you don't have one, then you can't ensure that your marketing plan will support your mission. I also emphasize the importance of doing research to get to know your audience well, so you can segment them more clearly. I try to ensure that all attendees have a firm grasp of these prerequisites (as I've done in this book) before we start writing the plans. (See the sidebar, "Things to Know and Do Before Writing Your Marketing Plan" on page 165.)

Once all my workshop attendees have the proper background information and they're in a marketing mindset, I start explaining how to write a simple marketing plan. One caveat is that nobody can write a complete plan in a few hours, especially without involving all the people who would have to have a hand in it (and especially where approvals are necessary). But what my students do leave with is a full outline, written in logical order that they can expand on when they get back to work.

Five Steps to a Basic Marketing Plan

Here are the five steps we go through in my workshops:

1. Choose and describe your target market.

2. Describe the services you offer for this group, in terms that really attract customers.

3. Identify your competition and how you can overcome it.

4. Pick a few promotional strategies that will reach your chosen target.

5. Establish measurable goals.

Things to Know and Do Before Writing Your Marketing Plan

- Be familiar with your parent organization's strategic plan.
- Have a strategic plan for the library and know it well.
- Consider your library's mission statement (and vision statement if you have one).
- Know the Four Ps and what each means.
- Understand the differences between marketing, promotion, publicity, and public relations, and realize what the cycle of true marketing is.
- Involve managers and colleagues to build support and to ensure buy-in later on.
- Think about what materials and resources you have available for your marketing project. (That includes not only physical materials, spaces, and money but also expertise and potential partners.)
- Finally, start working your way through the cycle of true marketing.

I think this is another mistake that many accidental marketers make: They try to jump right into writing a plan without realizing there are so many prerequisites to take care of. Now you know.

This all sounds simple enough, and it is, if you've done all the work you should've done before you reach the point of actually writing the plan. Let me explain a bit more about each step, then we'll see how they mesh with the overall marketing process.

1. Choose and describe your target market. You serve many markets, and you need to write a separate plan to fit each one that you want to reach. (However, basic elements of one plan can also work for others. The later steps are the ones that need to be the most customized.) I have each attendee choose one particular group that he or she wants to focus on in the context of the workshop.

(*Hint:* Don't start with your most difficult one!)

2. Describe the services you offer for this group, in terms that really attract customers. This is where you think about clear communication and avoiding lingo. And you can't just say, "We offer information." This is the time to think outside the box and to describe your services in ways that your potential customers will understand and value. It's a big bonus if you can talk with people in the target group and test your words on them to see what really makes sense to them and what actually attracts them.

(*Hint:* Here are two ways to say the same thing—which will really get through? "We can search full-text databases and get relevant results lists," or, "We're experts in excavating the exact data you need, when you need it.")

3. Identify your competition and how you can overcome it. You'll never be the first stop on the info train if your target audience isn't even riding the same rails you are. If you have a service that you know they need, but they're not using it, then what are they using instead? Do your potential patrons rely on friends and colleagues for information? Do they search the open web when they need something? Why do they work that way; why do they prefer it? What would make them change? This is where your customer research is essential.

(*Hint:* You can't overcome your competition without fully understanding it first.)

4. Pick a few promotional strategies that will reach your chosen target. Your research comes to the rescue here again: You need to know where your customers hang out and what they do. Will they read paper messages or only email? How do they think; how do they learn? One size does not fit all. Any message you want to put out should be written in different ways for different audiences.

(*Hint:* If you don't speak in the language and communicate in the format that your patrons already know and accept, they'll never hear your messages.)

5. Establish measurable goals. This is one step that untrained marketers simply skip all too often. It seems like extra work, yet it's the best way to find out whether your efforts are making a difference. And really, why bother doing anything if you have no way to find out whether it worked? More importantly, why bother if you can't learn from your first attempt how to improve subsequent ones?

(*Hint:* Make measurement easy; provide a simple way for target users to send feedback.)

Once you've worked your way through these five steps, you will have in mind a particular group of people that you know a lot about, along with a list of what you offer to those folks. You'll know something about how they might already be fulfilling their needs without you, and you'll have crafted a message that they will see and hear. You've set goals for how you want to affect this set of people, as well as for how you will measure the effect of your marketing campaign.

Workshop participants enjoy walking through the process in a group, especially because they get to brainstorm together after I explain each step. And I enjoy fluttering between groups to offer inspiration and to learn about their unique situations and challenges.

The Marketing Plan as Part of the Cycle of True Marketing

Now let's look at these five steps of writing a marketing plan in the context of the entire cycle of true marketing (from Chapter 9) to see how they fit together as a whole workflow—nay—lifestyle:

A. Do some in-depth research to learn about the people in your service area. It's essential to get demographic information; geographic data can be very useful too.

B. Acknowledge that there are many different target audiences that make up your unique user population. Use your research data to segment them into various groups.

C. Set initial qualitative and quantitative goals for your work with each group.

D. Get to know people from each group that you intend to reach out to; ask them what they want from you and how they want to get it.

E. Identify products and services you already have that will benefit each target market according to the wants and needs expressed. (If you don't have any already, decide whether you can create them.)

F. Identify what the target groups currently use to fulfill these wants and needs; realize that these alternatives are your competition.

G. Think about ways you can evaluate your success in delivering what the people want (by measuring how well you meet the goals set out in step C).

Now write your formal marketing plan, using the info you gathered in the previous steps.

H. Promote your products and/or services to their respective markets in ways that will definitely reach those specific groups. (In other words, begin to carry out your marketing plan.)

I. Deliver the products or services, making sure you have evaluative tools in place to determine whether people are hearing your message and using your offerings.

J. Get feedback; evaluate your success by comparing your results to the qualitative and quantitative goals you'd set earlier.

K. Given the evidence you've gathered in your evaluation process, note what you did well and what you could've done differently. Plan to implement whatever changes are necessary with your next round of projects.

L. Go back to whatever step in the process you could have done better.

M. From whatever point you started over, cycle through the rest of the process again until your next evaluation. Note what worked better this time, and keep adjusting to improve the products and services as you go along.

As you can see—actually, as I hope you've already figured out by this point in the book—there's a lot of work to be done before you even begin writing your marketing plan. My five steps for creating the marketing plan are meant for those who have already done research and who have many of the pieces in place. Unfortunately, though, many people try to begin with the marketing plan, ignoring (or simply ignorant of) all the work that needs to come before.

If you're an accidental marketer and you've been wondering why some of your efforts have failed, by now you probably have a good idea of what went wrong (or what never "went" at all). The good news, though, is that you also know how to start doing it better from now on.

How a Communication Plan Can Help

Since communication plans are the tools that enable you to spread your message to a large audience, I'll discuss them here briefly. Then I'm going to recommend that you check out Appendix A to read a case study that illustrates the idea clearly and simply.

As the name implies, a communication plan is created to organize the ways you'll tell your news to others. As with other types of plans, you'll need to do some research and then use your findings to create a set of steps to follow. Actually, it can be more of a flowchart, with lots of "if/then" scenarios: "If we want television coverage, then call Esmeralda. If we want a full-length newspaper feature, then do X, Y, and Z in the three weeks before the event."

One of the most basic things you can do is set up a simple list or database of all of your media contacts. This may seem obvious, but if you're accidentally doing promotion only once in a while, and if different people are promoting different things and there's no set person in charge, it's quite conceivable that no list exists. If everyone is just rushing around sending out little press releases or emails as time permits, then doing something as simple as creating this contact list could impose some order on your chaos.

You'll want to simply gather basic contact and coverage info for all the media employees who might broadcast your news. Make a chart or spreadsheet with a list of news organizations and their reporters/editors on one axis and headings for info on the other: phone numbers, email addresses, snail-mail addresses, contact preferences, beats covered, and deadlines. (Deadlines will vary with the medium. A newspaper that comes out every Thursday might have a deadline of 2 PM Tuesdays; nightly TV news might be 3 PM each day, etc.) The resulting chart will look something like the sample I've created (see Table 10.1).

One reason for compiling this list is to eliminate the need to scrounge around for contact data all the time; the other (more important) reason is to target your messages properly. You should

Table 10.1

Media Channel & Staff Member	Office phone #	Cell phone #	Email	Snail mail	Contact how?	Beat	Deadline
MLS-TV, Channel 6 Jane Miller, Sr. Reporter Jim Dirk, Community Reporter							
The Doe Report, newspaper Jane Doe, Chief Editor John Doe, Reporter							
82.3, WLIS, Radio Ben Exodus, Station Manager Gates Paul, News Director							

not be sending all of your messages out to all of your contacts every time. If you overload editors with all sorts of inappropriate messages, it'll be like crying wolf. If most of the messages your contacts get from you don't fit their needs, they'll start ignoring all of them. Then, when you really need their coverage, those over-loaded folks won't be there for you.

As you can imagine, a communication plan is more than just a media list. It's difficult to give advice on this topic because there are so many libraries that have vastly different communications needs and opportunities. Some will never use mainstream media, but that doesn't mean they shouldn't have these plans. Some librarians will rely more on intranets, wikis, or blogs to reach their target audiences. Some would never have a use for radio announcements, while others can simply rely on member newsletters and email blasts. The best way to handle your mass communication needs will always depend on what type of library you're in and who you're reaching out to, what tools they pay attention to, and what your message is. That's why communication plans come last. But any good library promoter should always have a complete list of available avenues on hand, so he or she is prepared to get a message out at a moment's notice.

That said, I'll now refer you to the aforementioned Appendix A, where you'll find a full-length article that Marsha Iverson wrote for *MLS*. It's a really useful case study in which Iverson details how she realized that her standard approach to media relations wasn't working, and how she and the community relations staffers at King County (WA) Library System did a three-step needs assessment, and then developed a communication plan in which they treated the media as a primary audience instead of just a tool. The detailed records of press coverage that Iverson keeps proves that the formal plan works.

A Word About Technology Plans

Technology plans aren't part of marketing plans, but they should inform them. Your library probably has a technology plan, and if you're not aware of one, talk to your info tech staffers and find out for sure. So much revolves around technology, and these days everyone simply expects your library (and every other organization under the sun) to have high-level tech tools. Those tools need to be factored into your marketing plan in several ways:

- You should be promoting the fact that you have technologies for customers to use and shouting about the benefits that people can reap from taking advantage of them.

- You should be using technology to gather and assess marketing data.

- You should be using technology as a promotional tool to carry your messages to target audiences that use those communication formats.

Don't forget that the way you use technology has a tremendous effect on the way people view your organization. Many librarians are working hard to shed old perceptions and the "we're all books" stereotype. Using technology intelligently is one of the best ways to change people's minds and to show them what libraries can be in this day and age. That's another major reason that you need to incorporate technology into your marketing.

So just as a strategic plan dictates the content of your marketing plan, a technology plan should affect both your marketing and communication plans. Know what's available, and when and how it will change, and use your tech tools and tactics to your greatest advantage.

Sharing Plans Among Friends

One of the best ways to study all sorts of plans is to get examples from colleagues. Many librarians, of all different types, have posted their plans on their websites for all to see. Sharing plans is also a frequent topic on ALA's listserv PRTalk, which is dedicated to "promotional activities and library PR issues." You can always ask there and be assured of a friendly, helpful reply. (If you're not already on PRTalk, join immediately; it's a wonderful resource! Just go to lists.ala.org/sympa/info/prtalk and click *Subscribe* on the left; you'll be prompted for your email address. There's also a list focused on higher-ed libraries called AcademicPR at lists.ala.org/sympa/info/academicpr.) Of course, you can't simply copy what others have done, because each plan is customized, but you can see how peers handled certain things or find formats or phrases that you like.

When an entire organization coordinates all of its plans at the highest levels, it helps ensure that everyone involved is working in concert toward the most important goals.

Recommended Reading

Dodsworth, Ellen. "Marketing Academic Libraries: A Necessary Plan." *The Journal of Academic Librarianship* 24:4 (1998): 320–322.

Donald, Roslyn. "Marketing: A Challenge for Corporate Librarians." InSite Pro. www.insitepro.com/donald3.htm (accessed January 27, 2009).

Kassel, Amelia. "How to Write a Marketing Plan." *Marketing Library Services* 13:5 (June 1999): 4.

Nelson, Sandra. *Strategic Planning for Results*. Chicago: ALA, 2008.

Owens, Irene, ed. *Strategic Marketing in Library and Information Science*. Binghamton, NY: The Haworth Press, 2003. Co-published simultaneously as *The Acquisitions Librarian* 28 (2002).

Chapter 11

Basic Rules for Producing Good Promotional Materials

So you have a marketing plan, you've chosen a target group to work with, and you've decided what you want to tell them. Now the fun of creating your materials begins.

This can be quite easy, really, provided that you know some basic rules and have some tools and talent at your disposal. And that might be the main thing that accidental marketers forget: Just keep it simple. People absorb messages better if they are short, clear, and easy to read. This chapter will help you assure that your messages are.

Craft Your Message Carefully

The first thing you need to decide is exactly what you want to tell people with the particular promotional piece you're creating. What's the main point? Whether you're working on a flier, poster, email message, web content, or brochure, your message is the most important part. You'll want to refer back to Chapter 2, which discussed the keys to clear communication and the ways to avoid library lingo.

Once you have your attention-getting, top-level message, decide what other info to add according to what sort of piece you're creating. Obviously for a poster, you'll just need to add the "who, what, when, where" and tell people how to get more information or buy tickets or sign up; whatever's necessary. If you're designing a general-interest brochure, you'll probably want to include info about each department or service, list your open hours and all contact info, etc. Web content has some rules of its own. So you need to realize that if you plan to promote one thing using various formats, you won't be able to use the exact same text in each instance. While your key message may remain the same, you're going to have to tweak and customize at least a little for each unique promotional vehicle.

Remember, too, that all the text you write needs to appeal to the potential customer or attendee. Don't write what you want to say; instead, write what they want to know. Always write with "WIIFM" in mind, to answer the attendees' unspoken question, What's In It For Me?

Here's a quick example of how to start with a vanilla message, then make it pop. Let's say you're planning a fundraising event and you want to use posters and email messages to get the word out. What are the first phrases that come to your mind? Maybe "Come to a fundraiser for the library!" That's what *you* want to say, but who really wants to hear another appeal for money? A phrase like "Support your library!" might sound better to patrons, but it's too vague. So ask yourself what the hook is—why would people want to come to this event? Then you'll get into phrases like "Come to the library's fundraiser and meet a movie star!" or "Enter to win a new TV at the library's fundraiser." Ah, now you're getting somewhere. (Note: If your fundraiser doesn't have a hook—something that will make people want to attend, other than their goodwill—then back up and rethink things a little. Redesign the event so it has some major attraction, or risk low attendance.)

For the event's poster, after your fascinating headline, you'll want to add only a few details, keeping them sparse enough to be read from a distance. (Most people don't read posters from a few inches away.) The most important things to include are the date, time, and location. People need this info immediately to judge whether they can even attend, so make that text big and bold. Then tell them what exactly is going on: "Movie star Jane Hotstuff will be there to sign autographs for anyone who donates $25 or more to the library's new building fund." End by giving folks a way to find out more details if they want; a short snappy URL is the best way. You absolutely do not want to use one of those way-too-crazy-long-overblown URLs like "http://www.yourtownlibrary.org/fundraiser/PRdept-December/infoforpatrons.Hotstuff.com." Seriously, who can remember that, especially if they read it on a poster or something, and they're not in front of a computer? Even if that's where your info has to live online, that doesn't have to be your URL. Ask your IT person to create an automatic redirect from a short, memorable URL that matches your message, like www.JaneHotstuff_at_library.org.

Now let's say you're writing an email announcing this same event. Take your catchy headline, "Come to the library's fundraiser to meet a movie star!" and shorten it to fit into the visible subject line of an email. Something like "Movie star at library fundraiser!" (But make sure it doesn't sound like spam.) The text of the message can be the same as that of the poster. I suggest you still have the date, time, and location at the top, large and bold, since people skim email quickly and want to get the gist in just a few seconds. Also make sure the sentence "Movie star Jane Hotstuff will be there to sign autographs for anyone who donates $25 or more to the library's new building fund" is near the top. If people decide the event is of interest to them, then they'll read the smaller print. So at that point you can include other details.

Crafting your message for maximum impact really isn't hard. Just think about the way you read and evaluate your own email messages. Ask friends what makes them read theirs. And there are plenty of studies about how people read email and what makes them act on it. But unless you're in the email marketing business, you don't need to study all the research. You'd be surprised how far you can get with a lot of forethought, a little common sense, and a descriptive, non-spammy subject line.

Design Rules for Creating Good Promotional Materials

Once you have your message written and have some idea how you want to present it, it's time to actually design the materials. In this section I'm going to concentrate on creating print materials. If you're an accidental marketer, chances are you're an accidental designer, too. Whether you're just struggling to put together words and clip art in a word-processing program or you're attempting to use some high-end software package, the same basic rules apply.

I've spent about 20 years in publishing and have worked with professional designers and graphic artists on countless projects, from fun birthday cards to full-color magazines to books to DVD labels. I've learned an awful lot from them, and I'll boil it down for you. But my first rule is, don't do this alone if you don't have to. If your library or parent organization has any sort of design department or publicity office, try to use it to the fullest extent allowed. And listen to the designers' suggestions. They've been trained in the best ways to piece things together, in how to use "white space" (leaving some areas blank so a piece doesn't look too busy), and in how to create items that are clean and readable. If you want a bookmark to be orange and purple, and your designer says "No way!" then you should listen. Professional graphic artists know their craft, and you should trust their judgment.

But let's assume for now that you do have to create something on your own. Here's what the experts would tell you:

- **Don't** go overboard. This means don't use lots of different fonts (typefaces) or colors. Just because they exist doesn't mean you should use them.

- **Do** pick just one or two fonts. That makes things easier to read.

- **Don't** crowd the page. Keep graphics and text to a minimum. People don't read things that look overwhelming. In print design, less is more.

- **Do** use a graphic element to add interest. Just one photo or piece of clip art (maybe two) can attract attention to your piece. You can also create graphic interest with a simple border, box, or shape, or even by adding one color or printing on colored paper.

- **Don't** put up handmade signs. In this day and age when computers make things so easy to create, handwritten work looks sloppy and very unprofessional.

- **Do** keep the audience in mind while designing. Use simpler or larger fonts for people who don't see very well; use pictures of kids if you're designing for parents, etc.

- **Don't** sacrifice clarity for cleverness. A font that's a beautiful, flowing, italic script might be fitting for a fancy event—but it might be very hard to read. Remember, people are likely to glance at your promo piece for just a couple of seconds before they move on. If they can't read the heading, you've lost them.

- **Never** throw together wacky rainbow colors, wild fonts, and fuzzy pictures, unless you're promoting a groovy '70s throwback event.

Even if this is all you know about graphic design, you'll avoid some of the biggest mistakes that amateurs make.

Consultant Pat Wagner of Pattern Research, Inc. wrote a wonderful article on this topic, complete with illustrations of what to do and what not to do. With her permission, I've reprinted it here: See Appendix B to read it in its entirety and to see her examples.

Her article also includes a short glossary of typography terms to help you work with designers and understand software options.

Speaking of software packages, there are a handful of excellent ones out there you might want to try:

- Adobe PageMaker/Adobe InDesign (www.adobe.com)
- Microsoft Office Publisher (www.microsoft.com)
- Corel Ventura (www.corel.com)
- Serif PagePlus (www.serif.com)
- QuarkXPress (www.quark.com)

Many library promo people like to use PageMaker for simple design needs. However, the latest version, 7.0, is now outdated and Adobe's website says the company is no longer supporting PageMaker (www.adobe.com/products/pagemaker). InDesign is Adobe's newer tool, and licensed PageMaker users can get a special deal on an upgrade. Microsoft Publisher is regarded as a good basic package. Corel Ventura specializes in "long, complex documents," according to its online description. Serif's PagePlus is a solid competitor that comes at a much lower cost than most of the other professional packages. QuarkXPress is very powerful tool, but can also be somewhat complicated for the uninitiated; many pros use it.

To use any of these tools well—certainly if you want to exploit their full potential—you should take classes. Learning the ins and outs will save you hours and hours of frustration. If you want to read more about their features and get help choosing a package, you might want to check out the great overview on About.com at desktoppub.about.com/od/software/f/software_list.htm.

One way to keep your print projects simple (especially press releases and everyday fliers) is to use a template. This means having a semi-blank document that contains all of your standard styles, fonts, and information. It saves you from having to start from scratch every time. Most of the software tools I just mentioned come with some starter templates built in.

Templates are particularly useful in situations where different people are creating materials, for several reasons. First, using a template speeds up the work. Second, it ensures that all the standard identification data is always present. Third, it ensures a consistent look, which is essential to your brand. (It also forces consistency on those renegades who'd do everything their own way if given half a chance.) Finally, it makes everything appear more professional.

Tracking Workflow for Promotional Materials

Tracking the flow of work for printed materials can be one of the most challenging aspects of the job. The process of creating, checking, and producing print projects is long enough as it is, and the more people you add to the mix, the harder it gets. I tend to favor a dictatorial approach to the process, but hey, that's just me. If you can't have total control of your projects, you must at least establish a set of steps that includes checks and balances, along with a hierarchy of who may or may not make changes. Having too many hands stirring the print pot just results in chaos.

These are the most basic steps of creating print materials:

1. Decide exactly what you're creating, and for whom.

2. Craft your message and write the text.

3. Choose graphics, colors, etc.

4. Put the piece together.

5. Get it approved by supervisors, event coordinators, etc.

6. Implement any changes or corrections.

7. Have one or more people proofread it.

8. Ask someone (other than yourself) to take a final look.

9. Send it to press with instructions and due dates.

10. Check an early proof if the printer allows it.

I advocate having lots of people looking at a piece but giving few of them the right to change it. Suggestions are one thing; edicts are another. You don't want to have the event organizer (the person who ordered the print piece) ask that it be done on blue paper to match the event's decorations, then have some manager decide it should be on yellow paper because she likes yellow better. Every step in this process should be focused on creating the best piece to do the job it's intended to do. Everyone involved needs to understand the importance of putting personal preferences aside. When I advise that lots of people look at a piece in progress, the purpose is to get different takes on whether the message is clear enough, to ensure the absence of typos, and to catch potential errors before printing. It's not to get lots of opinions about how something should look or how it should be worded. You need to establish that just a few people can make those decisions (preferably the ones who know the event and the audience best), and then stick to your procedures (and to your guns).

That said, there are various ways to track whatever workflow you ultimately agree on. Your choice will depend on countless factors, including how many printed pieces you produce each month, how many people are involved, whether you have staff members dedicated to this process, and whether those involved work full-time or part-time. At the very least, you should have a tracking sheet (paper is OK; online is much better) with spaces for all of these items:

- Job name

- What's being made (flier, brochure, etc.)

- Who ordered it

- Date job comes in

- Date by which it must be done

- Date by which it must be delivered (if it's going off-site)

- All of the steps in your process (like the previous list)

- Spaces for people to sign off on each step with their name and date

- Date due to printer

- Date that printer's proof is due to you

- Date that job is expected back from printer

- Any necessary shipping info (if it's going off-site)

As you can see, there are a lot of details involved, and having a tracking tool in place is essential for getting things done well, done on time, and done without losing your mind. Organization is the key.

Some pieces of software are designed to track things like this, if you want to go that route. Some good things about software packages are that they can do the job efficiently, and they usually allow people to access the records from different locations (branches). On the down side, there's always someone who will find it hard to learn the program or see it as a hindrance. In those cases, you might do just as well making your own checklist with a basic word-processing or spreadsheet program that you keep on your intranet or server.

One thing that's for sure about tracking workflow is that one person needs to be completely accountable for each job from start to finish. It's easy for a proof to languish on someone's desk or get lost in someone's in-box. Somebody has to be responsible for keeping the job moving and keeping it on schedule. That's part of why I like to see a sort of dictator, whip-cracker, or otherwise-forceful personality in charge, because it's not easy to get lots of small, multi-person jobs done in a busy organization. It's common for those involved peripherally to say, "Oh, that's just a little flier, what's the big deal?" But if that flier is promoting something that matters to the library's reputation, success, or bottom line, then it's not such a little thing after all.

All promotional materials are very important. If you're making some that aren't, then maybe you shouldn't be spending time on those. Concentrate on what really matters. Not every story hour or book club meeting needs its own printed announcements. (Instead make lists for a month or more at a time.) Printing materials for every little thing creates overcrowded, disorganized bulletin boards and leads to information overload. Prioritize!

Helpful Tips for Working With Print Shops

The final step in making your promo materials is, of course, having them printed. Again, if you already have in-house capabilities that are part of your organization, use them. If you don't, you'll need to find a print shop nearby. These are plentiful, so this usually won't be a problem. If you haven't worked with a printer before, ask around for recommendations. (*Hint*: This can be a great topic for a cold call to a nearby business you've been meaning to partner with. You can phone their PR person to ask for their opinions and expertise about print vendors, and later you'll have a reason to call them again to say how your job turned out. Instant relationship!)

The first thing to know about the printing business is that you should always get more than one bid for any print job. (When I say "print job," I mean something more than everyday photocopies.) Prices can vary a good bit from place to place, depending on various factors such as how busy each shop is at the moment, what types of paper each carries, and what sort of presses they run.

Sometimes you can get discounts if you have jobs that aren't time-sensitive, things that the print shop manager can do piece-meal between other jobs to even out the workflow. So if you don't need those posters back until next month, but your design is all done and ready to go, you could ask your printer about taking the job early. And while you don't need to know much about the various types of printing equipment, you do need to keep in mind that different presses imprint different products, so if your job involves anything other than standard paper, some vendors won't have the equipment to handle it. Also, certain shops can tackle folding or binding better than others. It's best to start calling around early so you have time to find a printer that can meet your needs.

Of course, once you've had experience with a few printers and you've found some that work for you, you'll know where to turn next time you have a similar job. You probably don't need to compare bids more than once a year or so.

Printing technology has come a long way in the past 20 years, so now you can get really nice work done just about anywhere. But if you want a special type of heavy card stock or seeded paper, or if you're printing onto a package or anything out of the ordinary, I'd advise you to call around and ask to see finished samples of other work. Specialty printers are not all created equal.

It All Reflects on Your Library

The last thing to remember about your promo materials, or anything you send out, is that they all reflect on your library. Using tasteful stationery says something about you. Having too-busy, over-crowded posters says something about you. Printing on cheap, thin paper says something about you. Anything that has your organization's name on it is a representation that others will see, evaluate, and judge. Treat everything you create with that in mind.

Chapter 12

Getting the Message Out

The thing about having an important message is that, if it doesn't get out to people, it doesn't do any good. And now that you've crafted important messages that are well-targeted to certain groups of people, it's time to get them out there.

The marketing plan that you've written should include strategies to reach each of your target markets—because, based on your research into those markets, you've learned how each one prefers to communicate. Some things are obvious. For instance, you wouldn't send Twitter messages to old folks or put ads in newspapers to reach children. You wouldn't post time-sensitive scientific data on hallway bulletin boards or post results from requested research on the open web. You know the basic channels to use to reach the different people you're dealing with. But your customer research should inform your communication decisions even further, and those details should be written into the mini marketing plans you've made for each specific outreach campaign. Now you're ready to put those plans into practice.

My Recommendations for Communication

While your customers have told you how best to communicate with them, I'd like to add some of my own recommendations to the mix. I want to get you thinking about communicating in ways that are more suited to the future than the past:

- Bulletin boards full of papers are passé. They easily become cluttered and unattractive. They are not a good place to post anything of real import. One possible exception is if you have one right by a service desk or a self-checkout machine—a place where people are likely to wait in line for a few minutes—if you have only a few pieces of paper on it at a time. Give people something they can read in three minutes while they have three minutes with nothing to do. But this should only be a back-up for real, targeted communication.

- Some libraries have already moved on to putting their in-house messages on flat-screen monitors instead of bulletin boards; this is definitely the wave of the very-near future. Create a few short headlines that can run in a loop on a system like this. It's not complicated for your IT department to set up this kind of system, and colorful motion on a screen definitely gets people's attention. I heard of one library that has a big screen mounted in the lobby so that passers-by on the street can see it. That's a great way to pull people inside.

- If you're still mailing announcements to outside organizations on paper, you're probably looking pretty old-fashioned. Of course you should ask your contacts how they want to hear from you, but I'm betting that most would rather get email these days. It's instant, and it's easier to share with others. And with more and more people jumping on the "green" bandwagon, it looks good to avoid sending paper.

- I know lots of you still use bookmarks as a way to tell or to remind customers about upcoming events. Personally, I hate bookmarks. I think they're a waste of money and they make you look bad. Remember, anything you give away with your name on it reflects on you. Think of the qualities of most paper bookmarks: colorful, yes, but also cheap, thin, flimsy, and disposable. I'd rather see librarians invest their precious money in something more lasting. If you must do bookmarks, then make sure they're printed on heavy cardstock and/or are laminated. And don't just silently stick them in books as you check them out; speak to the patron about the topic at hand. Better yet, hand the bookmark to the person so he can read it while you're handling his books, thus ensuring that he pays some attention to it. If you just put it into a book without saying a word, it's likely to be ignored. But if you hand it to the customer and he reads it then and there, two things can happen. He may realize it's not an event that matters to him, and he can put the bookmark back onto the desk (so you've not wasted one). Or, if he is interested, he can ask questions right on the spot, or better yet, sign up right away. Then you've made a real connection.

- If you put announcements on your website, that's a great start. But you need to make sure they're findable, clear, and organized. Many libraries have a section on their home pages with rotating headlines, which can be effective since readers' eyes are attracted to the motion. If your website has this feature, make sure there's an obvious link underneath to "Click here to read more" so people don't have to try to catch an interesting headline and click on it as it goes by. If you don't care for scrolling, then have a box listing a few headlines that stays in one set quadrant of the home page, or that says "Click here for current events" or some such thing. Setting up an RSS feed is even better; that way interested folks can subscribe to get updates on their own computers whenever something new is posted on your site.

- The fact that people search online in very different ways means that you need to plan to accommodate differing needs. So you need to make event info available through various paths. Your data should be set up in one behind-the-scenes format that can be served up different ways. This makes life easier for you and your patrons: It means that, whenever there are changes and corrections, you make them in only one spot (instead of correcting lots of individual pages). It also means that interested customers can choose to see listings by date, by branch or location, by topic, or by age group. Talk with your IT department or webmaster about keeping your data in one table so that it can be exported in various ways. This isn't rocket science and, once it's set up, it saves time and frustration for everyone.

So those are my thoughts on generic distribution through in-house sources. The underlying concept I want to get across is that I hope you'll abandon paper and use electronic tools whenever it's feasible. I hate to see libraries be the last to adopt new technologies, and if you haven't yet made the changes mentioned here, you're already overdue.

Working With the Media

In many cases, you'll need to do more than send out messages from your own physical and virtual sites; you'll need to rely on some form of mass media for wider distribution. Since I've been a member of the media for a couple of decades, I feel pretty darn qualified to advise you on this topic.

Even if you never had media training, you would probably figure out the basics quickly: Be nice to reporters, pay attention to their deadlines, and don't expect them to pick up every story you send. But you might be wondering how you can form more productive relationships with them and how you can convince (or even trick) them to pick up more of your stories. You're in luck, because there are some hard-and-fast rules to follow, in addition to some "soft" rules that you won't usually find in books. Read on.

Writing Press Releases

In Chapter 11, I talked about designing promotional materials, and many of those rules also apply to press releases (PRs). Here I'll give you some pointers about the actual content of a good press release:

- Use a template for consistency. It should include these elements (from the top down): the library's name and logo, the phrase *press release* or *media advisory*, the date, the name of and contact info for the PR person, and your library's address, phone number, and URL.

- Make sure you have a clear, informative headline.

- Include the "who, what, when, where, why" information.

- If photos are available, say what they are and how the reporter can get them.

- Don't be cute; reporters aren't giving points for creative writing. This is about communicating facts quickly and concisely.

That last piece of advice is perhaps the most important: You should always focus more on being clear than on being colorful. Remember, busy readers need to be able to evaluate your press release in only 15 or 20 seconds to determine whether it matters to them and whether to read the entire thing. But that doesn't mean you should write a clever headline—it means you should write a clear, descriptive one that immediately tells the reader exactly what's going on. As for the rest of the text, shorter and clearer is always better than longer and fluffier.

Communicating With Members of the Media

If you've been absorbing what I've been telling you throughout this book, then the next thing I say shouldn't surprise you. The best way to make sure that editors and reporters really hear your message is to customize it for each of them. Members of the media are, themselves, one of your target audiences. And they don't like mass mailings any more than anyone else does. So, as you would with your other target audiences, you need to spend some time with these folks, get to know them and how they work, ask how best to communicate with each one, then serve them as best you can, all the while evaluating your results and tweaking your outreach to become more effective.

In the case of the press, I can give you some specific advice based on my experience as an active member of this target audience:

- Find out who covers your "beat" so you can address your press releases by name rather than sending them to a general news address. When I see anything addressed to "Dear Editor" or "Dear Sir or Madam," I automatically discount it as coming from someone who doesn't know who I am or what my publication is about.

- Find out what the deadlines are for daily papers, week-lies, etc. Deadlines may vary for different sections of the same paper. Oh, and just because you get a press release in 15 minutes before the stated deadline does not mean it's on time. Usually, last-minute items make it into that edition only if they're terribly important, or if there's space that needs to be filled.

- Find out what sorts of things each publication does and does not cover. Don't send your list of events to a newspa-per that doesn't have a community calendar or to a radio station that doesn't announce common or ongoing events. Never send it "just in case they change their minds." Good publications have mission statements and policies just like you do; if they tell you they don't cover a certain sort of thing, take them at their word.

- Once you've identified contacts at each media outlet you aim to use, find out exactly how each person prefers to

receive PRs (mail, fax, electronically). Also, ask specifically whether they take phone calls, because many don't.
For those who want PRs sent electronically, ask for more
details: Do they want the text in the body of the message
or as an attachment? If they want an attachment, what
format do they prefer? Also, ask them to make sure you
are on their electronic "white list" so your emails won't be
blocked as spam.

- Make sure they know how to contact you when they want
  to. Every public relations person dreams of the day when
  a media contact that they've cultivated will call and say, "I
  want to run a big story about you." Don't make your communication a one-way street. Make sure your contacts
  know how to get in touch with you and that they understand there are reasons why they'd want to. You can be
  more than a space-filler when they need a quick human-
  interest story or a nice photograph of smiling kids. Tell
  them that you can help with their research, find statistics
  to back up an article, or help them spot trends. Contact
  them once in a while to ask if you can help on something
  they're working on; don't call only when you want a favor
  from them. Become as much of a reliable partner to them
  as you want them to be for you.

- Have basic information and general photos always available on your website. Paper and broadcast media want
  photographs, and with tight deadlines there's often no
  time to get any taken. So you should always have general
  photos of your buildings (inside and out) as well as of
  your director and other managers, so you're ready at a
  moment's notice. Likewise, everyday information such as
  addresses, phone numbers, staff listings, circulation data,
  resource lists, and more should be easily accessible in a
  Press Room section of your website. It's much easier for a
  reporter if she can find those details on her own when
  she's writing a story; having to email or telephone for

every little tidbit is annoying and time-consuming. I can't tell you how many times I've needed to check a library branch address or even just the spelling of a name, and I wasted time searching a website only to discover it wasn't there. That doesn't reflect well on an organization that claims it's all about disseminating information.

- When you're planning something really big, tell the press in advance and arrange for custom coverage. For an anniversary event, a townwide celebration, or anything major, don't just send your usual press release a few days ahead of time. Get in touch weeks in advance to let your contacts know what's going on and what sorts of opportunities will be available to them (interviews with the director, photo ops, celebrity appearances, etc.). This gives the reporters time to discuss your event with their editors, who can block out time for a reporter and photographer to attend if your event is deemed worthy of coverage.

- Don't expect to have every event mentioned by the press. While every little thing is important to you, you need to see things from their bigger point of view. A project might matter to you because you've put time and effort into planning it, but how much does it matter to the general population? For every request for coverage you send, the media probably has 50 other requests. What's news to you might be nothing to them. As you build relationships with these people, you'll learn more about their point of view. That will help you to write press releases that will be more appealing to them and to understand which things they choose not to cover and why.

I know that all of this just sounds like more work, and it is. But developing a relationship with a few key members of the media, whether reporters, editors, or editorial board members, makes everything easier in the long-term. It's not out of line to ask to have breakfast or lunch with your contacts, either, as long as you're not paying for them (which could be construed as a "gift"). Don't be afraid to invite them to chat over a meal or a beverage; don't act as if they're doing you a big favor. Remember, you're doing them a favor too, by giving them access to you and your expertise and your world of resources. Your relationship with a member of the media is an equal exchange between two professionals.

It's not out of line to thank a press person for good coverage, as long as there's not gift-giving involved (which could be construed as payment for coverage). Writers, editors, photographers, and managers work just as hard as anyone else, and often the only feedback they get comes when there's a problem. So getting a card or an email from someone praising their work is a rare and welcome treat. Wouldn't you be thrilled to get a note from someone who appreciated the research you did for them? And wouldn't you be more eager to serve that customer again, knowing that your work really matters to him? Treating others the way you'd like to be treated is never a bad idea.

Giving Good Interviews

Usually a public relations person is thrilled at the chance to be interviewed—unless, of course, he or she doesn't really know how to do it. While being interviewed isn't terribly difficult, it can be quite nerve-wracking to have cameras pointed at you or microphones held in front of your face. Oftentimes, library directors want to be the ones to speak to the press and to be the public face of the library. But if you think you might ever get tapped to do the job, you should be prepared with some basic knowledge.

A word about who should do interviews: Your library should have a designated spokesperson, for several reasons. The biggest one is that a reporter could call your library at a moment's notice, and you don't want to say, "Uh, well, I'm not sure who to send your call to; could you, um, hang on?" At the very least, you should know who to send this kind of call or request to. On some occasions it will be the director, other times the head of your public relations or marketing staff; in some cases it should be the library's legal counsel. If you're part of a larger organization, such as a university or corporation, you need to know whether you are supposed to answer questions that are specific to the library or whether someone else should handle them. Whatever organization you're in, it probably has a set of written protocols for handling these circumstances, and you should be familiar with them.

Let's say that you are cleared to talk with the media. What should you do to prepare yourself? The first rule is to know what you're talking about. Be very familiar with library policies and processes as well as with any hot topics that are likely to come up. While I've been working on this book, the most pervasive library-related topic has been how libraries help people get through tough economic times. Previous big issues have often been negative, for example discussions about privacy and pornography. So you need to understand what's going on in the world and how it relates to libraries.

One good way to prepare for such discussions is to have some "sound bites" or "talking points" at the ready. You've heard plenty of these during everyday TV and radio interviews. Remember in the 2008 U.S. presidential race, the way all the members of one political party would make the same comments no matter who was interviewing them (or what the question was)? That's what I mean by talking points. You know the main message you want to get across, and you make sure you say it at least a few times during the interview. (However, using the same talking point to answer every question, no matter what it is, is not really the way to go. Leave that to the politicians.) What we rely on more are sound bites, which are slightly different. A sound bite is a brief, quotable remark; it's a fact or a single idea that works well in or out of context. These are especially useful for media interviews that you know will be cut down to just a minute or so of air time. A sound bite will deliver your message clearly even if it's the only sentence that the public ends up hearing. As you can imagine, these types of phrases don't necessarily roll off your tongue. They need to be prepared and practiced so you can deliver them whenever you have the chance. See the sidebar, "Sample Sound Bites," on this page to help you see how they can encapsulate one major point.

Sample Sound Bites

Here are some examples of sound bites:

- Professional librarians are the best search engines around.
- Libraries put the world on your doorstep.
- Libraries save their companies money by gathering competitive intelligence.
- It ain't your grandma's library anymore.
- Medical libraries save lives.
- Libraries serve everyone, so they're part of the great American dream.
- Libraries ensure that everyone has equal access to information.
- Real librarians have masters' degrees just like other professionals.
- In a world that's information-rich, librarians are information-smart.
- Today's libraries are at the forefront of information technology.
- Librarians can teach you how to sort out the overload of information that's on the web.
- Libraries aren't just for reading anymore.
- Libraries are much more than books.

Even though you know a lot about the library business and your own main message, you should try to keep your answers short and simple. If you watch newscasts, you'll see that people edit stories down to try to pack the most punch into a few seconds. News managers don't like long, rambling answers. Print editors are the same way. If you babble on and on, someone will shorten your words, and that means there's a chance they will paraphrase your thought into something you didn't really mean. Another danger in being edited is that a piece of your message can end up being taken out of context. If, however, you learn to speak quickly and succinctly, no one will have to mess with your words.

So you need to deliver a coherent message quickly and concisely, perhaps while there's a recording device aimed at you. Gulp. How can you be sure of yourself? Practice! How can you practice being interviewed? Fake it! Work with anyone who will role-play with you. Have a partner ask you possible questions so you can answer. Once you think you've got it down, then make the game harder, or rather, more realistic. Ask your helper to turn a camera on you and shove a microphone (even a toy one will do) at you. You'll notice that it instantly feels different, even though it's not a real interview. Practice speaking under pressure, and get your partner to ask questions you didn't anticipate. If you can videotape the process (most cheap digital cameras can do it these days), you can learn even more by watching yourself after the fact. Do you stumble over words? Do you look nervous? Are you playing with your hair or shifting from one foot to the other? Actually seeing yourself on camera can do a world of good in preparing you for the real deal. You can even make it a fun game or competition among your colleagues.

Finally, remember to avoid using jargon. That's another reason for you to prepare sound bites and to practice them. It's only natural to talk about work the way you would at work, tossing around words such as *collections* and *resources*.

My final tip is that you shouldn't feel pressured to fill silent seconds. When you're done with your answer, stop talking. If you feel the need to blab on just because there are a few seconds of silence, you're likely to say something you didn't mean to say. Unless your interview is live, dead air can be cut out. Even if it is live, just allow the reporter a few seconds to respond to you or to come up with the next question. Learn to say what you need to say and then stop. Talk can be cheap; silence can be golden.

Crisis Communication

One thing everyone dreads is "crisis communication" or answering questions about problems or emergencies. Again, practice is the key. Not only will it enable you to know what to say and how to say it, but it will help you keep your cool if the interview is not a friendly one.

Even when there's not an emergency, sometimes a reporter will ask a question in a negative fashion. If you answer the question as it was asked, you'll inadvertently be making a negative comment. This is an important thing to be aware of and to practice your way out of. You need to learn to turn your answer around and use positive words. Try never to repeat the negative phrases. Here's a simple example:

> *Reporter:* "Yesterday, police nabbed a drug dealer who was sending emails from the library. Doesn't that mean your library is a dangerous place, especially for parents to bring their children to?"
>
> *Negative answer:* "No, the library is not a dangerous place. People should not be afraid to bring their children here."
>
> (Even though you're disagreeing with the reporter, this answer repeats the negative word "dangerous" and adds the word "afraid.")

Positive answer: "The library has always been a safe place. This was simply an isolated incident."

Another thing that can easily happen during an interview is that you'll get a question you're simply not prepared for. Rather than stumble, buy yourself time to think before answering. You can always repeat or rephrase the question, or use phrases like these so you still sound smart and in control while you stall a little bit:

- Let me make sure I understand the question. You're asking …

- I want to think this through so I can give you a clear answer.

- That's a good question …

If you get a tough question that feels like a trap, or a question that's off base, or one you don't want to answer, you can turn it around using these tactics:

- That's one way to think of it, but in reality, it's more like this …

- That's an interesting question, but a better question is, …

- That's one way of looking at it, although we prefer …

- That's a common misconception, but the truth is that …

And if you absolutely don't know the answer, it's better to admit that than to make something up out of panic or to say something you might regret later. You can always use responses like these:

- I'm not quite certain about that; let me check with the proper person and get right back to you.

- I'm sorry, but I'm not authorized to discuss that topic. Let me hook you up with the person who can help you.

- I'm really not the right person to answer that question. But I'm happy to find someone who can help you.

Whatever you do, never utter any of these sentences:

- This is off the record.

- No comment.

- I have no idea.

- You're wrong about that.

One last point about media relations: Building solid relationships with your main media representatives should decrease your chances of having to go through a hostile interview. If the press people know you and, more importantly, understand your library's work and its importance to your community, they're less likely to ask the threatening-sounding questions that are bred from lack of knowledge and respect.

A Good Answer for a Tough Question

Here's one way to answer a tough question that many of you might hear.

Reporter: "With our county [township/state/national] budget in crisis, why is your library still asking for more funding? In this bad economy, isn't it more important to fund things like emergency services and schools? People don't really need libraries anymore since everyone has internet connections at home."

Negative answer: "Our library needs more money to be able to operate. We don't want to lay off people like other businesses have had to do. Emergency services are important when people need them, but people need to use our library every day. The internet does not replace us."

Positive answer: "In times of budgetary crisis, libraries are more essential than ever. This fact has been proven again and again over the years by measuring our usage. [Add stats if you can.] Our services help people save money and help them find new jobs if they've been laid off. Not everyone has internet access at home; in fact, in our area, only [X] percent of the people do. Libraries are institutions that help people during tough times by providing them with internet access, by helping them rewrite resumes, by allowing them to borrow books and movies and music free of charge, and by being a safe place for community members to meet and interact. And since we offer a [X] percent return on investment of taxpayer dollars, that proves that funding our library during this financial crisis is one of the smartest things our county can do."

Notice that, in the positive answer, every sentence except the second one can stand on its own. So no matter how much the media needs to shorten this answer, it's still clear, positive, and sensible.

Choosing Which Medium to Use

Different publicity situations call for different media. I'm sure we'd all love to see libraries buying television commercials that would air during the most popular shows to reach massive audiences, but that's not realistic.

If your choice of which medium to use isn't obvious for one reason or another, then compare the strengths and weaknesses of each one to decide what will work best. Better yet, turn to Appendix C, where the work has already been done for you. I'm including a reprint of an *MLS* article where columnist Christie Koontz analyzes the pros and cons of television, radio, magazines, newspapers, posters/billboards, and the internet. This piece, called "Promotion Is Not the Same as Marketing," also discusses various types of advertising and explains the differences among them. She even includes the seldom-mentioned transit ads that run on buses and subway cars; that medium is wonderful for reaching huge numbers of folks in urban settings.

Spreading the Library's Message Through Partnerships

Your library and the media aren't the only institutions that can spread the word about your work, your resources, and your expertise. Plenty of other organizations and individuals can help if you give them the chance. These arrangements can be formal or informal, spelled out or implied.

I recommend forming partnerships with all sorts of groups, and there are plenty of reasons to do so. Partnering can spread your message, bring you money, give you access to resources, improve your standing in the community, make you more visible, and show off your business acumen. It's hard for any organization to make it alone these days, especially nonprofits. Working with others and trading for in-kind services can be incredibly beneficial. And any group that you partner with will learn more about your library (and vice-versa), which creates a whole new group of people who can talk about and talk up what you do.

One thing you can do, which you might not think of as a partnership per se, is to offer training for people in your community. In a corporate setting, this could mean working with another department to train its employees on searching smarter or on using particular databases that are suited to their work. Choose a group that can offer you something in return (a voice at companywide meetings, help with your annual report, tech support, etc.). Some municipal libraries have done training for government staffers and subsequently were allowed to include fliers for every resident in their government-related tax bills (at no cost).

Academics can partner with faculty members and offer library instruction to students in exchange for the professors sending students to the library or requiring them to use certain trusted sources (instead of the open web). Public librarians have partnered with schoolteachers, helping them find support materials for lesson plans in exchange for time to speak to their classes about the value of using a library.

One basic idea that I suggest to all types of librarians is to join their local Chamber of Commerce, Speakers' Bureau, Lions Club, Jaycees, or the like. This affiliation will introduce you to local leaders and give you opportunities to speak at their meetings. Even if you work in, say, a hospital library or a school media center, these groups can be valuable to you. Club members probably have no idea what media specialists do, and they probably never realized that hospitals have their own libraries. Simply introducing yourself to people in community organizations gives you a chance to educate them about libraries in general, and they'll surely want to know about yours in particular. It can make great fodder for their next water cooler conversations: "Hey, Joe, you'll never guess who I met at the club meeting last night. There's this librarian who says she works in a 'special library' right in the hospital and she researches treatments for the doctors there. Who knew?"

Another of my favorite recommendations is to contact college professors to see if they'll assign student projects that are actually work for you. Marketing classes can create simple marketing plans and promo materials for the library; design classes can create fresh logos for you to choose from. The professor gets a new and exciting class project that links students to the real world, and you get something done for free that would otherwise be high-priced. Don't forget about library schools! Think about how their students could help you catch up on work that your staff can never get to.

Zany Partnership Ideas

- Partner with grocery stores to hold storytimes there, to install a book drop or set up a branch there, or to get discounts on food and beverages. The Williamsburg (VA) Regional Library works with Ukrops Supermarket to have Saturday morning storytimes on site (www.wrl.org/feedmeastory). The store provides the space and the snacks. Parents love it because it's a place where they're already going anyway.
- Hold events in a nearby shopping mall to attract people who may not come to your location. The Delaware County (PA) Library System had a gigantic book sale in the center court area of the Granite Run Mall over a three-day period in 2005. It raised more than $13,000 dollars and got not only local but also national media coverage because of its size and unique location (www.infotoday.com/mls/nov05/gruber.shtml).
- Work out trade deals with small businesses; they often need all the publicity they can get. Build an alliance with a florist who will give you floral displays for your events in exchange for your free publicity. (Put out small signs that say "Flowers courtesy of Betty's Bouquets," thank the shop in your event program, have

a pile of business cards sitting out.) Or let the owner of an independent music store owner give a presentation (that may bring business to his store) in exchange for some CDs to expand your borrowing collection.

- Join with scout troops, which are always seeking out community service projects. To benefit the library, scouts could build wooden benches or creative book shelves, plant gardens, or read to younger kids.

- School librarians can form alliances with videogame stores, skateboard shops, or arcades. Ask if the management will help you promote young adult reading by giving coupons or game tokens to kids who read a certain number of books from your library.

- Try trading services with senior citizens. Suggest a program swap, where they give talks about their experiences or read to kids, and in exchange you go to their site to speak about something like health info or computers.

- Partner with parents to help them understand what librarians can do for their kids. Hold evening or weekend sessions that parents can attend to hear what you offer for their children. Be sure to have a kids' storytime simultaneously so the adults can listen to you without interruption. Ask the parents what programs they'd like to see. Treat them as partners in the processes of learning, reading, and researching to win their support.

- Form relationships with consultants. Look for local ones, especially small proprietorships, that specialize in things you could use help with—accounting, marketing, advertising, image building/branding, space planning, etc. Chances are these people need access to information and help with research when working for other clients. Sounds like a fair trade waiting to happen.

When considering prospective partnerships, once again, begin with the end in mind. What benefit do you want to get out of the deal? What are you lacking? Then think about who could provide it. And for goodness' sake, don't feel or act as if you're on the lesser end of any deal. Librarians' expertise is just as valuable as anybody else's, and it doesn't hurt to make that clear by starting conversations with words such as, "I'd like to propose a mutually beneficial idea" or "What would you think about trading some of my library's brain power for some of yours?" And don't overlook a great opening line like "I'm going to make you an offer you can't refuse!"

A Few Words About Word-of-Mouth Marketing

Word-of-mouth (WoM) marketing sounds self-explanatory, but it does entail a bit more than telling a friend something and hoping she'll pass it along. It's more purposeful than that, and it can be a powerful tool. What's better, WoM is basically free!

I recently joined Nancy Dowd, director of marketing at the New Jersey State Library, in a presentation about WoM. She's my inspiration on this topic, and I'll share some of what I've learned from working with her on it.

WoM really is true marketing (if you do it right) because it shares lots of the same steps. Here's a run-down:

1. Choose a target audience.

2. List the products, services, and programs you have for that group, along with what benefits they hold for the folks.

3. Decide what measurable outcome you'd like to achieve.

4. Find influential people whom others in your target market would listen to and recruit them to help you spread the word.

5. Create short key messages about the product you're pushing; work with your influencers to ensure that the messages will appeal to the intended audience.

6. Decide which communication tools to use (blogs, YouTube, etc.).

7. Put your message out via the chosen tools and let the influencers take over by commenting on the message and/or passing it along to others.

8. Evaluate your success by looking at how many people acted on the message.

This is a simplified version of the process, but now that you've read all the previous chapters in this book, you'll understand. The big difference between WoM and distributing other marketing messages is that here you are working through the influential people. You want to partner with the folks that other people look up to and follow (think team leaders, the cool teens, religious officials, etc.). Ask them up front if people like them really want what you're offering and how they'd react to the message; enlist their help in crafting and presenting it.

That's why WoM works, because you're involving leaders from your target audience, not only in shaping the message but also in spreading it. The only cost is the time it takes you to do it (unless you offer incentives to the influencers), and you'll find it's a great exercise for learning more about the people you intend to serve.

The Time Has Come for Mobile Marketing

A new avenue that I'm just learning about myself is mobile marketing. Despite its name, it's not about road trips; rather, the *mobile* alludes to mobile phones and other hand-held devices. If you're an iPhone junkie or have a personal relationship with a similar portable device, you can imagine what this is all about.

It's become the norm today to send customers messages via email, and the next thing that's already lit up the horizon is sending text messages to their mobile devices. Before you cringe at the thought of cramping your fingers typing out lots of individual messages, think about how you send mass email blasts. You can send text messages the same way. By subscribing to certain services (or setting up the technology yourself), you can push out mass texts that remind recipients of programs, welcome them to your building, or whatever you like. Of course, you can also send individual messages to tell people that their holds have come in or their research reports are ready.

With mobile devices becoming more prevalent, this is definitely a great way to go. Some Europeans are way ahead of the Americans in this field, with libraries and shops pushing out messages about events or sales that are automatically picked up by the devices that passers-by are carrying. Intrusive? Perhaps. It depends on what the message is and how it benefits those who receive it.

The same company that's publishing this book has a new one on this hot topic, *The Mobile Marketing Handbook: A Step-by-Step Guide to Creating Dynamic Mobile Marketing Campaigns*, by Kim Dushinski. If you're interested in practical, easy-to-follow advice on reaching mobile users, you can learn more about this title at books.infotoday.com/books/MobileMarketingHandbook.shtml.

I'm excited about this new vehicle that can reach library users and nonusers alike wherever they are, putting your messages right into the palms of their hands. This is what we all strive to do, and technology has made it easier than ever.

Recommended Reading

"A Communications Handbook for Libraries." American Library Association. www.ala.org/ala/aboutala/offices/ola/mediaspecific/mediaspecific.cfm (accessed January 27, 2009).

"Media Map: Charting a Media Relations Strategy." Association of Research Libraries and SPARC. www.arl.org/sparc/bm~doc/Media Map.pdf (accessed January 27, 2009).

Chapter 13

Using Your Website for Public Relations and Outreach

These days, anyone who's even a little internet savvy has high expectations when it comes to websites. The leading companies that have built their sites to be ultra-usable and über-intuitive have set the bar high for all other organizations. And while you probably can't afford to hire away any programmers from Amazon.com or Lands' End, you can still do a lot of simple things that will make a big difference.

First, I recommend that you have (or build) a good relationship with whoever maintains your website. Contrary to what some believe, technology people and PR people have (or should have) a lot of common concerns. Second, both you and your webmaster should read some of the excellent books and articles that have been published about website usability. (I've listed a few at the end of this chapter.) Third, if at all possible, do some small studies with your own website users. Ask them what they like and don't like about your site. What do they find intuitive, and what makes no sense to them? (Remember that different types of people will have vastly different opinions, depending on their own level of knowledge and on which portion of your website they're trying to use.)

In order to persuade the webmaster to make some PR-related changes, you might need to get management on your side. Fortunately, that shouldn't be too hard to do. If your administrators are at all susceptible to logic (here's hoping!), then they need only realize that the library's website is one of its major outreach and public relations tools. It is one of the public faces of your institution. It's senseless not to ensure that the website is as friendly and helpful as your in-person customer service. And if it's not, that needs to change, pronto. Oh, and the webmaster's opinion of whether the site works well enough is not the most important one here. It's the users who matter. Anyone who had a hand in building the site *knows* how it's supposed to work, so they can't possibly see it through the eyes of a person who's not familiar with it. Don't expect that announcement to go over well … that's why you need an edict from higher-ups that supports making changes based on users' reactions and needs.

What Do People Expect From Websites?

So how do you know what people expect from websites? If you're not an expert in usability, ask the folks who are. There are plenty of published studies to refer to and while I was editor of *Computers in Libraries* magazine (www.infotoday.com/cilmag), I read a lot about them, so I can give you a quick list of the big concerns:

- Pages shouldn't be so crowded and busy-looking that you can't find the topic you're seeking.

- Pages should download quickly.

- Get rid of all lingo; use the words that your customers will understand.

- Employ powerful "federated search" whenever possible. (One search box covers all the resources provided on the site, so users don't have to repeat the same search in every section of your site or for every resource you have.)

- Always have a way to log out and a way to get back to the home page.

- Don't leave broken links in your pages. Check them with a tool like Link Sleuth (home.snafu.de/tilman/xenulink.html).

- Provide an application for users to submit virtual reference questions or initiate online chat, so they can get
  help easily, at the moment of need.

- Make sure using your website from outside of your library
  is as easy as using it from inside your building.

- Check whether your site is accessible to differently abled
  people who use screen-reading software and other tools;
  there are various testing tools available. Learn more at the
  webpage, Evaluating Web Sites for Accessibility: An
  Overview, from the Web Accessibility Initiative (WAI) at
  www.w3.org/WAI/eval/Overview.html.

- Make sure your site works with different browsers. Try the
  tool BrowserShots (browsershots.org).

Serving Members of the Media via Your Website

Everyday users have plenty of their own concerns and demands
when it comes to websites, and particular user groups will each
have their own additional desires. But since this book is about
marketing, the one specific target market I'm going to cover here is
the media. (Again? Yes. Can you tell I'm a member of the media?)
Press people could (and should) be accessing your library online to
search for information on news stories or articles they're working
on. They could also be using your site to get background info for an
article about the library itself, and of course, you want to make that
as easy as possible.

   If you want the media to know about and cover your organization, then it only makes sense to facilitate that via your website,
because that's probably the first place a reporter will start looking
to learn the basics. Every library should have an online Media Kit.
Back in Chapter 3, I listed the sorts of things that press people want
to be able to find online.

You might be wondering if I have a personal pet peeve here. Why yes, I do, thanks for asking. In fact, since I like you so much, I'll share two.

First, I've been amazed at the number of libraries that don't have their street addresses on their websites. Maybe webmasters figure that if you're visiting online, you don't live nearby so you won't be visiting in person. But I've often sought street addresses so I could get driving directions online or so I could send things in the mail. You still need to link your virtual presence with your physical one.

Second, I can't count the number of times I've wanted to contact someone from a particular library and could not find a direct phone number or email address on the website. Maybe you think this is private information, but if you're working for a public entity, that's questionable. As a member of the media, I often read about a project that someone has done or an interesting paper they've written and want to contact the person to schedule an interview or ask a question. If I know the library they work for, I'll go to that website and search for "Jane Jones" so I can learn a bit more about her before making the call. The lack of staff info on library websites often makes that impossible.

You may think that posting staff data is just a matter of convenience, and wonder why reporters can't just call the general phone number and ask for Jane Jones. Well, we could. But we're very unfriendly people, and we hate to waste our time.

Seriously, though, put yourself in a reporter's shoes: You're on deadline, and you need to fill a space for tomorrow's paper with a quick story. You have a lead to follow about something in the library. Just a quick call to Jane Jones and you'll be on your way. You hit the website and ... well, there's no media page, so you don't know whether there's a press contact who could help you. So you look directly for Jones' name ... no staff directory. You search the site for "Jones" and of course get too many results. You look on the library's main contact page for an address and phone number, but the only contacts listed are "Ask a Librarian," the director, "Renew your materials," and the webmaster. "Never mind," you say to yourself. "This is too complicated. What other leads do I have that might fill my space?"

And so the library has missed an opportunity for press coverage. Members of the media should be one of the main target markets that you're serving. And they expect to be able to find individual contact information online. If you're doing marketing or public relations work, you never want to miss a chance for media contact.

But that's not the only reason to serve members of the media. You want to build relationships with reporters, newscasters, editors, etc., so they turn to your library for information no matter what they're covering. If you don't want them all doing their research on Google, then court them, be there for them, become the place they turn to for research help on a consistent basis. That will turn them into library users and advocates, and you never know when their support will come in handy down the road.

Make Sure Search Engines Can Find Your Site

The best way to ensure that people find and use your website is to make it as easy as possible for search engines to find. The fact is that few people will type in your URL as they begin a search. They're going to start at a common search site like Google, Yahoo!, or GoodSearch (my personal fave). When they type in their keywords, you want your library's site to come up in the first five or 10 hits of the results list. There are ways to do this without paying for those top-of-list positions.

Use Code to Its Full Potential

The practice of making your site as findable as possible is known as "search engine optimization" or SEO. Most people who design websites will already know the basics. But if your library has an "accidental webmaster" (there's a book in this series for that too![1]), then he or she might not be super-savvy. Hopefully, your webmaster knows these tips and has implemented them already, but it's worth sitting down with him or her to talk about it. (Just in case your webmaster is someone who "doesn't appreciate suggestions" from nontechies, you could approach this as "Please teach me about how you make our site findable." Then if he or she has missed any of the tips I'm about to give you, you could innocently say, "I heard something about XYZ … could we do that one too?")

The main idea is that you want search engines' "crawlers" or "spiders" to find your keywords when they're crawling across websites looking for matches for the search terms that someone has asked for. And having those keywords in the text of your pages isn't enough; you need to have them in the underlying code of your site as well. Here are some of the main spots that should be "optimized," rather than left blank, in the software code:

- Title tags

- Meta descriptions

- H1–H8 tags

- Photos and graphics

For instance, if you have a running podcast on your site, make sure it's not simply titled as "podcast episode1," "podcast episode2." That won't get it into search results lists. Software code's titles and tags need to be descriptive, so instead use something like "podcast1 storytime infant" and "podcast2 storytime 2to5years." Pay special attention to each page's title tag, because the search engines do. Make sure each page has a unique title tag that describes its content.

There are lots of tips, tricks, and tools that you can explore at Google Webmaster Central (www.google.com/webmasters). You will find tools for improving traffic, FAQs, statistics counters, and more. There's also a link there to a whole page on submitting your content so you know that Google will be picking it up. Also visit the similar pages for Microsoft Live (webmaster.live.com) and Yahoo! (siteexplorer.search.yahoo.com).

In fact, you should register with all of the major search engines just to make sure your site is available to each one's crawlers. This is a simple thing that any webmaster worth his or her salt should have already done, but it's worth checking on—and worth your knowing about if you're looking at all possible avenues to making your library's site as useful, and as used, as it can be.

Be Aware of Who's Discussing and Linking to Your Site

Aside from working with your tech staffers on search engine optimization, you should also take charge of how your library's website is used and referred to by everyone else online. One way is by making sure it's registered with other popular "finding sites," and another is by making sure that other sites where you're listed or discussed have the proper, correct information.

First, a few words about registering on "finding sites" (other than everyday search engines). You probably know about Wikipedia, the user-built site that has all sorts of basic info about all sorts of stuff. Is your library listed on Wikipedia? If not, make an entry, quick! If it is, then read the entry to make sure everything is true and correct. (You might also want to see who created the entry and thank that person for it.) In addition, there are a number of directories just for libraries, and you ought to check to see that you're listed on them:

- Libdex (www.libdex.com)

- Libraries411.com (www.libraries411.com)

- PublicLibraries.com (www.publiclibraries.com)

- Libweb: Library Servers via WWW
  (lists.webjunction.org/libweb)

Aaron Schmidt and Sarah Houghton-Jan, a pair of popular library speakers/bloggers, often address this topic. By checking their blogs—Schmidt's Walking Paper (www.walkingpaper.org) and Houghton-Jan's LibrarianInBlack.net (librarianinblack.type pad.com)—you can find lots more information. I asked the duo to write a round-up for *MLS* called "How to Drive Traffic to Your Website"[2] and in it, they name sites where you can list your local events, videos, and wireless network availability.

Schmidt and Houghton-Jan also recommend that you monitor local blogs to see what people are saying about your library when you're not listening. If you really want user reactions, uncensored, checking sites such as www.metblogs.com is one way to get them. If you read these sites regularly, you'll be able to respond to questions and address complaints, thereby showing people that you really care about serving them well. Another tip I really liked was that you can see who's linked to your library's site by using a special syntax in Google. Go to www.google.com and, in the search box, enter "link:http://www.[your library's URL]." It's fascinating to see what sorts of sites have linked back to yours!

Learning How People Search and See

Finally, as I've mentioned in various sections of this book, learning how people search is paramount in making your site the best it can be. So at the end of this chapter I list some resources you can consult when you're ready to learn more about that. A few of the books on the list might be a little heavy for beginning marketers, but if you decide that studying web usage is a topic you really want to dig into, then by all means, check them out.

The studies that I find most interesting are the ones on "eyetracking." This is where the testers employ specialized software that sits behind a normal-looking computer screen and can actually track where peoples' eyes look. Sounds Big-Brother-ish, I know. But it's a great way to study how people look at webpages, and it's an essential tool for discovering what parts they *don't* look at. Eyetracking studies have also proven that most people simply skim pages, which is bad news for people who design sites full of necessary data. However, once you realize that most surfers skim and you learn what attributes draw them in, then you'll know where to put your most important stuff.

Here are a few very basic findings from eyetracking studies that were done on people reading English (results would be different for languages that are read right-to-left):

- People start at the top left of a page.

- Their eyes look over the page in a pattern shaped like the letter E or F.

- They are attracted to bullet points with space in between them.

- Right-side boxes don't draw much attention.

- Attention drops off toward the bottom of the page.

Now ask yourself: Weren't your eyes drawn to the bulleted list on this page? And when you read, don't you get bored with long, text-heavy paragraphs? Ah-ha! See? Remember these basic truths when you're thinking about designing webpages, or even print, for that matter. In fact, I think I remember similar studies of newspaper reading habits from my journalism-school days. Before software, researchers simply observed people reading newspapers and found the same E-shaped patterns. I could try to look up these old studies so I could cite them for you, but they'd probably be on boring pages jammed with text that I'd barely want to skim anyway.

You Need the "Full Monty" Website

Even given this basic knowledge, nothing you read about web usability will be as enlightening as having librarians watch your very own customers read your webpages and perform searches to see how they view and use your own site. If your headings don't make sense to your user base, if the layout isn't intuitive for navigation, and if the users don't have basic search literacy skills, then your knowing a few tenets won't save the day. Great library websites are built purposefully by dedicated people who take into account the needs and habits of users, incorporating not only technical functionality and great content, but also usefulness and findability, usability and accessibility, and marketing and branding. To ensure satisfying experiences for your users, you have to go for the full monty!

Endnotes

1. Julie Still, *The Accidental Webmaster* (Medford, NJ: Information Today, Inc., 2003).

2. Aaron Schmidt and Sarah Houghton-Jan, "How to Drive Traffic to Your Website," *Marketing Library Services* 22, no. 6 (November/December 2008): 1, 5–6, infotoday.com/mls/nov08/Schmidt_Houghton-Jan. shtml (accessed January 27, 2009).

Recommended Reading

Usability/Accessibility

I recommend reading just about anything by web usability guru Jakob Neilsen. There's plenty on his site at www.useit.com. Also check out the following:

Brown, Stephanie Willen. "Test, edit, repeat: Steps to improve your web site." *Computers in Libraries* 22:10 (November/December 2002): 14–21.

"Evaluating web sites for accessibility." Web Accessibility Initiative (WAI). www.w3.org/WAI/eval/Overview.html

King, David Lee. "The Mom-and-Pop-Shop approach to usability studies." *Computers in Libraries* 23:1 (January 2003): 12–14, 71–72.

Norlin, Elaina and CM! Winters. *Usability testing for library web sites: A hands-on guide*. Chicago: ALA Editions, 2002.

Prasse, Michael J., and Connaway, Lynn Silipigni. "Current approaches to evaluation usability testing: Method and research." In *Academic Library Research: Perspectives and Current Trends* (ACRL Publications in Librarianship #59). Chicago: Association of College & Research Libraries, 2008.

Reynolds, Erica. "The secret to patron-centered web design: Cheap, easy, and powerful usability techniques," *Computers in Libraries* 28:6 (June 2008): 6–8, 44–47.

Wiley, Deborah Lynne. "Usability testing for library web sites: A hands-on guide." *ONLINE* May/June 2002: 85.

Wiley, Deborah Lynne. "Access by Design: A Guide to Universal Usability for Web Designers." *ONLINE* January/February 2006: 62.

Search Engine Optimization

Breeding, Marshall. "Winning the competition for attention on the web." *Computers in Libraries* 28:6 (June 2008): 31–33.

Search 101: A Guide for Webmasters and Search Engine Marketers. searchenginewatch.com/webmasters

How People Search

Cockburn, Andy, and McKenzie, Bruce. "What do web users do? An empirical analysis of web use." *International Journal of Human-Computer Interaction* 54 (2001): 903–922.

Eyetracking Overview. www.useit.com/eyetracking

Fallows, Deborah. "Search engine users." Report for the Pew Internet & American Life Project. January 23, 2005. www.pewinternet.org/pdfs/PIP_Searchengine_users.pdf

Michael, Alex, and Salter, Ben. *Marketing through search optimization: How people search and how to be found on the web*. 2nd ed. Oxford, UK: Butterworth-Heinemann, 2007.

Nielsen, Jakob. "How little do users read?" Alertbox. May 6, 2008. www.useit.com/alertbox/percent-text-read.html

Nielsen, Jakob, and Pernice, Kara. *Eyetracking web usability*. Berkeley, CA: New Riders/Peachpit Press: Forthcoming. www.useit.com/eyetracking.

Spink, Amanda, and Jansen, Bernard J. *Web search: Public searching of the web*. Dordrecht, The Netherlands: Kluwer Academic Publishers, 2004.

Weinreich, Harald, Obendorf, H., Herder, E., and Mayer, M. "Not quite the average: An empirical study of web use." *ACM Transactions on the Web* 2:1, Article No. 5 (February 2008). portal.acm.org/citation.cfm?doid= 1326561.1326566

Chapter 14

Finally, the Fun Stuff

Congratulations, you've made it to the last chapter! You didn't just skip back here to only read the fun stuff, did you? Be honest! If you've read all the way through, then by now you've accomplished (or at least learned about) the following:

- Endured my lectures about clear communication
- Assessed your entire organization
- Delved into demographic and geographic data
- Heard from marketing experts around the world
- Gotten buy-in from managers and coworkers
- Made some serious evidence-based decisions
- Faced the world of statistics
- Slogged through my sermons about true marketing
- Written or updated strategic and marketing plans
- Improved your promotional materials
- Learned more about getting your message out
- Found out how to make better use of your website

Wow. After all that, you deserve some light, fun reading. You've made it to the place where I'll share stories about cool, interesting things that other librarians have done, as well as some of my own ideas for activities.

You might think I placed this chapter at the end of the book to try to force you to read through the dry stuff—and I did—but there's a much bigger reason. In the cycle of marketing, that's where this fun stuff belongs, at the end. But far too many accidental marketers *start* here, trying to think of neat stuff to do to draw patrons in. Sadly, this is wrong, wrong, wrong. This is why your programs don't always attract crowds; this is why your publicity is hit-or-miss. If you start planning activities before you've made critical decisions about target markets and ways to reach them, you really haven't been "marketing." You've just been "promoting." By now (I hope), you understand the vast difference between those two terms, and you realize that promotion is just one little part of marketing. And I hope you'll join my quest to get all of the world's librarians to understand the difference and to use the words—and the actions—correctly.

But enough preaching for now—on to some creative stuff!

Fun Events and Success Stories

Here are some fun, successful things that your fellow librarians have done:

- Most of you have heard of book cart drill teams. They're just too much fun, and something that staff from *any* type of library can participate in. (If you're a solo, well, grab some friends!) Crowds just love watching costumed librarians perform little choreographed dances with book carts in front of them (or beside them, or behind them, or under them). Lots of teams perform in local parades, to great acclaim. What a super way to get peoples' attention and to smash some old stereotypes! Enjoy some of the videos I've found (see the sidebar, "Book Cart Drill Team Videos" on page 227 for URLs) and think about forming your own drill team.

- Having a party is almost never a bad idea. Having a party with a theme that relates to library usefulness is always a good idea. The staff members at Tunxis Community College in Farmington, Connecticut, are known for the parties they throw every fall, but they had an especially interesting theme party back in 2001 for the whole campus. It was based on Maslow's Hierarchy of Human Needs, the pyramid-shaped list of basic needs (food, drink, shelter, safety, recognition, etc.). Since the library's mission statement declares, "We make your life easier," this theme worked double duty. All invitations, gift bags, and food were based on a white clinical theme. What made it even better is that they invited *everyone*, from the college president and the faculty to the maintenance crew to the students. Everyone got to see the librarians wearing costumes, toasting, and serving food. The article in *MLS* about this particular party (infotoday.com/mls/jul02/lavoie.htm) has been cited numerous times. Other Tunxis themes have included a Faculty Survival Kits party, a French Cafe party, and a We Look Different costume party.

- A circulation assistant at the Wadleigh Memorial Library in Milford, New Hampshire, challenged patrons with overdue fines to out-dance her. The library brass agreed to waive fines for anyone who could beat her at Dance Dance Revolution during a 1-hour contest on its Patron Appreciation Day.

- Various libraries have drawn teens in by asking them to be tech teachers. Teenagers can be really useful in helping others figure out new technologies. Sometimes they help staff; sometimes they work one-on-one with senior citizens or others in computer labs. Projects like this not only show young people the value of libraries, but can also make them feel more important, giving them new confidence and some "work" experience. You can read one such story at seattletimes.nwsource.com/html/snohomishcountynews/2004065990_techteens12n.html.

- Some libraries have their own mascots, which just gives them more avenues to publicity. It's fun to have characters greeting people at your PR events or appearing at parties or marching in parades. You can read about how one such character, Smart ALEC (A Library Electronic Connection), was created to promote an electronic kiosk at the Iowa City (IA) Public Library (www.infotoday.com/mls/jan00/howto.htm). Another organization, the Public Library of Charlotte & Mecklenburg County, created a character called "Brarydog" ("brary" as in "short for library"), named for a personalized web application that allows patrons to customize a personal library webpage with their favorite resources. You can still see the zany blue character at www.brarydog.net or read about how it came to be in *MLS* ("Making a Customizable Site for Easy Access & Marketing Its Character," vol. 15, no. 2, March 2001).

- A Pennsylvania library system was able to serve the fastest-growing part of its area without building a new branch. Instead, the Adams Memorial Library in Latrobe, Pennsylvania, put a mini branch in a grocery store! A partnership with a local chain resulted in a 650-square-foot branch in the Davis Supermarket. The library paid monthly rent for the space, but the market covered utilities. One major benefit was that the market's shopping center location had plenty of parking, whereas there were few spaces available near the main library downtown. The special report "White Eggs and Milk, or *Green Eggs and Ham*?" in the December 1996 issue of *MLS* has all the details. Library staffers even created some book displays and put them in corresponding aisles, so you really could find the book *Green Eggs and Ham* near the eggs!

Book Cart Drill Team Videos

There are plenty of fun videos on YouTube and elsewhere; here are a few that I enjoyed.

Cleve J. Fredricksen Library Bookcart Drill Team, Camp
 Hill, PA
videos.pennlive.com/2008/08/fredricksen_library_book
 cart_d.html
 This was actually covered in a major local newspaper, *The Patriot-News*, in an article titled, "Library's drill team shelves staid image" (www.pennlive.com/patriot news/stories/index.ssf?/base/news/121771770331617. xml&coll=1). Another Fredricksen drill video on YouTube has gotten more than 1,500 hits!

Madtown Truckers and Baraboo Bookers, Middleton, WI
www.youtube.com/watch?v=c3OOf2XpRmI
 Two teams battled at the 2008 Wisconsin Library Association conference for the chance to compete at the Book Cart Drill Team World Championship at ALA '09 in Chicago. You won't want to miss the hammy guy strutting to Steppenwolf's "Born to Be Wild." One of the viewer comments says, "I think this sport needs to be fast-tracked to the Olympics!"

Des Plaines Public Library Cart Wheels Book Cart Drill
 Team, Des Plaines, IL
www.youtube.com/watch?v=_4P5nMNaiRA
 This video from the 2008 Fourth of July parade is nicely embellished with scenes from the set-up, the actual parade, and the happy crowd. It features music from *Grease*, which matches the team's theme of greasers, prom queens, and muscle cars.

"Wow Factor" Ideas You Can Try on Your Own

I'd like to share a number of ideas for what some people call "wow factor" stuff. These are the things that make people sit up and say, "Wow! That's cool! Libraries do that?"

Some of these are projects I've heard about over the years; some are from recent news, blogs, and lists. Wherever I can, I identify the ideas' origins or the projects' places. And I apologize in advance to anyone who sees his or her own work here without identification or credit. My brain can only remember so much!

These are in no particular order, nor are they grouped by type of library or anything else. I didn't want to compartmentalize these ideas because I didn't want any readers to think they could only tackle certain kinds of projects. With a little tweaking and creative thinking, many sorts of librarians can adopt most of these ideas in some form or another. Remember, this is the fun, adventurous stuff!

Have Bag, Will Travel

The Reader Services Department at University College Dublin (UCD) in, yes, Ireland, sells cotton book bags. That in itself isn't very "wow," but here's what is: UCD encourages bag buyers to carry their totes around the world and to take pictures of where they've been. The staff created The Book Bag Blog (ucdrsbookbagblog. blogspot.com), where they post photos that customers email to them. The blog is fantastic, showing photos of UCD Library bags in far-flung places like Ethiopia, Antarctica, and Australia. Oh, and there's a prize for best photo of the year.

Borrow a Person from a "Living Library"

Various European libraries have held events where customers could come in and "borrow" a person for a short time. The volunteers who are "borrowed" are not electricians or tutors, but rather people with interesting lifestyles that others may not understand.

At one such event in London, volunteers wore shirts asking "What's YOUR Prejudice?" and, upon being borrowed, went off for 30-minute chats with their patrons, where they answered questions about their lives. A newspaper article (women.timesonline. co.uk/tol/life_and_style/women/the_way_we_live/article 3790377.ece) written by one of the volunteers explained: "The human 'books' on offer vary from event to event but always include a healthy cross-section of stereotypes. Last weekend, the small but richly diverse list included Police Officer, Vegan, Male Nanny and Lifelong Activist as well as Person with Mental Health Difficulties and Young Person Excluded from School. I was there as Gay Man."

Santa Monica (CA) Public Library and Bainbridge Island (WA) Library have also sponsored Living Library events where the "books" loaned included Hunter and Military Officer. Bainbridge tied in its event with the nearby Kitsap Regional Library's One Community, One Book celebration, which centered on *To Kill a Mockingbird*. Promo info included character Atticus Finch's quote, "You never really understand a person until you consider things from his point of view ... Until you climb inside of his skin and walk around in it" (read stories at living-library.org/flying-start-in-santa-monica-los-angeles..html and at living-library.org/bainbridge-island-living-library-with-116-readers..html).

There's an organization to guide others who want to have Living Libraries; learn more at living-library.org.

Customized Library Cards

San Francisco (CA) Public Library and others have begun offering different designs on their library cards so each patron can choose a favorite. All four designs were created by young artists from local schools. During the initial period at San Fran, people could trade in their old cards for new ones; after that, the cost was 50 cents for kids and $1 for adults to upgrade to the cooler cards. The designs

are at www.sfpl.org/news/newcards.htm and more info is at www.
sfpl.org/services/librarycard.htm.

Adopt a Rare Book

Guests have chosen rare books to adopt at Princeton (NJ)
University and Folger Shakespeare Library in Washington, D.C.
Wine and cheese parties have served as backdrops for these cultural affairs where people could view rare books, maps, manu-
scripts, and coins. At Princeton, attendees could choose a favorite
item to "adopt" for anywhere from $100 to $1,650. The monies
were used to restore those items or to purchase others. Princeton's
event in March 2008 drew 90 people (www.dailyprincetonian.
com/2008/03/31/20625).

Students Believe Other Students

At some universities, librarians use photographs of current students in their "Ask a Librarian" promotional materials. Seeing a
real person that they know on a poster that says, "I asked a librarian for help and got an A on my paper" is more convincing than
faceless "Use the library" ads.

Make Your Own Trading Cards

Library vendor SOLINET created trading cards to share info about
staff members. In a blog post (cebuzz.wordpress.com/2008/
03/17/using-trading-cards-as-promotional-tool) Max Anderson
explained, "We created trading cards to give out—including some
fun facts about ourselves but also some relevant information that
would be useful to explain what we do and who we are, to people.
What we found was that some fellow staff members weren't always
sure who taught what—and who was responsible for what subject
matters." The post includes his own trading card with his photo on
the front and his stats (interests, bio, likes/dislikes, courses taught,
and trivia) on the back.

Wake Up and Smell the Runners

Wake Forest (NC) University had a Wake the Library 5K and 1 Mile Fun Run in October 2008. The 3.1-mile route started and ended in front of the library and wound through the campus' cross-country trail. Library staffers helped get sponsors to pay for T-shirts, prizes, and other items. The race got blog coverage (blog.zsr.wfu.edu/gazette/2008/10/13/wake-the-library-5k-and-1-mile-fun-run) and Flickr coverage (www.flickr.com/photos/zsrlibrary/sets/72157607936263426/detail).

CaddyStacks: Golf in the Library

Turn your library into a miniature golf course and have people come and pay to play. A cool grassroots organization called Library Mini Golf (www.libraryminigolf.org) will come set everything up for you. It all started in the Trumbull (CT) Library, quite by accident, with a hurricane-relief fundraising event called Golf for the Gulf that raised $10,000. (Nope, that's not a typo.) Money at that event and others that followed came from sponsorships (businesses paid $125 or $250 per hole and bought ads on the scorecards) and players (charging $3 per child and $5 per adult to play a round of 18 holes). The Trumbull event drew more than 400 players, and a later one at the University of Hartford (CT) Library had more than 1,000 players. People of all ages were drawn by the novelty of playing golf inside a library. The course has real tees, greens, and regulation holes, all built in portable pieces that are simple to set up and can easily wind around the stacks.

"Boo" Is in "Book"

Is your library haunted? If rumors abound, capitalize on them by seeing if you can get added to the list that one blogger has been keeping at www.britannica.com/blogs/author/geberhart. Or publicize the stories on your own. Enjoy the notoriety and attract folks who are interested in eerie stuff, whether it's Halloween or not. Become part of local "hauntings" tours in your area.

Build a Soapbox Derby Car

Staffers at Western Michigan University (WMU) Libraries broke some stereotypes (and maybe some speed records) when they entered the school's traditional Soapbox Derby in 2003. A team that included the dean of libraries, staff, faculty, and student workers entered WMU's 30-year-old derby. They built their car from the ground up, recruited a pit crew, created T-shirts, and even secured a faculty/staff sticker so they could park the car on campus. As some of the team members explained in an *MLS* article (www.info today.com/mls/sep05/KirkDennis.shtml), they came in second on race day, barely edged out by the Society of Physical Engineers team. They raced again the next year, when they made it to the quarter-finals. And they gained a lot of admirers along the road. Later, they displayed their car in the library rotunda to remind everyone how innovative and adventurous their library staff members are.

Have a Worldwide Open House

A solo librarian at a large global corporation, Time Customer Service, held a virtual open house during National Library Week so she could reach employees who worked different shifts all over the world. Within her intranet, she designed a six-page tour of the library's services and its recent website enhancements. The tour included a guest book to sign so she could send all "attendees" thank-you treats (custom-designed cookies!) and draw names for a few door prizes. The full details at www.infotoday.com/mls/dec00/bumgarner.htm show off her success.

Make the Library Loud!

More and more libraries are having concerts in their off hours, which is another great stereotype-buster. In fact, the Lancaster Music Library in Lancashire County (U.K.) won a 2007 Love Libraries award (www.lovelibraries.co.uk) for its Get It Loud in Libraries project (www.lancashire.gov.uk/libraries/services/getit

loud/about.asp). Staffers transformed the library into a rock venue for evening concerts with popular bands like Harry and The Potters. Teens who could scream in the library began to see it in a whole different light.

Patrons of the Arts

Numerous libraries loan works of art that people can hang in their homes or offices. Patrons can borrow paintings or sculptures for 3 or 4 weeks at a time to brighten their homes or to impress clients. Some loaning libraries require credit card numbers, just in case.

Today, the University of California–Berkeley's (UCB) Morrison Library is reviving its Graphic Arts Loan Collection program where students, faculty, and staff with valid UCB IDs can peruse art on a website and then reserve pieces online (galc.lib.berkeley.edu). Items include framed original lithographs, etchings, and wood-block prints. The rules allow two items per person for a semester for free. (If a work comes back damaged, or doesn't come back at all, the borrower must pay the value of the piece plus appraisal costs.)

Keep Kids Truckin'

The Ashland (OH) Public Library had a Touch-a-Truck event for kids. A newspaper article (www.times-gazette.com/news/article/ 4223041) reported that "Trucks from construction companies, emergency responders, and the city of Ashland were lined up in the city and county parking lots off Main Street for kids to climb on and examine." Children really enjoyed exploring the vehicles, especially climbing inside them and honking the horns. Earplugs recommended.

Promises, Promises

Librarians all over, just like school administrators, sometimes find themselves promising kids that they'll do wacky things if the youngsters read enough books. Seemingly tame summer reading programs and reading contests lend themselves to escapades that make headlines. Librarians have cut off long hair or shaved their heads, eaten insects, sat atop dunking tanks, and taken pies in the face. Such promises are great motivators for kids. And even though making good on them might not be pretty, they are practically guaranteed to get you on the evening news. And they cost almost nothing. Free publicity!

Become Download Central

Some libraries have been able to acquire freestanding kiosks where patrons can download materials they want. At DOK, the library concept center in Delft, the Netherlands (www.dok.info), there is a download station that uses Bluetooth technology. Librarians choose content (which changes frequently) such as magazines and audio books to install on these "Tank U" stations. People with Bluetooth applications on their cell phones can download the content they want and then play it while commuting on the train or wherever they please. Read more about DOK's innovations at www.infotoday.com/mls/mar08/Boekesteijn.shtml.

Go *Wherever* the People Are

Mobile libraries can change lives, and minds. There are lots of examples if you look around. A public library in Lima, Peru, the Biblioteca Comunal de Santa Cruz, won an award for pushing grocery carts full of books through crowded marketplaces. This allowed the library workers to sign out books to the market's vendors and their children, who often had to accompany their parents to work.

A "Bieb in the Box," a tiny library on wheels, has been set up in cemeteries in the Netherlands so grieving people could access data on death, bereavement, funerals, spirituality, etc., on-site, where and when they needed it. (See a photo at www.infotoday. com/mls/sep07/Koontz.shtml.)

Many have heard of the Camel Public Library that carries boxes of books to nomadic peoples and refugees in Kenya (www.ifla.org/ V/press/pr0228-02.htm). It even has a blog at camelbookdrive. wordpress.com.

Wrestle Mania?

The Podium Library in Bath, U.K., held wrestling matches to mark the National Year of Reading in 2008. A newspaper article (www.thisisbath.co.uk/news/Second-library-wrestling-bout-planned/article-444693-detail/article.html) promoting the second match said, "[T]he library will be transformed with a temporary arena and seating. The match will feature full scale wrestling bouts from UCW [Ultimate Challenge Wrestling] regulars The Gangster and Checkmate as well as Hubert, Shabazz, T.K., and 'Gentleman' Gilligan Gordon." The library sold tickets and donated the proceeds to charity. In the article, council cabinet member for libraries David Hawkins said: "Wrestling in the library is a fun and entertaining evening which helps to publicise libraries to our community and on this occasion raise money for a respected local charity."

Create the Unexpected

A consultant named John Stanley (www.johnstanley.cc) led a group on a Library Study Tour through New Zealand in 2004. One of the surprising things they discovered was a library with a coffee shop that also served wine (www.infotoday.com/mls/mar05/ StanleyEmberton.shtml). This library, at Botany Downs in Manukau (south of Auckland), had a liquor license so it could offer wine to customers. Many people like to enjoy a glass of wine with a good book at home—maybe even with a good book they got from your library. So why is it so hard to imagine that happening in your building?

The Union County Public Library in warm, sunny Florida had a Snow Party as a summer kick-off event for residents in June 2007.

Staffers created a mini winter wonderland in their tropical sur-
roundings with a little money and a lot of imagination. They rented
a snow-making machine for just $1,200 that blew four tons of ice
into a big snow pile in the library's parking lot. They also prepared
wintry crafts and activities (like building snowmen out of marsh-
mallows) and promoted the whole thing by putting a giant inflat-
able snowman on the lawn during the week before the party. A
snow cone machine from a party rental store churned up tasty,
cold treats for the nearly 500 people who attended. Since
Floridians almost never see real snow, this event offered residents
something wonderfully unusual.

Focus Group Increases Success in New York

We wanted to do focus groups. It was a struggle to
get participants but we finagled people by doing
something that felt underhanded at the time—
stereotyping. We looked at who doesn't use us and
then zeroed in on hobby groups, sports enthusi-
asts, professionals, police/fire/EMT, senior living
facilities, etc., and contacted people through their
group affiliations to get them to attend.

This was for a project we were working on to
help our libraries win their votes and, based on
our findings, we've started a new project called
"Building Your Base" to continue to reach out to
those who are unfamiliar with a modern library
(midhudson.org/byb).

The major finding (surprise, surprise!) was that
most people don't understand what a modern
public library offers today. They think we're just
books. We heard great suggestions for things we're

already doing (having an online catalog, reserving items from home for later pick-up, offering DVDs, holding adult programs). What it did was point out our PR holes and drove home the need to repeat the basics. We often see our librarians announce a new service and then never mention it again. Now we advise them to remind people, and to keep in mind that there's always someone new or someone who missed the announcement the first time.

—Rebekkah Smith Aldrich, Coordinator of Member Information, Mid-Hudson Library System (midhudson.org), Poughkeepsie, NY

The product that Smith Aldrich mentions above, Building Your Base: Tools for Connecting with Your Community, is a fantastic toolkit packed with clear information about how to determine target markets then reach out to them. This is a success story about taking a project one step further to create something that will encourage proper marketing going forward. I encourage everyone to check out this site!

Promotion That Doesn't Feel Like Promotion

There are plenty of things you can do to promote your library's resources and resident experts. Lots of casual outreach activities are really promotional opportunities in disguise. For instance, do you think of giving a presentation as a form of promotion? It certainly is, even if your presentation isn't about the library. Anytime you're talking to a group, be sure to mention where you work and why you love it. (No need to read off a boring list of resources—

you can simply say why you enjoy being a librarian and let your enthusiasm do the work for you.) Likewise with teaching classes, inside or outside your building. Just live the love you have for your profession.

When you're comfortable with speaking, then think of ways to use that skill to the library's advantage. Offer to speak at meetings anywhere and everywhere. You can talk about the library or about your other hobbies or, being a librarian and all, you can do research to speak on just about anything. Everyone has meetings; consider all the groups you could appear for:

- Faculty members
- CEOs and vice presidents
- K–12 teachers and administrators
- Law firm partners or paralegals
- Nurses and doctors
- County commissioners
- Deans and administrators
- Incarcerated men and women
- Gym members
- Sports teams
- Patients with illnesses
- Disaster victims
- Salesmen
- Business owners
- Job seekers
- Pet owners

Think of creative ways to use your expertise. Let's say you're a medical librarian who specializes in kinesiology (the study of muscular movement; sometimes called "exercise science"). Outside of work, you could arrange to address members of fitness clubs or high school sports teams, groups of trainers or coaches, or maybe people taking physical therapy. By giving them the most up-to-date information and mentioning that you know how to search specialized sources at the library, you make yourself and your profession look good.

Once you have some public speaking under your belt, you can do higher-level outreach, such as lobbying politicians, raising money, or formally advocating for libraries. If you want to sway politicos, a great way to start is to mark National Library Legislative Day by attending ALA's annual Library Day on the Hill, when you go with other librarians, get briefed on talking points, then visit your area's representatives to explain why libraries matter. In 2008, ALA added a Virtual Library Legislative Day in Second Life (the virtual world). There's plenty of info on ALA's website. Speaking of which, if you don't know about ALA's Legislative Action Center, get to capwiz.com/ala/home right away. The Action Center makes it easy to identify your representatives and send them form letters about topics related to our field. Plus it explains the issues; gives tips on calling, writing, or emailing your reps; and even has a calendar of what topics are coming before both the House and the Senate every day. It's your one-stop shop for contacting elected officials, and you don't have to be an ALA member to use it.

One other thing that people don't often consider as a promotional opportunity is entering contests. Think about it: What better way to get other people to announce your greatness than to win a contest, then ride all the free publicity? Of course there are plenty of library-related contests out there, but don't limit yourself to them. Enter the local and regional stuff too. Look for ways to win games, customer-service awards, races, quiz shows, photography contests, team sports, whatever floats your boat. In fact, the less conventional, the better.

And never, ever forget the simplest unofficial promotional trick of all—just being yourself everywhere you go and striking up conversations with strangers. You'd be surprised how easy it is to work in a little library talk while you're waiting in line or sitting in a crowd. I make it a point to do this whenever I can, partly because I try to live a life of changing attitudes toward libraries, but also partly because I love seeing people's reactions. And the more unusual the situation, the more fun it is. In fact, sneaky advocate that I am, I like to spring the word on people when they least expect it from me.

One of my favorite stories is from a train ride from upstate New York to New York City. I'd just done a presentation at a big library conference and was dressed in business clothes. I ended up sitting with a young guy who was all decked out in his punk-rock gear (black clothes, piercings, the works). He seemed friendly enough, and I thought, "Ooooh, this is somebody I want to shock and educate." So I asked where he was riding to, and was he leaving home or returning. When he then asked me the same, I told him I was going home from a conference full of librarians. Of course he wondered what they'd have conferences about, and I was only too happy to tell him. We chatted for a good while, finding common ground on some fronts (especially computer topics), and had a great time. We both learned from each other. And I knew that, as soon as he got home and saw his friends, he'd say, "Man, you'll never believe—I was talking to this librarian chick on the train and she told me that libraries actually …"

In my off-time (such as it is), I'm an avid volleyball player, and all of my long-time teammates know what I do for a living. Newbies and opponents, however, don't. So I like to chat with people after a long night of slamming balls into their faces and seeming all mean and nasty. Then I shock them. It's so easy, really—I just ask what kind of work they do off the court, and once they tell me, they automatically return the question. I love the looks on their faces when I tell them I'm a librarian. It really does change their perception! And, if they're interested enough to continue the conversation, that's my chance to get into the "Libraries aren't what you think anymore" speech, quickly rattling off a few highlights and benefits.

This strategy also worked especially well back when I still worked on *Computers in Libraries* magazine. When techies asked my vocation, I'd say that I was the editor of a technology magazine. They'd get excited, thinking it was *PC World* or some other big title they'd heard of. When I'd say it was called *Computers in Libraries*, they might be a bit let down for a minute, then they'd look at me as if to say (or they'd just blurt out), "Wow, bet there's not much to read in there." That, of course, was my cue to retort, "Actually, you'd be surprised. Libraries always try to be on top of the latest technologies. It makes my head spin, trying to keep up with them all. *CIL* covers all sorts of networks, RAID arrays, internet stuff, webpages, RFID chips, client/server stuff, social networks, databases, and all the hardware too. Plus, libraries run on very specialized software packages that enable them to track all the books and things they loan out. It's really very complicated." It was great watching their mouths drop open until their jaws hit the floor. It would blow their minds—and their old-fashioned notions. God, I just *love* doing that to people.

Snappy Comebacks for That Awful Question, "Now That We Have the Internet, Why Do We Still Need Libraries?"

The question "Now that we have the internet, why do we still need libraries?" is still coming up, and I have to admit, it's one of those things that totally infuriates me. As far as I'm concerned, no discussion of library promotion would be complete without some discussion of this disturbing trend. Because if unenlightened people are still asking the question, it means that we all have more work to do.

What Do People Really Think of Librarians?

As I'm fond of saying, Why wonder when you can ask? Well, some *have* asked. Yes, there are actual studies of the public's perceptions of librarians. Check them out when you have a chance; they make for fascinating (and occasionally infuriating) reading.

I especially recommend one by Maura Seale from Grand Valley State University in Allendale, Michigan. It's called (wait for it …) "Old Maids, Policeman, and Social Rejects: Mass Media Representations and Public Perceptions of Librarians." It was published in the Spring 2008 issue of the *Electronic Journal of Academic and Special Librarianship*, and you can find the full text at southernlibrarianship. icaap.org/content/v09n01/ seale_m01.html.

This part of the abstract explains why this study and others like it are important enough to be mentioned in this book:

> [A]lthough librarians are often described in posi-tive terms, there is nearly no awareness as to the knowledge, duties, skills, and education of librari-ans and, as a consequence, public perceptions draw more heavily on stereotypical representa-tions of librarians' personalities. *Ultimately, librarians and libraries tend not to be effectively utilized, as users remain unaware of librarians' abilities and responsibilities.* [emphasis mine]

So tell people, tell people, tell more people, then tell them some more. They need to know what your skills are and what you can do. They need to know what you have that can benefit them!

At the end of the "Old Maids" article is a list of lots of other studies and articles you can explore. Then, if you want something a little more light-hearted, go enjoy Ruth Kneale's site You Don't Look Like a Librarian (www.librarian-image.net) or read the book (Information Today, Inc., 2009). For years, Kneale has been gathering talks, articles, and images that show librarians as they're perceived in popular culture. This site is what led me to hire her to write the fun little department for *MLS* that we call "Spectacles: How Pop Culture Sees Librarians," which you can find in every issue.

Then, if you're mad as hell and you're not going to take it anymore, you can learn to connect with your community via current pop culture. Try the blog Pop Goes the Library (www.popgoesthelibrary.com), which was started by Sophie Brookover in 2004. At the end of 2008, she and Elizabeth Burns published a book by the same name (Information Today, Inc.), which explains how to create your library's own pop culture niche. And it includes a great big chapter called "Advocacy, Marketing, Public Relations, and Outreach." Gotta love that! The book and the blog are both lots of fun, and you may accidentally learn a few things while reading them.

As you saw earlier in this chapter, I have my own little elevator speeches in my head, as we all should. We need to have snappy comebacks too. I have a few personal favorites, but for the wide audience of this book, I decided to ask some PR-savvy colleagues what they like to say. In the same survey discussed in Chapter 1, I also asked respondents for their best retorts to the "why do we still need libraries" question. I think you'll enjoy some of their answers as much as I did, and I hope you'll find—or create—occasions to use them! (All are printed here with permission.)

- "Because librarians are the best search engine around!" —Shelley Civkin, communications officer, Richmond Public Library, Richmond, British Columbia, Canada

- "With more information than ever, you need a professional to sort it out for you." —Amy Guyette, academic librarian, Indianapolis, IN

- "To ask why we need libraries at all, when there is so much information available elsewhere, is about as sensible as asking if roadmaps are necessary now that there are so very many roads." —Jon Bing, professor of Information Technology Law, University of Oslo, Norway (found at www.bs.dk/publikationer/english/nnpl/html/chapter03.htm); used as the signature file of Andrea Avni, information center librarian, Sound Transit, Seattle, WA

- "Now that we have the internet, why do we still have doctors, teachers, sales associates, hospitals, schools, and retail stores? The internet improves these services too, but can never replace them." —Mary Odom, research librarian, Paul V. Corusy Memorial Library, International Association of Assessing Officers, Kansas City, MO

- "How many clicks does it take you to find the information you are looking for?" —Paula Watson-Lakamp, communications manager, Fort Collins Regional Library District, Fort Collins, CO

- "It's true, there's lots of information available via the internet … but most scholarly content is not *freely available* on the internet." —Melissa Gonzalez, community resources/history reference librarian, John C. Pace Library, University of West Florida, Pensacola, FL

- "Libraries and library staff members are an integral part of the community." —Nancy Fletcher, PR and special needs librarian, Waukesha County Federated Library System, Waukesha, WI

- "I have heard hospital administrators say, 'It is all free and on the internet.' My response: 'When you get coin-operated mammogram machines that require no technicians to run them nor any radiologists to interpret the results, that is when you can close the library and lay off the librarian.' I promise not to ask you, a health professional, how to suture myself if I get cut—I will come to you directly for your expertise. Please promise that you will ask me, the information access expert, the next time you need to do a search." —Teresa (Teri) Hartman, associate professor/head, Education Department, McGoogan Library of Medicine, University of Nebraska Medical Center, Omaha, NE

- "While public libraries used to be gatekeepers of information, we've moved toward becoming gateways. The internet is just one of the many lifelong learning and research tools available at your library." —Cortni O'Brien, librarian, Avon Public Library, Avon, CO

- "We have an average of over 3,600 visitors come into our library *every day*, and the number keeps growing. Those folks clearly feel we still need libraries!" —Joanne Hinkel, community relations, Boise Public Library, Boise, ID *[Author's Note: The number quoted here is a daily average*

*for April–September 2008 for one main building and two
small branches.]*

These answers were quoted in the media:

- Following a news story on flood damage at the Cedar
  Rapids (IA) Public Library in July 2008, some people left
  comments along the lines of "Who needs a library anyway?" Someone left this "gotcha!" response: "I'm assum-
  ing 32,000 books having been checked out at the time of
  flooding indicates that at least a few people appreciated
  the resources the library had to offer." (Cited online in
  American Libraries Direct, link.ixs1.net/s/ve?eli=
  l223607&si=y164207364&cfc=3html)

- "No matter how smart and helpful search engines get,
  they're never going to replace librarians." —Gary Price,
  founder and editor of the ResourceShelf blog and former
  director of online resources at Ask.com (quoted in *New
  York Times*, September 2006)

- Even employment studies show that people are going to
  keep using libraries. In fact, in September 2008, CNN and
  CareerBuilder.com created a list of 15 jobs you could get
  into that will pay between $50,000 and $59,999, and
  "librarian" was on the list. In fact, they projected a 4 percent increase in the need for librarians by the year 2016.

And, finally, here are some of my own comebacks:

- "Believing that the internet can replace libraries is like
  believing that email can replace the postal service."

- "Even though sites like WebMD are great, we don't shut
  down doctors' offices. Why would we shut down
  libraries?"

- "Just a small fraction of the world's knowledge is online.
  To find the rest, we still need librarians."

- "If libraries don't matter anymore, then why does one of the smartest men in the world, Bill Gates, spend millions of dollars to keep building and improving them?"

- "If you really want to be green, use libraries. Buying a few copies of each book for hundreds of people to share is greener than everyone buying their own copies."

- "Employees who aren't well-trained in searching can waste hours of company time looking for information that trained librarians can find in minutes. Information professionals can actually *save* an organization time and money."

- "Now people can book their own flights online, but that hasn't meant the end of travel agents or airline agents."

- "If your accounting department thinks it can save money by putting Google on every desktop and eliminating the need for the library, suggest that it could also put spread-sheet software on every desktop and eliminate the need for the accounting department."

The Final Lesson

The final lesson here is that you should always be ready to respond to anyone, anytime, anywhere if you hear people question the existence of libraries. You understand their value—heck, you *live* their value! All you need to do to help in a big way is have a sentence or two in mind so you're always ready to spring into action. You don't need a special occasion. Always remember: You can be an advocate at any moment, even while waiting in the queue at the post office or while sitting on the train. Never pass up a chance to talk about the value of libraries!

Improving Our Media Relations via Strategic Communications Planning

Marsha A. Iverson

This article was originally published in Marketing Library Services, *November–December 2007, Volume 21, No. 6. Reprinted with permission.*

The King County Library System serves more than 1.7 million people over a 2,100-square-mile area in western Washington. Over the years, we've added new libraries, expanded and diversified the collection, developed and implemented computer and technology strategies, and grown with the population we serve. KCLS is consistently one of the busiest library systems in the nation, now with 43 libraries and a staff of about 1,200.

For the past 13 years I have been the public relations specialist for KCLS. I'm the ".6" part of a 9.6-member Community Relations and Graphics staff. It is my job to get media coverage and to establish community partnerships for the benefit of our patrons. How hard could it be? Surprisingly so, until I changed my approach and became a strategic planner. In this article I'll explain a few different models for communications planning, then share my own success story to illustrate how these plans can work.

Understanding Planning Models

Strategic planning is just another name for asking yourself a bunch of questions about what you're doing and why. Whether you're launching a new service, reaching out to an underserved group, or planning a development campaign, strategic planning can help you focus and concentrate your communications efforts to get better results.

If your resources are limited, using a planning process—no matter how informal or homegrown—will help you make the best use of your time, energy, and budget. There are as many planning structures as there are planners. I tend to rely on three slightly different models, depending on the problem I'm trying to solve.

1. The no-frills model: The most basic communication model of all identifies the fundamental parts of a communication interaction: A sender, a message, a recipient, and a channel to carry the message. If all else fails, cover these four elements and you're still off to a good start.

I learned the value of this simple model early on, when I was nearly finished with a set of radio public service announcements—promoting services for the deaf and hard-of-hearing. I had my message. I had my audience. I'd miscalculated the channel.

After many years of conducting and scrutinizing communications campaigns, I'm frequently amazed at how often the message is more of an afterthought than a fundamental part of the plan. If you don't have something important to say, be quiet and listen.

2. The mid-size plan: When I need *more* detail to develop a strategic plan, I use a different model that helps clarify specific pieces.

- What is the current situation? (What am I doing and what results am I getting now?)

- What is the desired situation? (What results do I want and what do I need to do to get them?)

By knowing where you are and where you want to go, you can figure out how to get there.

3. My favorite plan: My favorite way to develop a strategic communication plan is following the four-step process required for entering the John Cotton Dana Library Public Relations Award contest.[1]

1. Needs assessment: Why are you communicating? What's the underlying need?

2. Planning: How will you meet the need identified in Step 1?

3. Implementation: Carry out your plan.

4. Evaluation: Review the results. Did you reach your goals? What did you learn?

This simple structure is a great way to develop a strategic plan, and the lessons you learn during your first project will help you plan the next.

By choosing an approach at the beginning, you can make your process as simple or as complex as your project requires. Sometimes you'll find it helpful to go through several iterations in different phases of a larger project. As you apply these planning steps to different projects, you'll find out what is most helpful to you and you'll develop your own style.

My Own Story: Rethinking Media Relations

The KCLS service area is a media-rich environment: There are four daily newspapers, five local TV stations, three interview-format radio stations, and dozens of weekly community papers, all of which would make excellent venues for library news. Despite the abundance of channels—both print and broadcast—our coverage never met our expectations.

I schmoozed. I wheedled. I occasionally pleaded. I tried every trick I could think of: neon envelopes for the press kits, cover letters to the editors to tell them how important our library programs are. I wrote context reports to explain the communitywide need for literacy and library services. I made tempting offers of exclusives and photo essays. We were awash in eye-catching graphics and meaningful programs, but there didn't seem to be any correlation between our efforts and resulting column-inches of news or feature coverage.

Who had time to plan? Not me. I was too busy trying to keep up with the workload: writing and faxing press releases and PSA scripts, creating eye-catching press kits about library events, and wondering what it would take to actually get the media coverage our wonderful libraries deserved.

Then one day 7 years ago, the books editor for a local daily paper responded to my terribly clever release for a pending author visit: "You may think this is a big thing. To us, this is NOT a big thing." Where had I gone wrong? Our traditional PR strategy had been to seek media coverage of KCLS programs and special events. We wanted front-page, above-the-fold feature coverage—with color photos—for everything. We didn't get that coverage, and I wanted to know why.

Performing Our Needs Assessment

We knew that libraries were crucially important to the quality of life in our communities. All of our marketing efforts—the promotions and fliers and posters and banners and special events—were very successful in reaching the folks who came to our libraries and signed up for our mailing lists. We also knew that there were many county residents who didn't know what library resources were available. We wanted to reach them.

Year	Features	News Briefs	Mentions	Calendar	Photos	Editorials	Other	Friends	Year Total	% < yr Summary
2002	129	77	184	771	29	24	14	NA	1,228	36%
2003	169	104	187	1,093	49	66	8	NA	1,676	36%
2004	210	108	78	1,743	71	54	21	NA	2,285	37%
2005	84	105	127	2,272	45	17	34	NA	2,684	17%
2006	192	211	170	4,591	23	94	106	1	5,388	101%
5-year totals	784	605	746	10,470	217	255	183	1	13,261	339%

How could we reach people who did not use the library? Through the media, of course. But the media wasn't doing its part. Why? It was time to do a multistep needs assessment.

Step 1: Gather Data. We looked closely at our output—press releases and media advisories—and the coverage we received for our efforts. For this I used the mid-size planning model.

Current Practice: We promote individual programs and special events. All PR, marketing, and advertising are based on events and special programs. We were competing with the wrong market (commercial event venues in a major market). We sought separate media coverage for individual events with unique graphics, which lacked continuity and obscured the core value of the library system.

Current Results: We had unpredictable coverage, unreliable media people, and no strategic messaging. We got solid coverage of calendar events (valuable to patrons, but limited strategic results), but only occasional, unpredictable mentions for some major events. The media rarely ran features on blockbuster programs. Sometimes we were surprised by coverage of minor programs. Finally, the rare stories about our libraries generally did not identify KCLS as a system.

Step 2: Analyze Communications With Current Data. Here's the overall picture we saw:

Our Message: Libraries are important.

Our Audience: We targeted the public, especially everyone in the county who did *not* use the libraries.

Our Channel: We wanted to use reporters and editors.

Our Error: We assumed that our media contacts understood how important our libraries are to the community, and we relied on them to cheerfully, faithfully, and consistently seize upon each of our press releases and race to tell every one of our stories to their audiences, for free.

Step 3: Gather More Data. A simple follow-up email query of key media contacts indicated that our assumptions had been wrong. We found that the reporters most likely to cover library issues didn't use the library, and they didn't even know that there are two large neighboring library systems in the same territory!

I needed to know more about these media folks. Who were they? What did they know already, and what was I trying to tell them? How could my messages be important to them? More to the point, why weren't these reporters and editors eager to tell our story to their audiences?

Then came the first big conceptual whack upside my head: Reporters and editors are an audience, not a channel! If they didn't know how wonderful the libraries are—and understand how important we are to the community—why would they want to tell our story?

The second conceptual whack upside the head came when I learned that my media contacts knew nothing about KCLS. They bought the books they wanted. They thought of libraries as just repositories for the collected works of Dr. Seuss, Thucydides, and Miss Manners. They were certain that libraries had nothing they needed.

I had to find a way to change their minds. Thus began my conversion to being a true believer in strategic communication planning.

Using Data to Develop Our Plan

How could we get skeptical reporters and editors to learn about the library? First, we needed to get their attention. We had been told—quite firmly—that our events weren't "news," no matter how important we thought they were. We had expected the media to serve us. Now we had to learn how to serve the media. I would find out what they needed from the library and find a way to meet them on their terms.

It was time to get strategic: I tried thinking like my target audience. What would I want from the library if I were a reporter? I'd want information for whatever story I was working on at the moment. We changed our approach by focusing our major media efforts on core library services. We aimed to increase the strategic impact of media relations by doing these three things:

1. Treating media contacts as a key audience

2. Enhancing awareness of KCLS through existing basic PR

   • Continuing calendar coverage

- Focusing on community weeklies for possible photos/local features

- Seeking specific mention of King County Library System in all stories about KCLS libraries

3. Enhancing the perceived value of KCLS through new PR initiatives

- Increasing our chances of news coverage by linking KCLS resources to significant issues

- Expanding the visibility of our library system as a key player in important discussions

- Establishing partnerships with key community entities for collaborative cross-promotion

- Positioning the library system as leader in community-building

Implementing Our Communications Plan

We realized that the best way to improve our media coverage was to provide a valuable service to reporters and editors. So in 2000 we identified all the media contacts we could find and made a database (which we now update regularly). Then we asked what information they wanted from us, when they needed it, and what format they preferred. (We continued sending our calendar releases to the calendar sections, now entirely by email.)

For issues of major importance, we started to use a staged release process:

1. Offer exclusive features to selected contacts well in advance, with a reply deadline.

2. Send a media advisory throughout the region.

3. Post briefs to the media folks' Web sites for their online calendar listings.

4. Follow up the media advisory with a general press release.

Evaluating the Results of Our New Strategy

Two years after we implemented our new approach to the news media, we began keeping detailed records of our press coverage in community weeklies and regional daily newspapers. The findings surprised us. (See the chart on page 253.)

While our first round of strategic communication planning for media relations coincided with an upsurge in coverage, it would be misleading to claim that all of the increased coverage was due to our revised approach to serving the media. We made a few other changes that likely affected the results:

- We had begun a strategic branding process back in 2000, which set the foundation for the revised approach to media and made a significant impact on communitywide visibility.

- We began tracking an entirely new category of print coverage we call "mentions." (That's when KCLS is mentioned in stories about something else.)

- The upsurge in calendar listings reflects some growth in the system and perhaps the recent addition of automated event calendar scheduling.

Even with all of these other external factors, our revised approach is at least part of the reason for the continuing rise in print coverage.

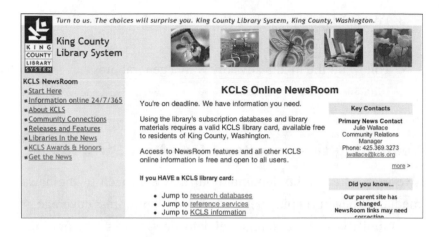

Our Resulting Solution and Further Progress

Our quest to serve the media as a professional resource led us to create our Online NewsRoom in 2005. By then we had learned several lessons:

- Reporters rarely read details unless directly related to the story they're writing at the moment.

- Reporters who were not familiar with our online resources would not look for them.

- To serve media contacts well, we needed to provide an easy, convenient way for them to get information anytime, from anywhere.

Explore our resulting solution at http://kcls.mediaroom.com.

After 2 years in operation, the KCLS Online NewsRoom averages 45 to 60 visitors per day. Our media advisories and press releases get a significant number of visits from journalists. And, according to the tracking reports from PR NewsWire, people access our NewsRoom site from more than 80 different countries!

Now it's time to begin the media relations strategic planning process all over again—this time for the Online NewsRoom. We'll begin with a user survey that will start our next needs assessment.

Planning is a process that helps structure your thinking. No plan will be perfect and even the best plans will be modified as you use them. Each plan you work through will help you focus your work more effectively and will give you better information for your next communication challenge. That's why I remain a planner.

Marsha A. Iverson is the public relations specialist at the King County Library System offices in Issaquah, Wash. She has been a public relations/communications professional since 1974. She holds a B.A. in cultural anthropology from The University of California–Santa Barbara, and has done post-baccalaureate study in scientific and technical communication and interdisciplinary studies at the University of Washington. Iverson is the immediate past chair of the ALA/LAMA Public Relations and Marketing Section, and has been a juror for the John Cotton Dana Library Public Relations Awards for the past 5 years. Her email address is iversonma@aol.com.

Endnote

1. Another advantage of using this four-step structure is that when you're done with your communication campaign, just summarize what you've done, display the results in an eye-catching, cohesive presentation, and you'll have a strong entry for the annual JCD Award competition sponsored by H.W. Wilson Co. For details on the award, go to www.hwwilson.com and scroll down to the John Cotton Dana Award Link.

Designing Promo Materials That Are Legible

Pat Wagner

This article was originally published in Marketing Library Services, *March–April 2006, Volume 20, No. 2. Reprinted with permission.*

What's the difference between a promotional flier that looks pretty and one that is actually read and acted on by a library customer or employee? Often, it's simply legibility.

Over decades, graphic designers have developed a set of principles that work according to how the human eye sees a printed page and delivers its information to the brain. These principles are easy to apply, no matter what kind of software programs you use to create your print material. Most simple word-processing programs are more than adequate for what the average librarian needs to create most printed promotional pieces.

The Principles of Legibility

When we are applying the principles of legibility, we are trying to do two things: 1) make it easier for the eye to see the type and communicate the information to the brain, and 2) guide the eye so it reads everything on a page. My experience tells me that if we are successful, the reader will be much more likely to act on the information.

Why can designing for legibility seem so hard? It is easy to get carried away by computer capabilities! Pale lavender ink is pretty, but will people need to squint to read it? That jazzy-looking poster with the tiny white type on the black background looks, like, way cool, but will people find the date and time of the YA author luncheon before they give up and move on?

Principle One: Size counts. The most common mistake I see is type that is too small. To make room for bigger type that has a larger point size, phrases will have to substitute for full sentences, and use one- or two-word "bullets" for phrases.

Here are a few simple guidelines to ensure that your type is large enough to coax your target audience to read it and to act on it.

- To test a flier that will sit on a table and advertise an event, hold the flier at arm's length. Can you easily read the words that say what you are promoting, the date, and the location?

- For a brochure that is folded, follow the same rule: Can someone read the main headline at arm's length?

- For a poster that's meant to be tacked to a bulletin board or wall, stand at least 5 feet away and see if you can read the headline, location, and time of the event.

- If your poster is going to be pinned to the wall of a corridor (as in most school, academic, or institutional settings), try to read the main points on your poster from the middle of the hallway, because that is where many people walk.

Definitions of Typography Terms

Body copy: The actual text of a piece, written in paragraphs.

Boldface: A thicker, darker variation of type, used for emphasis. Most fonts have a boldface variation.

Font: A family or group of type styles that share a specific design.

Italic: A slanted, lighter variation of type, originally designed to fit more words into a space than regular type. Most fonts have an italic variation.

Leading: The thin lines of white space between lines of type.

Pixels: The tiny dots that make up the images you see on your computer screen.

Point: A measurement of the height of a type character (letter or number). There are 72 points in one inch.

Sans Serif: French for "without serif," it refers to type designed without strokes, mostly more modern type fonts that have been better suited to the machine and computer ages. Popular sans serif fonts include Helvetica, Comic Sans, Arial, Futura, and Gill Sans.

Serif: The small strokes at the end of lines of type. Originally part of the physical creation of the individual letter (the tip of a chisel, the flick of a brush), it was included as part of the design of raised metal type. Finally, serifs are now part of the accepted design of a whole class of font styles. Popular serif fonts include Times Roman, Garamond, Palatino, Bodoni, Baskerville, Century Schoolbook, and American Typewriter.

Subheads: Smaller headlines, usually only one or two words, used to break up body copy.

Usually, I have to edit out at least 50 percent of the words on a library flier or poster to make space for a type size that is legible for the average person. What are left are the bare facts: one compelling headline that is funny, timely, provocative, or interesting; a pithy description; and one simple graphic, such as a line drawing or cartoon.

Principle Two: Just because you can do it doesn't make it right. Most computer programs come with infinite bells and whistles. You can apply hundreds of type fonts and thousands of colors to your work. This professional's advice? Don't.

First, please do not use more than two type fonts for any one-page printed piece or single page of a newsletter. You can actually use just one type font for a poster or flier and still have something that is attractive yet easy to read.

For a newsletter or brochure with more text, stick to one font for the body copy (such as Garamond) and one for the headlines (such as Helvetica). You can still use different sizes as well as *italic* and **boldface** for variation and emphasis. Please use these variations sparingly, otherwise they lose their impact.

Only two fonts—Good!

Carnegie Library Newsletter, Our Town, CO   May, 2006

We See Dead People!

Do you have precious family photos stuffed in drawers and boxes? Do you worry that they may come to harm? Please join us for a fact-filled free program by some of our area's leading experts on photograph conservation **Tuesday, June 6, 2006** from **1 pm to 3 pm** at the Carnegie Library, 1234 Main Street, Our Town, CO. You will learn how to clean, repair and store your photos safely. You can also bring photos for evaluation: Are they worth anything? What can you do to stop the damage and safely repair and mount them? For more information, **call Marge or Fred at the library at 303-555-1212.**

New Fines Start June 1

Library boss Pat warns users that the library board is going to raise the fines for overdue CDs from two cents per day to $10.00. After months of heated public meetings, the board has decided that if the library was going to continue to stay open and circulate books, CDs, DVDs and other materials, something had to be done to get the public to return items to the library in a timely fashion.

A proposal to require hard jail time on road crews on lonely mountain passes was rejected by a 32-31 vote.

Library boss Pat contemplates fines during last board meeting. Because the proposal to require jail time was defeated, he has since shaved off his beard and removed his toupee.

Page 4

Too many fonts & colors

We See **Dead** People!

How to Preserve
Your Precious Family Photos

Tuesday, June 6, 2006
1 pm to 3 pm – Free admission

Carnegie Library – 303-555-1212
1234 Main Street, Our Town, CO

Bring Your Photos for Evaluation

Second, just because you can print every word in a different color doesn't mean it is a good idea. Color can distract as much as it can focus the eye on the page. Stick with three colors: the color of the paper, black ink for the body copy and most headlines, and one accent color to emphasize important items.

A little color goes a long way. You can use a line of color between the headline and the body copy in a flier or poster, a color border around an important paragraph in a newsletter, or a small graphic of a flower to pull the reader's eye to the information about the garden club meeting. If you insist on using colored type, please ensure there is sufficient contrast between the type and the paper to make it readable. Dark red ink on light blue paper can be read with ease, but pale yellow type on creamy orange paper cannot.

Principle Three: The designer's job is to move the eye down the page, so that everything is read. Conventional wisdom is that the eye starts reading at the upper left-hand corner of a page. This will be true of most people who learned to read most Western languages.

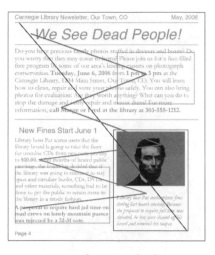

When someone reads a book, they read to the end of the line and return to the beginning of the next line, until they have read every word. But when they are reading a page with many different design elements—headlines, art work, photos—their eyes will tend to drag right and down (see red line). This diagonal path, which acts like a psychological magnet, means that words that are outside that path will probably not be automatically read unless we, the designers, take action.

The most common technique is to place headlines, graphics, and bolder design elements so as to entice the eye away from the gravitational pull of the diagonal. The result is that the eye zigs and zags down the page. By the time the reader gets to the bottom, most of the text has been read, or at least scanned.

Typical strategies include putting a headline or photo in the upper right-hand corner of the page and a graphic or a boxed paragraph in the lower left-hand corner. Smaller subheads, photographs, and design elements draw the eye back and forth.

What about centering all of the type like the layout of a formal wedding invitation? There is nothing wrong with that kind of layout. It is simple to do, and if there are only a few design elements, it can work: one headline, one drawing that illustrates the topic, a short line of type, and the appropriate facts. However, this is a very formal layout and does not suit less formal events or announcements. And it doesn't work if there is a lot of body copy, such as the biography of an author or detailed directions to the library building.

Principle Four: The details count. Here are four of my favorite tweaks.

Serif versus sans serif

This is a serif font.

This is a sans serif font.

Capital letters versus upper and lower case

THIS HEADLINE IS ALL-CAPS.
This headline is upper and lower case.

1. I am a fan of serif fonts for most print body copy. Those serifs send the eye more information so that the eye moves faster and retains more, according to rules I learned 40 years ago.

Two exceptions are worth noting. First, sans serif type fonts are more legible on a computer screen, because pixels on the screen tend to break up in the curves and skinny lines of serif fonts. Second, people have grown up reading sans serif body copy for a few decades now; a teen-oriented flier can probably get away with sans serif.

2. Convert occurrences of all-capital-letter headlines and text, even in larger posters, to upper- and lowercase letters. Words are less legible when printed in capital letters; reserve all caps for the occasional funny or provocative one-word headline.

3. The third tweak applies to the space between the lines of type, which is called leading, pronounced like the lead in "lead pencil." If you must use small type in the body copy, add an extra point of space between. One or two points of leading between lines seem to work best in body copy of eight to 18 points.

4. Watch how many words are in a line of type. The hardest print media to design is the standard three-fold brochure or a newsletter with three columns. The columns are too narrow to squeeze in more than three or four words per line. Our eyes move to read the line, and then, just as things are getting interesting, we have to skid to a stop and start over. A minimum of six words (an ideal range is eight to 14 words) is a better length for a line of type. Consequently,

Which is easier to read?

If you have any questions about this program, please contact
Marge or Fred at the reference desk of the library. Although
this is a free program and we welcome you to drop in at any
time, we are more than happy to answer any questions you
might have about the program. Or call us at 303-555-1212.

If you have any questions about
this program, please contact
Marge or Fred at the reference
desk of the library. Although
this is a free program and we
welcome you to drop in at any
time, we are more than happy to
answer any questions you might
have about the program. Or call
us at 303-555-1212.

I encourage clients to use one or two wider columns for newsletters and to stick to fliers that use one or two columns instead of folded brochures. These formats are much easier to lay out and are more legible for average readers.

Simple Design Is the Best Design

These principles simplify the design process and shorten the time it takes to turn out a quick flier. Try one or two, and see if you don't get some compliments and more attention. And to make designing easier, just remember this: Simple works better!

Pat Wagner has consulted on personnel, management, leadership, marketing, and planning issues for libraries since 1978. She has been a printer, graphic designer, book publisher, editor, book reviewer, columnist, and radio journalist. She can be reached via her company, Pattern Research, Inc., in Denver at http://www.pattern.com or pat@pattern.com.

Graphic Arts Resources

Books
Robin Williams is my favorite writer of books on design. You can read her
    advice and find out about her latest books at: http://www.eyewire.
    com/magazine/columns/robin or http://www.ratz.com/robin/books.
    html.

Web Sites
Cool stuff about legibility
    http://cgm.cs.mcgill.ca/~luc/readability.html
"How to Rescue Your Graphic Design Project When All Else Fails"
    http://www.allgraphicdesign.com/articledesign4.html

Creative typography resources
   http://desktoppub.about.com/od/typeart
User-centered design article
   http://www.stcsig.org/usability/topics/articles/ucd%20_web_devel.html
"The voice of typography" article
   http://www.graphic-design.com/Type/ voice/index.html
Poster Design, illustrated
   http://www.soe.uoguelph.ca/webfiles/ agalvez/poster
Legibility
   http://www.webstyleguide.com/type/legible.html
Type Legibility and Readability resources
   http://desktoppub.about. com/od/typelegibility

Promotion Is Not the Same as Marketing

Christie Koontz

This article was originally published in Marketing Library Services, *January–February 2006, Volume 20, No. 1. Reprinted with permission.*

Almost 10 years ago, during the summer of 1996, I stood nervously at the podium in room 214 of the Library and Information Studies School (now the College of Information) at Florida State University. It was a Tuesday night, and the first class meeting of Marketing of Library and Information Services.

My initial assignment for the nine students was fun, but critical. I asked them to descend the stairwell to the Goldstein Library, delve into the print version of *Library Literature*, and find the term "marketing" in the indexed hierarchy. Thirty minutes later, each returned to room 214 and stated that "marketing" was housed under the heading "publicity." I told them that we would revisit this exercise at the end of the semester so they could better understand the gravity of the august publication's mistake.

To this day, many professions (not just ours) confuse publicity with marketing. Marketing is comprised of four major steps, and promotional tools are only active in the third. The four are 1) marketing research, 2) marketing segmentation, 3) marketing mix strategy, and 4) marketing evaluation. (I've covered all of these in previous *MLS* columns.) The third step, marketing mix strategy, is the one with the four P's—product, price, place, and promotion.

It's the step in which you develop the offer (*product/services* based on marketing research and marketing segmentation), assess *customer costs* (*prices*) for the offer, identify *places* of distribution, and *promote* the offer to targeted customers. This shows just how far down the food chain of marketing *promotion* really is. Promotion is only *one* of the important tools of marketing. It's sort of like the index finger is to the human body—it's an essential, strategic part, but still greatly reliant on the whole.

Promotion Can Be Misused

There is always a tendency, as my old advertising professor once said, "to fall in love with your own ideas and immediately espouse them." This is why many organizations produce promotional materials first, without conducting marketing research and segmentation.

For example, let's say you spot a great brochure at the Swap & Shop at the annual American Library Association Conference. You come back to your library ready to reprint it (with permission, of course) and wrap it around one of your own similar services. But this goes against all marketing precepts. Promotional tools must be built upon knowledge of *your* customer markets, *their* media habits, and the *nature* of the product or offer. The message is affected by these important factors. Your customers may be (and likely are) different from any other library's. In short, emulating another library's promotional tools can be risky.

Major Promotional Tools for Nonprofits

These are the major tools you can use for promotional messages: 1) paid advertising, 2) unpaid or public service advertising, 3) joint advertising (a partner pays for your message), 4) promotions, 5) publicity, and 6) personal selling (Andreasen and Kotler, 2003,

Strengths and Weaknesses of Alternative Media for Nonprofits

Strengths	Weaknesses	Strengths	Weaknesses
TELEVISION		**NEWSPAPERS**	
High impact Audience selectivity Schedule when needed Sponsorship availabilities Merchandising possible	High production costs Uneven delivery by market Upfront commitments required	Large audience Immediate reach Short lead time Market flexibility Good upscale coverage	Difficult to target narrowly Highest waste High cost for national use Minimum positioning control Cluttered
RADIO		**POSTERS, BILLBOARDS**	
Low cost per contact Audience selectivity Schedule when needed Length can vary Personalities available Tailor weight to market	Nonintrusive medium Audience per spot is small No visual impact High total cost for good reach Clutter with spot markets	High reach High frequency of exposure Minimal waste Can localize Immediate registration Flexible scheduling	No depth of message High cost for national use Best positions already taken No audience selectivity Poor coverage in some areas Minimum 1-month purchase[1]
MAGAZINES		**INTERNET**	

Audience selectivity
Editorial association
 	
Long life
Large audience per insert
 	
Excellent color
Minimal waste
Merchandising possible
	Long lead time needed
	Readership accumulates
	    slowly
	Uneven delivery by market
	Cost premiums for regional
	    editions
		Reach upscale markets
		E-messages and newsletters
		    inexpensive
		Possible to track performance
		Messages can be changed
		    quickly
			Only reach those online
			E-messages can be lost among
			    e-mails
			A hit does not tell you much
			Medium is not fluid

		PERSONAL SELLING	

		Direct contact likely elicits
		    response
			Uncomfortable/time-
			    consuming[2]

1. Source for 'Television through Posters': A Program Manager's Guide to Media Planning (Washington, D.C.: SOMARC, The Futures Group, 1988.) Reproduced with permission.
2. Source for 'Internet through Personal Selling,' Andreasen and Kotler, 2003.

p. 441). By contrast, public relations is considered a management communication tool that seeks to influence the attitudes and awareness of targeted publics toward the library organization (as opposed to *promotion* of library programs and services). Let us take a look at the six major promotional tools.

1. Paid advertising—This is almost nonexistent in our field. Few libraries have the designated funds for using paid advertising mediums (except for employment ads). Television is prohibitively expensive. Radio ads must be frequently placed on the right channels to even begin to hit your markets, and thus can also become expensive. A quarter-page newspaper ad in a mid-sized market can cost upwards of $1,000 for one ad running only 1 day. An Internet banner is around $10 per 1,000 banner impressions, with an average click-through rate of 1 percent. A billboard that could benefit a library is probably not affordable (and in a college town like the one I live in, it will probably already be taken by Budweiser). So what is a librarian to do? Many turn to public service announcements—with mixed results.

2. **Public service advertising**—Some years ago I wrote a report, "Free Air Time: Can You Afford It?" while working as a communications intern for a state health department's public information office. Here is a quick review, with timely updates for each of the media. This is very important information. Since much time and energy is invested in public service announcements, we must always consider, "What is the impact for our effort?" The media are intrinsic to the utility of this tool, so let us scrutinize the possibilities.

- **Television** is in more homes than plumbing—no wonder we are drawn to it as a media choice. Along with enjoying its obviously wide appeal, the advertiser can control ad placement and reach (how many people are likely to see it). Yet most studies indicate these are not necessarily the key ingredients for successful campaigns. Successful television campaigns do four things: 1) avoid complicated message themes that get lost in clutter, 2) target specific audiences, 3) pre-test ads and assure relevance to the viewer, and 4) provide messages that suggest clear action (at least for the motivated!). The good news is these four aspects can be controlled by an organization that creates a PSA. But two factors remain: You cannot place it at the exact airtime you desire, and the production is expensive.

- **Cable television** in the early '80s was an advertiser's dream as far as reaching specific markets. Black Entertainment Network had 4.5 million viewers, and Spanish International Network served half a million Spanish-speaking people. These numbers, as well as cable choices, have grown exponentially. Cable allows advertisers to not only target specific markets, but to also create longer messages at lower rates. While cable continues to not be bound by any FCC commitment to PSAs the way broadcast TV is, the increased number of stations offer nonprofits more opportunities. (But the caveats of placement and expense remain.)

- **Print** continues to be one of the top PSA choices. For libraries and other nonprofits this is good news, as many print media allow and even desire articles that can attract broad and diverse community support. When I worked in Bainbridge, Ga., at the regional library, the local paper permitted my column, Off the Shelf, to run for all the years I worked there. Magazines also will run stories—but critical time can be lost if they are not frequently published. Getting to know editors and what they value for their readers is key.

- **Radio** was once called "the triumph of illiteracy" by John Dos Passos. This may appear to be true as our teenagers and young people listen to their personal radios and iPods. Radio accompanies many people in their cars, to the beaches, schools, and just plain old walking around. Most studies agree that radio reaches more people than television. As the table suggests, radio is an excellent medium for very selective markets. I recently had the honor of being a judge for the California Library Association PR awards. One of the winning candidates had developed 26 PSAs in Spanish. Now that is truly targeting your market! (Again the caveat is that placement and timing are not controlled by the organization creating the PSA.)

- **Transit** can be used quite well in markets with high ridership on buses or subways. Posters developed initially for in-library or other facility use can be reused effectively in this manner. Often transit companies donate a space or two because many folks who depend on bus transportation are targeted for public information campaigns. Posters and banners (or brochures), whether placed on transit or display boards in the community, can back up radio and television messages. Yet posters lack selectivity, even while offering high exposure. Brochures are often disregarded if they are poorly designed or ill-placed for distribution. Depth and clarity of message are always critical.

- **The library Web site** is characterized by the constraints of the Internet listed in the table. People must have access, be online, and be motivated to read the message. Problems of clutter can also occur.

- **Personal communication** is still "top shelf," whether it's delivered via your staff or a speakers' bureau. An informed staff and/or key supporters can take well-honed messages to the community. Keep your best communicators informed about the programs and services the library is hawking. One of my personal beefs is going to a store and asking the clerk about a hot sale item that is in the paper, only to get a blank look. Do not overlook the importance of internal communication and keeping your staff informed.

3. Joint advertising—This is a real boon, but you can rarely control the message. Just as the partnership must be scrutinized, so must the message be. Remember, before eagerly agreeing to any opportunity, ask to do a final review of the message, whether it is on an Internet banner, on the radio, or through another group's speakers' bureau. Remember, the audiences will likely be whomever your partner usually tries to contact—not necessarily your desired audience.

4. Promotions—These cover a wide array of techniques. You should select the tool to "promote promotion," if you will, when you are trying to build interest or to encourage usage of a service or product during a specified time period. One that's familiar and acceptable to us is the summer reading club (SRC). SRCs often entail the proverbial contest for number of books read, a coloring contest, and a certificate of completion in the fall. Libraries are reticent to use this tool, but there are additional successful examples of promotions, such as "Fine Free Friday" for book returns, or unlimited Internet usage during off-peak periods.

5. **Publicity**—This means unpaid coverage by the media, and is a wonderful gem. Developing opportunities for publicity takes time and commitment. Staff must develop a list of media contacts and get to know them. You must ask what type and length of stories editors seek, as well as deadlines and format. This is time well-spent when compared to what you can reap.

6. **Personal selling**—This is a bonus of our professional training. We are not staffed with 2-hour trainees. Our staff members are the most valuable conduit of information about library programs and services—to our *actual* customers. Our *potential* customers, by contrast, require additional use of a mix of the other five tools in order for us to reach them. Good staff members are the eyes and ears of the library via in-person, on the phone, e-mail or live chat

Now How Do You Choose Media?

With an understanding of promotional tools, you are now ready to select media. Remember the key here is to do your homework—identify, segment, and prioritize the library's customer groups. Your market research must also identify customers' media habits. Ask them what media they consume. Andreasen and Kotler offer the example of radio, television, and the Internet as the best choices for teenagers. By contrast, Florida snowbirds may best be reached at the senior center. Direct mail is also a good option for customers such as the parents of children who may attend story hours and summer reading clubs.

Secondly, various mediums are best for certain products. If you are trying to demonstrate a product or create an emotional effect, perhaps television would work best. Third, the complexity of the message dictates media. Instructive and detailed messages may be better communicated in print. Messages that entice listeners to imagine are better communicated on radio. And finally, there's that old bug-a-boo we cannot get away from—cost. Consider who you are trying to reach and how best to reach them with the funds you have. Be realistic.

The best approach is to use "integrated marketing communications," which simply means a mixture of tools and media that can accomplish your promotional objectives (Solomon, 2000). Again, the foundation is research and segmentation—they lead to successful and targeted promotion.

You should evaluate your chosen promotional tools by pretesting the messages with your target market. You can accomplish this by having your customer respond to a quick checklist regarding the message via a face-to-face interview, through online feedback, or in a focus group. You can further evaluate after the messages are released by noting an increase in usage or attendance, or by measuring response to direct mail. Promotional activities must always be tied to the program's objectives.

Good Promotion Is Based on Solid Marketing

Given all you've just read, I challenge you to review all of your library's promotional pieces and ask, "Are these based on customer research?" Then create a pile of "good promotion" and another pile of those pieces you consider *not* effective. If there are any pieces you cannot decide on, ask your customers if they ever laid eyes on them or heard of them. The answer will quickly determine which pile to put it in!

Christie Koontz, Ph.D., is a faculty member of the College of Information and director of the GeoLib Program (http://www.geolib.org/ PLGDB.cfm) at Florida State University in Tallahassee. Koontz teaches marketing and conducts workshops for colleagues around the globe. She also serves on the committee for the IFLA Marketing Award. Her email address is ckoontz@admin.fsu.edu.

References

Andreasen, Alan R. and Kotler, Philip. 2003. *Strategic Marketing for Nonprofit Organizations*, 6th ed. Prentice Hall: Upper Saddle River, N.J.

Koontz, Christie. 1980. "Free Airtime: Can You Afford It? A Report of Public Service Advertising." Written for the Department of Health and Rehabilitative Services, State of Florida.

Solomon, Michael R. and Stuart, Elnora W. 2000. *Marketing: Real People Real Choices*, 2nd ed. Prentice-Hall: Upper Saddle River, N.J.

About the Author

Kathy Dempsey has been a fan of libraries all her life. After getting her first card in elementary school, she tore through the whole series of Nancy Drew mysteries. In high school, she joined the Library Club so she could work there during study halls. In college, she chose the campus library for her work-study job. After graduation, she worked at several libraries as a paraprofessional for a total of 6 years (Temple University in Pennsylvania, Shenandoah University in Virginia, Handley Public Library in Virginia) in the late 1980s and early 1990s. In 1994, she combined her journalism degree and library experience to get the perfect job with New Jersey-based Information Today, Inc. (ITI), a publishing company that specializes in serials, books, and conferences for the library and information industry. Since joining ITI, Kathy has been the sole Editor of the *Marketing Library Services* (*MLS*) newsletter, which covers not only marketing but also related topics, including promotion, advocacy, public relations, fundraising, and outreach.

During the 15 years that Kathy has been monitoring, learning from, and participating in the field of library marketing, she's been called on to speak about the topic many times, beginning with EBSCO's Executive Seminar Series back in 1995. She's also presented library marketing and promotion workshops, conference sessions, and keynote speeches for organizations around the country, including Special Libraries Association regional groups, the New Jersey Library Association, the Library Public Relations Council, the Medical Library Association, the South Jersey Regional Library Cooperative, Dartmouth College Biomedical Libraries, the Pacific Northwest Library Association, the State

University of New York (SUNY) Council of Library Directors, the Association of College & Research Libraries' New England Chapter, and the Associated College Libraries of Central Pennsylvania. She has also spoken for The Partnership (Canada's national network of library associations) and at a symposium organized jointly by DOK and the Technical University of Delft in The Netherlands.

Kathy also worked on *Computers in Libraries (CIL)* magazine, beginning as Associate Editor in 1995 and working her way up to Editor in Chief in 2003. She resigned from *CIL* at the end of 2007 to devote her full attention to the marketing/promotion side. In 2005, she officially started her consulting firm, Libraries Are Essential, which provides "advice and consulting on library marketing, promotion, and public relations." As her Libraries Are Essential persona, she has partnered with Dr. Christie Koontz to research and write complete marketing plans for two large organizations (one state library and one 20-branch public library system). She currently consults and speaks part-time while she continues to edit *MLS* part-time.

Over the years, Kathy has written countless articles as a staff member for *Marketing Library Services, Computers in Libraries,* and *Information Today*. She was also a regular freelance writer for *Information World Review*, the U.K.-based information-industry newspaper, from 1997 to 2003. In addition, she wrote the forewords for two books in 2003: *The Accidental Systems Librarian* and *The Visible Librarian*. In 2008, she served as Project Editor for the unique book/movie combo *ShanachieTour: A Library Road Trip Across America*, created by three Dutch library employees who drove across the U.S. visiting libraries and spreading best practices to inspire librarians around the world.

Kathy is an active member of the New Jersey Library Association and has served in its Technical Services section, its Public Relations committee, and its Newsletter Editorial Board. Most recently, she became a contributor to The 'M' Word, Nancy Dowd's blog about library marketing. Kathy continues to devote her life to educating weenies who think that the internet can replace libraries.

Index

A

Abram, Stephen, 91–93
Academic Libraries: 2006 First
    Look (research study), 100
academic partnerships, 204–205
AcademicPR (ALA listserv), 173
acronyms, instant message lingo,
    23–24
addresses, gathering customer, 65
addresses, website, 177
advertising, 16, 18, 81
advocacy, 17, 18, 239
Aerni, Sarah E., 141–142
alert services, 33
Amazon.com, library marketing
    compared, 94
Anderson, Max, 230
AOL Instant Messenger (AIM)
    website, 23–24
approval, strategies for gaining,
    105–108
arcades, partnering with, 206
archive, document, 2–3
art, lending, 233
Ashland (OH) Public Library, 233
"Ask an Expert" services, 96
assessing data, 117–118

B

Bainbridge Island (WA) Library,
    229
Become the Brand of Choice, 125
benches, library, 29
Biblioteca Comunal de Santa Cruz,
    234
"Bieb in the Box", 234
bike racks, library, 29
blogs, library, 28–29, 30–35, 218,
    228
The Book Bag Blog, 228
book cart drill teams, 224, 227
book contests, 233–234
book display areas, library, 30
bookmarks, 188–189
book return, library, 29
branding, 16–17, 18, 35–36,
    125–126. *See also* logos
"Brarydog", 226
broken web links, 34, 212
Brookover, Sophie, 243
browsers, website use on, 213
BrowserShots, 213
Building Your Base: Tools for
    Connecting with Your
    Community toolkit,
    236–237

bulletin boards, library, 30,
   187–188
Burns, Elizabeth, 243
business, partnering with, 205–206
business cards, 163–164
buy in
   from management, 104–108,
      109–111
   from staff, 111–115

C

cafés, library, 30, 133
Camel Public Library, 235
cards, business, 163–164
cards, library, 229–230
cards, trading, 230
cell-phone areas, library, 28
cell-phones, marketing via,
   208–209
Census Bureau data, 67, 69–71,
   149
change culture, 154
chat lingo, 23–24
circulation desk, library, 30
cleanliness, library, 29, 30
clip art in promotional material,
   179
coat area, library, 30
Coffee, MaryGail, 137, 139
colors in promotional materials,
   178, 179
column inches of media coverage,
   33, 35
committees, disadvantages, 105
communication
information, organizing for,
   189–190
   with library staff, 113
   of marketing ideas, 105–108

   with media, 187–190, 191–195,
      202–203
   through partnerships, 203–207
communication plans, 161, 162,
   170–172
community information
   analyzing, 73–76
   geographic, 68–69, 71–73, 149
   importance of gathering, 149
   sources, 67–73
community organizations, partner-
      ing with, 204, 206
competing organizations, 154–155,
   166
computer area, library, 30
consultants, partnering with, 206
contests, 225, 233–234, 239–240
cool words, 23
Cooper, Julia, 27
Corel Ventura software, 180
cost/benefit analysis
   cost of, 143–144
   described, 135–136
   examples, 137, 139, 140–143
   value calculator, 136–137, 138,
      143
crisis communication, 199–202
cultural understanding, 149
"Customer-Based Marketing" col-
      umn (Koontz), 68
customer feedback. *See also* focus
      groups; surveys
   evaluating, 84–85, 157–158
   methods, 152–153, 155–156
   planning for, 167
   secret shoppers, 28, 37–40
   suggestion box, 40
   website form, 40, 211, 220
customers
   categorizing, 149–150
   complaints from, 131–132

gathering information on,
      48–49, 65
goals, setting, 151–152
needs, identifying, 83
reaching, 156–157
requests from, 153–154
research on, 96
customer service environment,
      37–40
customized library cards, 229–230

D

dance contests, 225
data, gathering/using, 96, 117–118,
      129–135. *See also* customer
      feedback
databases, online, 96
Delaware County (PA) Library
      System, 205
del Tufo, Theresa, 122
demographics. *See* community
      information
display areas for books, 30
DOK (library concept center, the
      Netherlands), 234
Dowd, Nancy, 207
download materials service, 234
drawings for incentive gifts, 47,
      48–49, 59
drill teams, book cart, 224, 227

E

Economic Benefits of Libraries
      (webpage), 140
email, 45–46, 177–178, 188
entrance, library, 29, 38

Evaluating Web Sites for
      Accessibility: An
      Overview, from the Web
      Accessibility Initiative
      (webpage), 213
evaluation, reasons for new mar-
      keting, 159–160
evaluation forms on library pro-
      grams, 84–85
event ideas
   art, lending, 233
   book bags, 228
   book cart drill teams, 224, 227
   book contests, 233–234
   concerts, 232–233
   contests, winning library,
         239–240
   dance contests, 225
   haunted libraries, 231
   living libraries, 228–229
   mascots, 226
   miniature golf, 231
   parties, 224–225, 235–236
   partnerships, 203–207, 226
   races, 231
   rare book adoption, 230
   refreshments, serving, 235
   soapbox derby car, 232
   technology mentoring
         programs, 225
   Touch-a-Truck, 233
   travel, 228
   virtual open houses, 232
   wrestling, 235
exteriors, library, 28, 29
eye-tracking, 219

F

failures, evaluating program, 90
feedback, customer. *See* customer
      feedback

fees, customer complaints, 131–132
"finding sites", 217
fines, customer complaints, 131–132
focus groups
  basic steps, 53
  collecting data, 61–62
  goals, 54, 152
  holding, 59–60, 61
  importance, 52–53
  incentives to participate, 58–59, 60–61, 62
  invitations to, 60–61
  moderators, 54, 56, 61
  multiple, need for, 66
  nonusers, involving, 64–65
  participants, recruiting, 56–58, 236
  questions, 55–56
  quotes from, 62–63
  refreshments, 60–61
  responses, collecting, 62–64
  suggestions, 65
  target audience, 54–55
Folger Shakespeare Library, 230
fonts in promotional materials, 178–179
Four Ps, 17, 19, 161, 165
Four Ws, 123
Franklin Park Public Library value calculations, 138
fundraisers, library, 176–177, 235, 239

G

geographic data, 68–69, 71–73, 149
GeoLib program, Florida State University, 68–69, 72, 87

Get It Loud in Libraries project, 232–233
gifts, incentive, 47, 48–49, 59
Godin, Seth, 93–94
golf events, 231
Google tools, 33, 96, 217, 218
Graphic Arts Loan Collection program, 233
graphics in promotional material, 179
greeters, library, 29, 39
Griffiths, José-Marie, 141–142
grocery stores, partnering with, 205, 226

H

hand-held devices, marketing via, 208–209
Harrington, Julie, 141
haunted libraries, 231
The Hollywood Librarian (documentary), 3
home pages, 31–32, 34. *See also* websites
Houghton-Jan, Sarah, 218
"How to Conduct a Focus Group" (Radford), 53
"How to Drive Traffic to Your Website" (Schmidt & Houghton-Jan), 218
"How to Evaluate Your Library's Physical Environment" (Cooper), 27
"How We Built a New Library Identity" (Yun), 126
"How We Proved Our Library's Value with an ROI Assessment" (*MLS*), 136–137, 139

I

IM (instant messaging) reference
    lingo, 23–24
incentive gifts, 47, 48–49, 59
incentives for student behavior,
    233–234
InDesign software, 180
in-library activity, tracking,
    133–134
instant messaging (IM) reference
    lingo, 23–24
interlibrary loans, 136
internet and libraries, 1, 100–101,
    241–242, 244–247. *See
    also* websites
"Internet searches: Librarians do it
    better", 109
interviews, media, 195, 196–202
Iowa City (IA) Public Library, 226
Iverson, Marsha, 172

J

jargon, 81–82, 198

K

kewl words, 23
King, Donald W., 141–142
King County (WA) Library System
    communication plan, 172
Kneale, Ruth, 3, 243
Koontz, Dr. Christie
    on Census data, 69–70
    as GeoLib director, 68–69
    on library closures, 71, 72
    on market research, 68, 86–87,
        149, 151

on media types, 203
Kupersmith, John, 22

L

Lancaster Music Library, 232–233
landscaping, library, 29
language, using appropriate, 23–24
Latinos & Public Library
    Perceptions (research
    study), 101
legislation, library-related, 239
Legislative Action Center, 239
LibrarianInBlack.net (blog), 218
librarians. *See also* staff, library
    becoming accidental marketers,
        3–5, 11
    intentions to market, 6–8
    marketing activities, job per-
        centage, 6
    marketing training, lack of, 2,
        8–11
    presentations by, 134, 237–239
    public perceptions, 3, 242–243
libraries
    closures, 71–72
    competition, 94
    cost benefits, 136–137, 138,
        140, 143
    cost of using, 19
    customer service environment,
        37–40
    geographic data, coordinating
        with library use, 71–73
    haunted, 231
    internet connectivity, 100–101
    living, 228–229
    mobile, 234–235
    online environment, 28–29,
        30–35, 96
    physical space, 27–28, 29–30

libraries (*cont.*)
    printed materials, 35–36
    public perceptions, 1–3, 25–27,
        95–97, 240–241
    relevance, 241–242, 244–247
    research on, 95–97, 98–99,
        100–101
    signage, 28, 29, 36, 39, 179
    staff spaces, 28, 30
    web listings, 217–218
Libraries Connect Communities:
    Public Library Funding &
    Technology Access Study
    2007-2008 (research study),
    100–101
library cards, 229–230
Library Marketing That Works!
    (Walters), 123
Library Mini Golf, 231
Library Public Relations,
    Promotions, and
    Communications (Wolfe),
    94–95
Library Terms That Users
    Understand (website),
    22–23, 31
lighting, library, 28
lingo, library, 20–24
Link Sleuth, 212
living libraries, 228–229
lobbying, 239
log-in to library website, 32–33, 34
logos, 122–125
Long, Sarah, 136
Luther, Judy, 142–143
Lynch, Thomas, 141

M

mailings, library, 188

"Making a Customizable Site for
    Easy Access & Marketing
    Its Character", 226
marketing. *See also* cost/benefit
    analysis; marketing plans
    author survey on, 6–9, 10
    cycle, basic steps, 14–16,
        145–149, 168–169
    data assessment, 117–118
    defined, 6, 13–14, 16, 17, 81,
        87
    described, 86, 87–89
    by email, 45–46, 177–178, 188
    evaluations, new, 159–160
    goals, 90–91, 92, 119–122, 167
    importance, 11
    language, 23–24
    learning, 11–12
    librarian training, 2, 8–11
    message, developing/communi-
        cating, 94–95
    mistakes, 79–85
    mobile, 208–209
    options, listing, 118–119
    by phone, 208–209
    priorities, 5, 91
    problem areas, 87–90
    research studies, 97–101
    review of process, 158–159
    strategy example, 18
    Sweet Soda example, 19–21
    targeting, 82–83, 166
    terminology, 81–82, 198
    by text message, 208–209
    word-of-mouth, 207
Marketing: A How-To-Do-It
    Manual for Librarians
    (Walters), 95, 114–115
Marketing Library Services, 3, 5
marketing plans
    basic steps to writing, 163–167
    example, 18
    in marketing cycle, 168–169

preparing to write, 168, 169
promotion in, 156–157
purpose, 161
sharing, 173
time span, 163
timing, 162
"Marketing Research is a Useful
    Tool for Libraries"
    (Koontz), 68
"Market Segmentation: Grouping
    Your Clients" (Koontz),
    151
mascots, 226
Massachusetts Library Association
    (MLA) value calculator,
    136–137, 138, 143
Massísimo, Angels, 87–89
The Measure of Library Excellence
    (Wilson, de Tufo &
    Norman), 122
Measuring for Results (Matthews),
    139–140
media. *See also* communication
    plans
    choosing, 187–190, 202–203
    communication with, 190,
        191–195
    contact information, organizing,
        170–171
    contacts, identifying, 192–193
    coverage by, 33, 35, 135, 194
    interviews, 195, 196–202
    press releases, 35–36, 83, 191,
        192
    relationships, building,
        192–195, 201
    website resources, 33, 34, 35,
        193–194, 215
meeting rooms, library, 30
Melanson, Robert, 137, 139
message, developing/communicat-
    ing, 94–95
metblogs.com, 218

Microsoft Live, search engine
    information, 217
Microsoft Publisher software, 180
Mid-Hudson Library System,
    236–237
miniature golf events, 231
mission statements, 120–121, 122,
    123, 164, 165
mobile libraries, 234–235
mobile marketing, 208–209
*The Mobile Marketing Handbook:
    A Step-by-Step Guide to
    Creating Dynamic Mobile
    Marketing Campaigns*
    (Dushinski), 209
monitors, displaying messages on,
    188

N

names, product, 20–24
National Library Legislative Day,
    239
natural language search tools, 22
Neilsen, Jakob, 220
networking, 240–241
Norman, Anne E. C., 122

O

"Old Maids, Policeman, and Social
    Rejects: Mass Media
    Representations and Public
    Perceptions of Librarians"
    (Seale), 242
online databases, 96
"Online Librarian" services, 97
online libraries, 96
open house, library, 232

Outsell, Inc., 136
outside-library activity, tracking, 134

P

PageMaker software, 180
PagePlus software, 180
parents, partnering with, 206
parking lots, library, 29, 38
parties, library, 224–225, 235–236
partnerships, 203–207, 226
patrons. *See* customers
Pattern Research, Inc., 89
"Perceptions of Libraries and
  Information Resources"
  (OCLC), 95
phone, library service via, 38
phones, marketing via, 208–209
photos in promotional material,
  179
Place, defined, 19
plans, formal, 161, 162–163, 173
PLGDB (Public Library
  Geographic Database),
  68–69. *See also* geographic
  data
Pop Goes the Library, 243
presentations, staff, 134, 237–239
preservation, document, 2–3
press releases, 35–36, 83, 191, 192
Price, defined, 17
price of library services, 19
Princeton (NJ) University, 230
printed materials. *See* promotional
  materials
print shops, working with,
  184–185
Product, defined, 17

programs, library. *See also* event
  ideas
  asking for existing, 97, 153
  delivery, 157
  describing in marketing plan,
    166
  download materials, 234
  failures, evaluating, 90
  identifying/creating, 80,
    153–154
  mobile, 234–235
  reasons for, 15–16
  for senior citizens, 206, 225
  success, measuring, 84–85
  for teens, 206, 225, 233
project proposals, 108–109
promotion
  defined, 16, 19, 81
  described, 5–6
  email, 177–178
  example, 18
  ideas for, 237–241
  in marketing plan, 156–157
  prioritization, 5–6
  strategies, choosing, 167
  of technology tools, 172–173
  What's In It For Me?, 176
promotional materials
  branding, 35–36
  content, 175–178
  design, 175, 178–181
  evaluating, 35–36
  examples, 229–230
  importance, 185
  production, 184–185
  software, 180
  templates, 180–181
  types, 175–176
  using students in, 230
  workflow, tracking, 181–184
"Promotion Is Not the Same as
  Marketing" (Koontz), 203

proposals, project, 108–109
PRTalk (ALA listserv), 173
publicity, 16, 18, 81
Public Library Geographic
    Database (PLGDB), 68–69.
    See also geographic data
Public Library of Charlotte &
    Mecklenburg County, 226
public relations, 16, 18, 81

Q

"quantitative worship", 89
QuarkXPress software, 180
quiet areas, library, 28
*Quotable Facts About America's
    Libraries* (ALA), 129–130

R

Radford, Marie, 53
rare book adoption, 230
recycling areas, library, 28, 29, 30
reference desk, library, 30
Research Library International
    Benchmarks (research
    study), 98–99
research studies
    branding, 126
    Information Management prac-
        tices, 99
    libraries, 95–97, 98–99, 100–101
    marketing, 97–101
    web page use, 219–220
restrooms, library, 30
return on investment (ROI). *See*
    cost/benefit analysis
returns, book, 29
review of marketing process,
    158–159

RSS feeds for library announce-
    ments, 189

S

Santa Monica (CA) Public Library,
    229
Savard, Réjean, 86
Schmidt, Aaron, 218
scout troops, partnering with, 206
scribes, focus group, 61
Seale, Maura, 242
search engines, online, 33,
    215–218
searching for content, 22, 34,
    109–110, 212, 218–220
seating areas, library, 30
secret shoppers, 28, 37–40
self-check stations, library, 30
senior citizen programs, 206, 225
Serif PagePlus software, 180
Service, defined, 17
services. *See* programs, library
Serving Non-English Speakers in
    U.S. Public Libraries
    (research study), 98
shopping malls, partnering with,
    205
sidewalks, library, 29
Siess, Judith, 91
signage, appearance, 28, 29, 36,
    39, 179
skateboard shops, partnering with,
    206
Smart ALEC, 226
Smith, Leif, 89
Smith Aldrich, Rebekkah, 236–237
Snow Party, 235–236
soapbox derby car events, 232
social networks, tracking use, 133

software for promotional material,
180
sound bites, 196–197
Special Libraries Association, mission statement example,
121
"Spectacles: How Pop Culture
Sees Librarians", 3, 243
spokespersons, selecting, 195–196
stacks, library, 30
staff, library
buy in from, 111–115
communication with, 113
posting information online, 214
presentations, 134, 237–239
spaces for, 28, 30
Stanley, John, 235
statistics, gathering/using, 96,
117–118, 129–135. *See
also* customer feedback
strange acts, as student incentive,
233–234
strategic plans, 161, 162, 163, 165
Strause, Roger, 136
studies, research. *See* research
studies
SurveyMonkey, 46
surveys
basic steps, 41
deadlines, 50
distribution and return, 44–46,
50
email, 45–46
goals, 41–42, 152
importance, 52
incentives to participate, 47–49
on marketing, 6–9, 10
multiple, need for, 66
nonusers, involving, 64–65
questions, 43, 44
range, 40
reminders, 50–51

suggestions, 65
tabulating, 46–47, 51–52
target audience, 42–43
telephone, 46
tools, 46
uses, 40
website, 45, 46, 156
Sweet Soda example, 19–21
SWOT analysis, 73–76

T

talking points, 196–197
talking with people about libraries,
240–241
target audience, 42–43, 54–55,
82–83, 150–151, 166
*Taxpayer Return-on-Investment
(ROI) in Pennsylvania
Public Libraries* (Griffiths,
et al.), 141–142
*Taxpayer Return on Investment in
Florida Public Libraries:
Summary Report* (Griffiths,
et al.), 141
technology mentoring programs,
225
technology plans, 172–173
technology use/availability,
100–101, 134–135
teens, 48, 83, 206, 225, 233
telephone, library service via, 38
telephone surveys, 46
templates for promotional material,
180–181
terminology, library, 20–24
terminology, marketing, 81–82,
198
text messaging, 23–24, 208–209
Time Customer Service, 232
Tomer, Christinger, 141

tools to help library patrons, 22, 34, 109–110, 212, 218–220
Touch-a-Truck events, 233
trading cards, 230
traffic flow, library, 29
training, librarian marketing, 2, 8–11
training for community organizations, 204
trash areas, library, 28, 29, 30
Trumbull (CT) Library, 231
Tunxis Community College, 225
typefaces, 178–179

U

Union County Public Library, 235–236
University Investment in the Library: What's the Return? A Case Study at the University of Illinois at Urbana-Champaign (Luther), 142–143
University of California-Berkeley's (UCB) Morrison Library, 233
University of Hartford (CT) Library, 231
unusual acts, as student incentive, 233–234
U.S. Census Bureau data, 67, 69–71, 149
users. *See* customers

V

value calculator, 136–137, 138, 143

Value For Money: Southwestern Ohio's Return from Investment in Public Libraries (Levin, Driscoll & Fleeter), 141, 142
"The Value of Libraries: Justifying Corporate Information Centers in the Year of Accountability" (Strause), 136
Ventura software, 180
videogame stores, partnering with, 206
vision statements, 120, 122, 165
Volk, Ruti, 109

W

wacky acts, as student incentive, 233–234
Wagner, Pat, 89–90, 179–180
Wake Forest (NC) University, 231
Walking Paper (blog), 218
Wallace, Linda, 120–121
Walters, Suzanne, 95, 114–115, 123
websites
    addresses, 177
    announcements, 189
    AOL Instant Messenger, 23–24
    assessing, 32, 34
    browsers, 213
    errors on, 34, 212–213
    evaluating, 28–29, 30–35
    features expected, 212–213, 214–215
    feedback on, 40, 211, 220
    home page contents, 31–32, 34
    links to, 217–218
    logging in, 32–33, 34

websites (*cont.*)
  making findable via search
      engines, 215–218
  media resources, 33, 34, 35,
      193–194, 215
  navigating, 32–33, 34
  organization, 31–32
  parent organization, as part of,
      31, 34
  searching, 22, 34, 109–110,
      212, 218–220
  staff info, posting, 214
  surveys, library, 45, 46, 156
  technology people, working
      with, 211–212
  tools for improving, 215–218
  usability, 211, 212–213
  usage statistics, 96
Western Michigan University
    (WMU), 232
What Executives Think About
    Information Management
    (research study), 99
What's In It For Me? (WIIFM) in
    promotion, 176
"Why Public Libraries Close"
    (Koontz), 71
Wikipedia, 217

Williamsburg (VA) Regional
    Library, 205
Wilson, Despina Dapias, 122
Wolfe, Lisa A., 94–95
word-of-mouth (WoM) marketing,
    207
worldwide open house, 232
"Worth Their Weight: An
    Assessment of the Evolving
    Field of Library Valuation"
    (ALC), 143–144
wrestling matches, 235

Y

Yahoo! search engine information,
    217
You Don't Look Like a Librarian
    (website), 3, 243
youths, 48, 83, 206, 225, 233
Yun, Sejan, 126

Z

Zaytseva, Liudmila N., 90–91

More Great Books from Information Today, Inc.

Pop Goes the Library
Using Pop Culture to Connect With Your Whole Community

By Sophie Brookover and Elizabeth Burns

You loved the blog—now read the book! Whether you regularly follow entertainment and gossip news, or wondered "Corbin Who?" when you saw the recent ALA READ poster, *Pop Goes the Library* will help you connect with your users and energize your staff. Sophie Brookover and Elizabeth Burns define what pop culture is (and isn't) and share insights, tips, techniques, and success stories from all types of libraries. You'll discover practical strategies and ideas for incorporating the pop culture passions of your users into collections, programs, and services.

320 pp/softbound/ISBN 978-1-57387-336-9   **$39.50**

Library Partnerships
Making Connections Between School and Public Libraries

By Tasha Squires

Connecting to share ideas, resources, and programs offers school and public libraries an exciting means of achieving their own goals as well as those of the community at large. Tasha Squires delves into the many possible avenues for partnership, from summer reading programs to book talks to resource sharing and more. Her advice is designed to help librarians appreciate, communicate, and build on the benefits of these relationships to make the most of tight budgets, create resource rich environments, and promote the development of lifelong learners.

224 pp/softbound/ISBN 978-1-57387-362-8   **$39.50**

The Mobile Marketing Handbook
A Step-by-Step Guide to Creating Dynamic Mobile
Marketing Campaigns

By Kim Dushinski

In this practical handbook, Kim Dushinski
offers easy-to-follow advice for firms that want
to interact with mobile users, build stronger
customer relationships, reach a virtually unlimited number of prospects, and gain competitive
advantage by making the move to mobile
device users. *The Mobile Marketing Handbook*
will help you put your message in the palms of
their hands.

256 pp/softbound/ISBN 978-0-910965-82-8 $29.95

You Don't Look Like a Librarian
Shattering Stereotypes and Creating Positive New
Images in the Internet Age

By Ruth Kneale

Librarian stereotypes have persisted for
generations, yet their practical impact has rarely
been studied. In this book, Ruth Kneale presents
the results of a 1,000-plus-respondent survey
and shares interviews with opinionated librarians
across the spectrum, drawing on published
literature and lively discussions from her website.
The result is an eye-opening look at librarian
stereotypes and their real-world consequences in
the Internet Age.

216 pp/softbound/ISBN 978-1-57387-366-6 $29.50